W9-BAF-251

RECLAIMING THE REPUBLIC

RECLAIMING
THE REPUBLIC

How Christians and Other Conservatives
Can Win Back America

Robert G. Marshall

Foreword by Professor Robert A. Destro

TAN Books
Charlotte, North Carolina

Copyright © 2018 Robert Marshall

All rights reserved. With the exception of short excerpts used in critical review, no part of this work may be reproduced, transmitted, or stored, in any form whatsoever, without the written permission of the publisher.

Excerpts from the English translation of the *Catechism of the Catholic Church* for use in the United States of America © 1994, United States Catholic Conference, Inc.—Libreria Editrice Vaticana. Used with permission.

All excerpts from papal homilies, messages, and encyclicals copyright © Libreria Editrice Vaticana. All rights reserved.

Unless otherwise noted, Scripture quotations are from the Revised Standard Version of the Bible—Second Catholic Edition (Ignatius Edition), copyright © 2006 National Council of the Churches of Christ in the United States of America. Used by permission. All rights reserved.

Scripture texts noted as NABRE are taken from the New American Bible, revised edition © 2010, 1991, 1986, 1970 Confraternity of Christian Doctrine, Washington, D.C. and are used by permission of the copyright owner. All rights reserved. No part of the New American Bible may be reproduced in any form without permission in writing from the copyright owner.

Cover design by Caroline Green

Cover images: Hand pointing finger © Christos Georghiou, ShutterStock and Fourth of July Background © vasosh, ShutterStock

Library of Congress Control Number: 2017961467

ISBN: 978-1-5051-0940-5

Published in the United States by
TAN Books
P.O. Box 410487
Charlotte, NC 28241
www.TANBooks.com

Printed and bound in the United States of America

To Our Lady of Guadalupe, the Patroness of the Americas, and to my loving family and friends who have encouraged me in my advocacy for our nation to return to the "Laws of Nature and of Nature's God"

CONTENTS

What Is At Stake

In the November 2017 general elections, progressives were testing out various tactics in Virginia and New Jersey to see if they could convince Democrats who normally voted only in presidential year elections to vote in a governor's year election. This effort was to prepare a voter turnout model in the 2018 congressional races for all fifty states.

Progressive groups targeted Virginia state legislative districts that had voted for Hillary Clinton in 2016 but were represented by Republican state legislators. Their "test" succeeded in defeating fifteen members of the Virginia House of Delegates in November of 2017. Even though I had amassed a record good enough to get into a Super Bowl, with wins in thirteen prior elections in a state legislative district that Obama had won twice, this time, I was one of the casualties.

How did this happen?

Largely, their success was accomplished by using the techniques described elsewhere in this book but which were carried out by a very large nationwide network of left-leaning organizations. My opponent, a male who claimed to be female after taking female hormones, was able to secure a massive number of door-to-door volunteers from LGBTQ supporters and groups, many from out of state. Over seventy volunteer door-knockers showed up from the Human Rights Campaign on one day alone! My wife, Cathy, and I personally ran into six pink-T-shirt-clad Planned Parenthood door knockers in one precinct on one day.

I am very grateful for the prayers of my many supporters and their generous financial backing. We raised more money than ever before, had more volunteers than ever before, and received 12.5 percent more votes than ever before in the current version of the Thirteenth House District, but we still fell short because the opponent had more money, mostly from out of state, more volunteers, and the support of the liberal media.

Many of my supporters were thoroughly convinced that my opponent, who supported teaching kindergartners they could change their sex, could not possibly win in conservative Virginia. But my opponent raised $808,000 with outside groups assisting and probably spending another $150,000–200,000 to my $300,000. The losses proved that out-of-state hit jobs can succeed.

Roem was funded almost entirely by the homosexual lobby. The *Denver Post* explained, "Roem outraised Marshall 3-to-1 thanks in part to large donations from lesbian, gay, bisexual and transgender advocates across the country. This was possible because Virginia is one of just a handful of states that imposes no limits on who can contribute, or how much, to a political candidate."[1]

---

[1]   Luke Wachob, "Danica Roem's win proved the value of unlimited campaign contributions," *Denver Post*, November 15, 2017, http://www.denverpost.com/2017/11/15/danica-roems-

Exit poll surveys found that 41 percent of voters were Democrat, 30 percent of voters were Republican, and 28 percent were Independent.[2] Republicans failed to turn out for Republican candidates perhaps because the Republican Congress failed to keep its promises to repeal Obamacare, defund Planned Parenthood, or follow through on any number of policy intentions. Democrats were prompted, in part, by their anti-President Trump animosity.

The *Washington Post* reported, "Virginia Del. Robert G. Marshall . . . is facing what could be his toughest reelection battle, with Democrats gunning hard for his seat this November as part of their strategy to . . . launch what they hope will be a national resurgence for their party following the election of President Trump. Marshall's opponent, Danica Roem, would be the state's first elected official who is openly transgender, an identity that the incumbent describes as 'against the laws of nature and nature's God.'"[3]

Bloomberg News detailed how progressives intended to mobilize the anger of the Left against Trump in Virginia and New Jersey state legislature races. As the *Post* pointed out, my race was literally dead center for the entire democratic

---

win-proved-the-value-of-unlimited-campaign-contributions/.

[2] "Exit poll results: How different groups of Virginians voted," *Washington Post*, November 8, 2017, https://www.washington-post.com/graphics/2017/local/virginia-politics/governor-exit-polls/?utm_term=.9726c5e2e9a3.

[3] Antonio Olivo, "Del. Robert Marshall: Conservative warrior fights to preserve 'laws of nature,'" *Washington Post*, October 21, 2017, https://www.washingtonpost.com/local/virginia-politics/del-bob-marshall-conservative-warrior-fights-to-preserve-laws-of-nature/2017/10/19/d650d876-a857-11e7-b3aa-c0e2e1d41e38_story.html?utm_term=.5ecb933df410.

comeback effort nationwide beginning with progressive recruitment of my opponent in September 2016:

> A new generation of progressive entrepreneurs and activists have quit their jobs to . . . identify and turn out supporters, especially . . . millennials and minorities.
>
> . . . The staff of MobilizeAmerica . . . was crammed into a dressing room backstage at an Arcade Fire concert at Capital One Arena in Washington. . . . They'd brought along Danica Roem, the first transgender candidate to run for Virginia's House of Delegates. . . .
>
> . . . The 13th District race between Roem and the 13-term GOP incumbent, Bob Marshall, is like the 2016 presidential election. . . .
>
> . . . Roem . . . is exactly the sort of candidate Democrats must find a way to push to victory. . . .
>
> . . . Virginia's elections will serve as a testing ground for MobilizeAmerica. . . . The vital question for Democrats is this: Can they harness the energy of the resistance and steer its members to the ballot box in 2018? Control of Congress, and the future of Trump's presidency, hangs in the balance.[4]

With fifteen Virginia Republican delegates losing, the progressives did succeed in nationalizing local state races. But even more disturbing is the impeachment threat to Donald

---

[4]   Joshua Green, "Can Democrats Harness the #Resistance? The party's fortunes hinge on turning anti-Trump energy into votes. A wave of new startups aims to help." *Bloomberg Businessweek*, November 2, 2017, https://www.bloomberg.com/news/features/2017-11-02/the-democrats-must-go-local-to-win.

Trump's presidency if the leftist progressives gain control of Congress.

You and I must take this larger threat seriously. Inaction, imprudence, or timidity on our part in the face of this growing threat is morally unacceptable, politically unwise, and socially suicidal.

I sincerely hope that the November 2017 elections in Virginia will be a wake-up call for those who believe that the founding principles of our nation must be not be abandoned, that we cannot allow local elections to be decided by hundreds of thousands of out-of-state dollars and scores of out of state LGBTQ (Lesbian, Gay, Bi-Sexual, Transgender, Queer) activists. The only way we can match the effort of the Left, who are clearly energized by their hatred for our President, is by more prayer and involvement in civic affairs. We must not enable the Left to succeed without even putting up a fight.

I simply do not believe that the great majority of Americans think abortion should be legal throughout all nine months of pregnancy, that taxpayers should turn over $500 million a year to Planned Parenthood (leaders of which were caught on tape discussing sale of baby body parts from their abortions), that taxpayers and insurance companies must fund risky sex-change operations and life-long hormone treatments, or that public schools should teach starting in kindergarten that one's gender can be changed without consequence.

We must provide good reasons for voters to support conservative candidates and convince more conservative-leaning individuals, who may have lost faith in politicians or lost interest in the "dirty" business of politics, to reengage or register to vote and express their love of country and of their neighbor by caring about policies that affect us on so many levels.

If conservative Christians do not fight back in the political arena, Second Amendment rights will be weakened or lost, religious freedom will be dismantled, and those who do not fully embrace the agenda of the LGBTQ activists will be denied jobs or professional accreditation or marginalized for their alleged "hate speech." I predict our public schools will provide transgender counseling and tax-funded birth control and abortion pills behind parents' backs. More institutions will embrace euthanasia as a duty and cost-saving measure. This is not far-fetched. It is the proud ideology and agenda of the political Left.

Hope is a virtue. We can neither give up nor be intimidated by fear of people calling us names. We know the Truth, and the Truth makes us free. We must continue to pray and work together for the sake of our children, grandchildren, and welfare of our country.

First, because success in human endeavors is not solely in our hands, we must work hard at being faithful to God. You are commanded to "love the Lord your God with all your heart, and with all your soul, and with all your mind" (Mt 22:37). We must "render to Caesar the things that are Caesar's" (Mk 12:17) and recognize that "the sons of this world are wiser in their own generation than the sons of light" (Lk 16:8).

We will be judged by how we use the talents God gives us, how we love our neighbor, and how we work in the vineyard.

We will reap what we sow. And we won't reap what we do not sow. If progressives work in the political vineyard and we do not, progressives will reap the harvest.

When I was in elementary school in the 1950s, America still recognized Christian social, economic, and political assumptions of right and wrong. The entire social framework was based on Old and New Testament ethics. We even read the Bible in public school home room with no objections from students or parents.

Our Declaration of Independence acknowledges that our inalienable rights come from God, yet policies largely imposed by the courts have totally rejected millennia of religious social norms especially in the area of marriage and family life.

As the media and Hollywood elites declare that people can choose which sex they prefer to be simply by stating such, those who disagree with this rejection of nature and the findings of straightforward biology are marginalized, bullied, and criticized. The ability of so many persons in position of authority and influence to deny the obvious regarding human sexuality and criticize the rest of us if we do not share their self-deception is a type of mass hysteria that will precipitate serious consequences to political, social, and economic institutions.

Those marked with the sign of faith must become the leaven of the body politic. The children of Israel were not brought out of Egypt on magic carpets. Soldiers and sailors in the Catholic fleet at Lepanto prayed but also fought in battle to successfully blunt further Islamic inroads into Europe by the Ottoman Turkish Empire. Christians today

must be willing to fight in the political arena to defend
our inalienable rights, including religious freedom and free
speech. Should Christians decide instead to withdraw from
civic affairs or to just roll over for the progressives, we will
clearly be targeted for social irrelevance. LGBTQ billionaire
mega donor Tim Gill, who has donated more than $440
million to legalizing same-sex marriage and securing passage of so called LGBTQ non-discrimination laws, has been
quoted as saying, "We're going to punish the wicked."[5] Gill
is referring to you and me, and all serious followers of Moses
and Christ.

This endeavor to reclaim America will take a permanent
commitment. Every time you leave your home, you should
think of yourself as a missionary. I advise keeping voter registration information with you every time you leave home.
Strike up conversations. Any time you meet a favorable citizen, inquire if they are registered, or if they vote in all elections or just some. We have to get more people who think
like us to be registered voters who do not miss any elections.
And even missing one opportunity to grow the ranks of our
supporters can have a bad outcome. The other side is committed; we must be more committed.

---

[5]   Andy Kroll, "Meet the Megadonor Behind the LGBTQ Rights
        Movement," *Rolling Stone*, June 23, 2017, http://www.rolling-
        stone.com/politics/features/meet-tim-gill-megadonor-behind-
        lgbtq-rights-movement-wins-w489213.

"Ordinary" Americans and the "Politics of Power"

By Professor Robert A. Destro

Introduction

Though there is no *official* ruling class in the United States, there is plenty of evidence that America's cultural elites do, in fact, think that the rest of us are either too dumb, racist, self-centered, homophobic, xenophobic, or devoted to our respective faith traditions to be trusted with the actual levers of power. Robert "Delegate Bob" Marshall's book is written for "the rest of us."

In 2008, then-Senator Barack Obama, speaking at a San Francisco fundraiser, "took a shot at explaining the yawning cultural gap that separates a Turkeyfoot from a Marin County", and famously observed that people in "these small towns in Pennsylvania and . . . a lot of small towns in the Midwest" have grown weary of the failed economic promises of both parties. "And it's not surprising then they get bitter, they cling to guns or religion or antipathy toward people who aren't like them or anti-immigrant sentiment or anti-trade sentiment as a way to explain their frustrations."[1]

On September 9, 2016, Hillary Clinton made explicit what Mr. Obama implied. Speaking before an LGBT for Hillary gala in New York City, the former secretary of state neatly divided the 62.9 million Americans who voted for Donald Trump into two "baskets": 31.45 million "deplorables" and 31.45 million "people who feel that the government has let them down."

> You know, to just be grossly generalistic, you could put half of Trump's supporters into what I call the basket of deplorables. Right? The racist, sexist, homophobic, xenophobic, Islamaphobic—you name it. And unfortunately there are people like that. And he has lifted them up. . . . Now, some of those folks—they are irredeemable, but thankfully they are not America.
>
> . . . But that other basket of people are people who feel that the government has let them down, the economy has let them down, nobody cares about them, nobody worries about what happens to their lives and their futures, and they're just desperate for change. It doesn't really even matter where it comes from.[2]

[1]   Mayhill Fowler, "Obama: No Surprise That Hard-Pressed Pennsylvanians Turn Bitter," *The Blog, HuffPost,* November 17, 2008, http://www.huffingtonpost.com/mayhill-fowler/obama-no-surprise-that-ha_b_96188.html (accessed July 30, 2017).

[2]   Angie Drobnic Holan, "In Context: Hillary Clinton and the 'basket of deplorables,'" *Politifact*, September 11, 2016, http://www.politifact.com/truth-o-meter/article/2016/sep/11/context-hillary-clinton-basket-deplorables/. James Barrett, "How Many Votes Did Trump and Clinton Get? The Final Vote Count," *The Dailywire*, December 21, 2016, http://www.dailywire.com/news/11777/how-many-votes-did-trump-and-clinton-

It is therefore no accident that much of the social engineering that America's social and cultural elites believe to be necessary legal and cultural reforms are accomplished through the courts, government regulations, and other informal means. One does not need Supreme Court intervention in "periods of ordinary lawmaking." In those political contexts, ballot box victories translate directly (or nearly so) into legislation that has, or will acquire, broad-based public support.

It is only when the voters send a clear message *rejecting* specific candidates, programs, or policy directions that those seeking a different policy direction need the courts to do the heavy lifting for them. These are, in the words of Professor Bruce Ackerman, "constitutional moments" in which the court, with or without the acquiescence of Congress and the executive branch, substitutes its own judgments for those of the people and their elected representatives.[3]

It is precisely because constitutional litigation neatly avoids the rough and tumble, logrolling, and compromise inherent in the processes of democratic self-governance that my friend and political comrade Robert "Delegate Bob"

---

get-final-james-barrett. The vote totals are compiled from official sources by David Wasserman @Redistrict, Cook Political Report @CookPolitical, https://docs.google.com/spreadsheets/d/133Eb4qQmOxNvtesw2hdVns073R68EZx4SfCn-P4IGQf8/edit#gid=19 (accessed July 31, 2017).

[3] See Bruce A. Ackerman, *We the People*, vol. 1, *Foundations* (Cambridge, MA: Belnap Press, 1991), which distinguishes periods of ordinary lawmaking from "constitutional moments" in which the courts, acting with or without the tacit approval of the legislative and executive branches, effect a major reallocation in the operational distribution of power.

Marshall wrote this book. As a veteran of the political fray at both the national and state (Virginia) levels, "Delegate Bob" knows from experience that we cannot stand idly by while our rights as citizens are diminished by judicial and factional usurpation of the political order. We must actively resist every such effort.

It is a difficult process, to be sure, but it is worth doing. Even if efforts to demand political accountability from the courts, the executive branch, and Congress fail, the attempt will be duly noted—at least for a short time. Writing in 1941, shortly after the politically-disastrous, but enormously influential, "court-packing plan" proposed by Franklin Delano Roosevelt as an explicit way to reign in the Supreme Court, then-Attorney General and future Supreme Court Justice Robert H. Jackson spoke plainly about "the politics of power":

> Constitutional lawsuits are the stuff of power politics in America. The Court may be, and usually is, above party politics and personal politics, but the politics of power is a most important and delicate function, and adjudication of litigation is its technique.[4]

Delegate Marshall's book is about the other—far from delicate—side of what Jackson called "the politics of power": the legislative process. He rightly concludes that legislation is the only process that can get the courts and executive branch under control. His book is essential reading for anyone who really wants to know (or to be reminded about) how the

---

4   Robert H. Jackson, *The Struggle for Judicial Supremacy: A Study of a Crisis in American Power Politics* (1941). 287–88.

game of power politics is *really* played in America.

Delegate Marshall makes two main points. The first is explicit: among its other guarantees, the Constitution of the United States contains two provisions that expressly confirm that the most basic right we have as Americans is the right to govern ourselves.

- Article IV provides that the "United States shall guarantee to every state in this union a republican form of government."[5] Its "plain language" is straightforward: The United States *government*—including the Supreme Court—is obligated to guarantee to the people of each state that laws will be made *by their elected representatives* in accordance with the division of powers set forth in each state's constitution.

- In keeping with that guarantee, the First Amendment explicitly guarantees the right of every citizen "to petition" Congress and his or her state "government for a redress of grievances."[6]

Because Delegate Marshall's second point is implicit, I will take the liberty to put it bluntly: the politics of power are not for the faint of heart. The fictional Mr. Dooley's famous observation that "politics ain't bean-bag"[7] is as true today as it was when he first pontificated from a Chicago pub back in 1895. Since that time, however, the stakes have

---

[5]   U.S. Const. art. IV, §4, cl. 1.

[6]   U.S. Const. amend. I.

[7]   The phrase was first uttered by the fictional Mr. Dooley, created by political columnist Finley Peter Dunne (1867-1936) in the Chicago Evening Post, October 5, 1895. Excerpted in Charles

grown infinitely higher.

Every citizen must understand that the politics of power are played *for keeps* on a variety of fronts in every venue in which an American citizen has the right "to petition for a redress of grievances": in the courts, in the media, in the millions of dollars spent every year on lobbying at the federal, state, and local levels, in the hundreds of millions raised and spent in political campaigns at every level of government, and in the ever-present gaze of both mainstream and social media.

And, thus, we return to the main points discussed in Delegate Marshall's excellent book. Even though there was no national consensus on abortion in 1973 (and there is none today), the Supreme Court legalized it nationwide for the entire duration of pregnancy.[8] Although the voters in twenty-five states overwhelmingly rejected same-sex marriage, the Supreme Court legalized it in all fifty states.[9] Though the nation has been traumatized by the evil of race discrimination since the first slave landed at Jamestown, Virginia, in 1619, the court has consistently held that racial discrimination is permissible whenever elite social conventions demand it.[10] And now the courts are poised to hold that the Constitution and laws of the United States require government

---

Fanning, *Finley Peter Dunne and Mr. Dooley: The Chicago Years* (Lexington, KY: University Press of Kentucky, 1978). Mr. Dooley's full statement: "Sure, politics ain't bean-bag. 'Tis a man's game, an' women, childer, cripples an' prohybitionists 'd do well to keep out iv it."

[8]   Roe v. Wade, 410 U.S. 113 (1973).

[9]   Obergefell v. Hodges, 576 U.S. ___, 135 S. Ct. 2584 (2015).

[10] The court has long approved the use of racial discrimination to accomplish social goals. In Plessy v. Ferguson, 163 U.S. 537

affirmation of those who self-identify as transgender. The list can be multiplied over many years and issues, but one theme is clear: America's cultural and political elites of both parties much prefer the court's approach to the politics of power than the bare-knuckled variety suggested by Delegate Marshall. But "Delegate Bob's" approach is nothing other than that envisioned by the Founding Fathers of this great country.

(1896), which approved the concept of "separate but equal", the court found it "reasonable" that Louisiana would legislate "with reference to the established usages, customs, and traditions of the people, and with a view to the promotion of their comfort, and the preservation of the public peace and good order." 163 U.S. at 550. In Brown v. Board of Education, 347 U.S. 483, 492-93 (1954), the court *rejected* the plea of Louise Brown and her parents that she be admitted to the public school closest to her home without regard to her race.

In approaching this problem [of school segregation], we cannot turn the clock back to 1868 when the Amendment was adopted, or even to 1896 when Plessy v. Ferguson was written. We must consider public education in the light of its full development and its present place in American life throughout the Nation. *Only in this way can it be determined if segregation in public schools deprives these plaintiffs of the equal protection of the laws.* . . . We conclude that *in the field of public education* the doctrine of 'separate but equal' has no place. Separate educational facilities are inherently unequal. (Brown I, 347 U.S. at 492-93, 495, emphasis added)

See Gomperts v. Chase, 404 U.S. 1237, 1240 (1971) (opinion of Douglas, J., sitting as circuit justice denying a motion for preliminary injunction pending the filing of a petition for certiorari) noting that "Plessy v. Ferguson has not yet been overruled on its mandate that separate facilities be equal." Today, racial discrimination is *permissible*: "A university may institute a race-conscious admissions program as a means of obtaining 'the educational benefits that flow from student body diversity.'" Fisher v. Univ. of Texas at Austin, 136 S. Ct. 2198, 2210 (2016).

Power Politics in Practice:
Voter Apathy and Political Stasis

As these words are written in late July 2017, the received wisdom is that the American electoral and political systems are "broken."[11] While it is unclear *why* Americans have soured on the process, their "negativity toward the election process does not seem to be based on the view that there is a dearth of good candidates."[12] It therefore seems implausible—if not impossible—for "ordinary Americans" to win in the game of power politics. Hillary Clinton correctly observed that at least some part of the electorate is comprised of

> people who feel that the government has let them down, the economy has let them down, nobody cares about them, nobody worries about what happens to their lives and their futures, and they're just desperate for change. It doesn't really even matter where it comes from.[13]

---

[11]   See Clare Foran, "How Can the U.S. Fix a Broken Government?", *The Atlantic*, July 16, 2016, https://www.theatlantic.com/politics/archive/2016/07/trump-clinton-washington/491426/ (accessed July 31, 2017); Mark Hensch, "Poll: 66 Percent Think Presidential Election Process is Broken," *The Hill*, March 25, 2016, http://thehill.com/blogs/ballot-box/presidential-races/274281-poll-30-percent-think-presidential-election-process-works (accessed July 31, 2017), citing 2016 poll data from Frank Newport, "Republicans Sour on Way Election Process Is Working," *Gallup*, March 25, 2016, http://www.gallup.com/poll/190292/republicans-sour-election-process-working.aspx?g_source=Election%202016&g_medium=newsfeed&g_campaign=tiles.

[12]   Newport, "Republicans Sour on Way Election Process Is Working."

[13]   Holan, "In Context"; see also Barrett, "How Many Votes Did Trump and Clinton Get?"

Delegate Marshall's book is a reminder that there is no such thing as "the government" or "the economy." In a representative democracy (a republic), *we the people* are the government. In a market economy, *we the people* are the economy. Unless ordinary citizens take charge of their own futures and make it clear that they *do* care "where [change] comes from," the tyranny of the elites Marshall so steadfastly decries will endure.

Marshall points out that it is implausible to expect short-term victories, but they are not impossible. The Hyde Amendment, adopted annually since 1976, is Exhibit A. Like the foundation of a building, short-term successes lead to long-term behavior and personnel changes. The long term is, therefore, where the action is, and the local level is where the battles over taxes, Supreme Court appointments, and foreign policy begins—and must be won.

Marshall reminds us that it all starts in the precinct—in the neighborhood. Quoting Frank Kent's almost ninety-year-old description of the function of the precinct and its importance in American politics, "Delegate Bob" reminds us that:

> Despite computers, television, automated calls, the Internet, social media, and other technical and cultural changes, the precinct is still the fundamental building block of all elections. It remains the place where votes are counted, where voters live and are registered, and the vehicle by which the system identifies voters. "Working the precinct" either by walking door to door or by making live phone calls is still the most efficient and effective way to win elections. Frank Kent's almost ninety-year-old description of the function of the

precinct and its importance is still relevant today: "No clear idea of a party organization can be had unless you start from the bottom. To discuss Presidential politics without understanding precinct politics is an absurdity. It is like trying to solve a problem in trigonometry without having studied arithmetic."[14]

Chapter 13, entitled "The Building Block of American Politics: The Precinct, or All Politics is Local," is thus the beating heart of the book. If you read *nothing else* in the book, read this chapter.

Conclusion

"Delegate Bob" Marshall has written both a playbook and a manifesto for all who dissent from the politically correct view on any number of hot-button cultural issues, including race, gender identity, and the proper role of religion in society. Today, elites demand that the rest of us affirm whatever gender identity a person declares[15] and that we remain silent in the face of such demands because "[t]he place for religion" and moral judgments "is in the private realm of our lives, in our homes, businesses, and places of worship."[16] Tomorrow, they will demand the right to censor speech on the grounds that the stress caused by exposure to ideas or arguments with

---

[14]   See p. 183.

[15]   City of New York, Human Rights Commission, "Gender Identity/Gender Expression: Legal Enforcement Guidance," http://www1.nyc.gov/site/cchr/law/legal-guidances-gender-identity-expression.page#1.

[16]   Erwin Chemerinsky, "The Court after Scalia: The 2016 election and the fate of the wall separating church and state," *SCOTUS-*

which we vehemently disagree means "that speech—at least certain types of speech—can be a form of violence."[17]

My hope, of course, is that "deplorables" like me will read Bob Marshall's book, adjust their conduct, and develop long- and short-term strategies that take aim at the court and the "establishment" politicians who gerrymander their way into safe congressional or state legislative seats and then strive to avoid any vote that will make them take sides on hotly-disputed issues. American voters need to understand that the Founders put the "right to petition for a redress of grievances" into the First Amendment because they knew from bitter experience that "politics ain't beanbag." It is serious business. Those who hold power are determined to keep it. If the 2016 election and its aftermath have taught us anything, it is just how ugly things can get when the elite power structure believes that its power is threatened by candidates and political movements from outside the "mainstream."

Delegate Bob Marshall is one of those outsiders. Read this book, give it to your friends, and get out there and demand change! The Founders built the foundation. It's our job to keep it in repair.

Politics, after all, "ain't bean bag."

Arlington, Virginia, July 31, 2017

blog, September 12, 2016, http://www.scotusblog.com/2016/09/the-court-after-scalia-the-2016-election-and-the-fate-of-the-wall-separating-church-and-state/ (accessed July 30, 2017).

[17] Lisa Feldman Barrett, "When is Speech Violence?" *Sunday Review, New York Times*, July 14, 2017, https://www.nytimes.com/2017/07/14/opinion/sunday/when-is-speech-violence.html (accessed August 4, 2017).

The Present Circumstance

America faces serious moral, legal, and economic decay. Just under 41 percent of all births in the United States now occur outside of marriage.[1] As of 2008, roughly 110 million Americans were reported to have one or more venereal diseases, with nearly 20 million new infections annually.[2] Our national defense establishment is rejecting personal behavioral standards our armed forces had upheld since George Washington was commander of the Continental Army. We are failing to protect the first right in our Declaration of Independence, the right to life.

---

[1]   "Unmarried Childbearing," Centers for Disease Control and Prevention, last modified March 31, 2017, http://www.cdc.gov/nchs/fastats/unmarried-childbearing.htm.

[2]   "CDC Fact Sheet: Incidence, Prevalence, and Cost of Sexually Transmitted Infections in the United States," Centers for Diseases Control and Prevention, February 2013, http://www.cdc.gov/std/stats/sti-estimates-fact-sheet-feb-2013.pdf.

On October 6, 2014, justices of the US Supreme Court decided behind closed doors to overturn the votes of nearly 51 million Americans in thirty-five states who cast the winning votes in referenda to affirm the traditional under-standing of marriage as a union of one man and one woman.[3] The justices' secret decision affirmed, as good, gravely destructive behaviors rejected by Scripture for thousands of years, behaviors that contradict the "Laws of Nature and of Nature's God." Our Founders wove these laws of nature into the fabric of the Declaration of Independence.

The Supreme Court's decisions on life and marriage and the inaction of Congress in allowing these judicial power grabs to proceed as if Congress has no power to stop the shredding of America's social fabric will, perhaps fatally, undermine the bonds of trust and allegiance between the most patriotic of citizens and their government. Actions by officials that destroy the institutions of self-government are not reflective of the America the Founders envisioned, nor an America under God.

Archbishop Charles Chaput of Philadelphia put it this way: "Catholics need to wake up from the illusion that the

---

[3]   Obergefell v. Hodges, 576 U.S. ___ (2015). On Writs of Certiorari to the United States Court of Appeals for the Sixth Circuit Brief of Amici Curiae Public Affairs Campaign And Opinion Expert Frank Schubert and National Organization For Marriage in Support of Respondents, John Eastman, Counsel of Record, Center for Constitutional Jurisprudence, Fowler School of Law, Orange, CA, 92866, April, 2015, votes were cast from 1998–2012, the total votes in favor of man/woman marriage at 51,483,777, versus votes against at 33,015,412. Collectively, that is a margin of 60.93 percent to 39.07 percent, *id.*, an over-whelming landslide in American politics.

America we now live in—not the America of our nostalgia or imagination or best ideals . . .—is somehow friendly to our faith. What we're watching emerge in this country is a new kind of paganism, an atheism with air-conditioning and digital TV. And it is neither tolerant nor morally neutral."[4]

Pope Pius XI wrote an encyclical in 1937 to German Catholics regarding their duties in a Germany growing ever more pagan and more militant toward those opposed to its paganism and racial programs. Speaking of Nazi efforts to divert the youth from the Faith, he wrote:

> It is not enough to be a member of the Church of Christ, one needs to be a living member, in spirit and in truth, i.e., living in the state of grace and in the presence of God, either in innocence or in sincere repentance. . . .
>
> . . . The violation of temples is nigh, and it will be every one's duty to sever his responsibility from the opposite camp, and free his conscience from guilty cooperation with such corruption. The more the enemies attempt to disguise their designs, the more a distrustful vigilance will be needed . . . . Yet do not forget this: none can free you from the responsibility God has placed on you over your children. None of your oppressors, who pretend to relieve you of your duties can answer for you to the eternal Judge, when he will ask: "Where are those I confided to you?" May every

---

4   Charles Chaput, "Disability: A Thread for Weaving Joy," *Public Discourse*, The Witherspoon Institute, January 24, 2012, http://www.thepublicdiscourse.com/2012/01/4575/.

one of you be able to answer: "Of them whom thou
hast given me, I have not lost any one" (John xviii. 9).[5]

The immoral policies of the Nazis were carried out in the
name of the German people. And today, all the moral
offenses promoted and/or countenanced by America's rad-
ically secularist public officials are accomplished and carried
out in the name of the people of the United States.

Simply observing the moral collapse of America is not
an option for persons of faith if only because there are no
"safe" zones; increasingly there is nowhere to hide from or
avoid complicity with the growing demands for allegiance
to and support for the secular policies and practices being
imposed on us by our government. This pernicious demand
for acquiescence extends overseas wherever the United States
goes, even when dispensing charity or foreign aid.

For example, a Catholic bishop in Africa has stated that
the United States government is subjecting his country to
an "ideological colonization" that is seeking to destroy the
African family through extortion-like practices. Because the
government of Nigeria has refused to abandon the moral
teachings of the natural law regarding marriage and the family, the United States, under Barack Obama, declined serious
assistance to Nigeria in its fight against the Islamist terror
group Boko Haram. These strong words came from Bishop
Emmanuel Badejo of Oyo, Nigeria, who stated, "Recently I
was alarmed when I heard Hillary Clinton, as Secretary of
State, say that the United States government was committed
to anything that would push the population control agenda.

---

[5]   Pope Pius XI, Encyclical *Mit Brennender Sorge* (1937), nos. 19, 39.

The United States actually said it would help Nigeria with Boko Haram only if we modify our laws concerning homosexuality, family planning, and birth control. It's very clear that a cultural imperialism exists."[6]

Boko Haram is the Nigerian terror group that kidnapped 276 school girls from a remote boarding school in mid-April 2014. Several months later, the "leader" of Boko Haram, Abubakar Shekau, announced via a video that more than 200 of the school girls had been married off and "converted" to Islam. He added that, "You people should understand that we only obey Allah, we tread the path of the Prophet. We hope to die on this path . . . . Our goal is the garden of eternal bliss"[7]

The US Department of State designated Boko Haram as a terrorist group in November 2013, noting, "Boko Haram is a Nigeria-based militant group with links to al-Qa'ida in the Islamic Maghreb (AQIM) that is responsible for thousands of deaths in northeast and central Nigeria over the last several years including targeted killings of civilians."[8] Yet the Obama administration's main concern in terror-plagued

---

6   Diane Montagna, "US Won't Help Fight Boko Haram Until Nigeria Accepts Homosexuality, Birth Control, Bishop Says," *Aleteia*, February 17, 2015, http://www.aleteia.org/en/religion/article/us-wont-help-fight-boko-haram-until-nigeria-accepts-homosexuality-birth-control-bishop-says-5344466437144576.

7   "Boko Haram leader says kidnapped girls married off, converted to Islam," Fox News, November 2, 2014, http://www.foxnews.com/world/2014/11/02/boko-haram-denies-truce-kidnapped-girls-married/.

8   "Terrorist Designations of Boko Haram and Ansaru," US Department of State, November 13, 2013, https://www.state.gov/j/ct/rls/other/des/266565.htm.

Nigeria was to ensure teen access to birth control, abortion, and homosexual marriage!

Domestically, things are no better for cultural conservatives: Obamacare[9] compels all Americans to pay for abortion pill coverage in their individual family insurance policy, including for minors who will be provided abortifacient birth control behind their parents' backs due to privacy laws, birth control that will be paid for by the parents' own insurance policy! The attempt by the Obama administration to compel Catholic and other religious institutions to provide insurance coverage with provisos which clearly violate their tradition's religious teaching shows how little respect President Obama and his supporters had for individual conscience and faith.

In the United States today, there is a "full-court press" to promote practices that many Christians find abhorrent. It is not just a hostile government that is doing this. Businesses, both small and large, are either lining up behind or being forced to support the LGBTQ agenda as a condition of staying in business. For example, the Colorado Civil Rights Commission ruled that Masterpiece Cakeshop owner Jack Phillips must comply with requests from homosexual couples to make cakes for their "weddings" despite his religious objections to such legal unions. In the 2012 case, Colorado did not recognize same-sex marriages but did recognize same-sex civil unions. Phillips was ordered to submit quarterly reports for two years to demonstrate his change of policy. His employees will have to undergo sexual attitude

---

9   With the election of Donald Trump as president, efforts are underway to repeal Obamacare.

restructuring. Phillips also has to provide the names of any bakery clients he turns away.[10] As of June 2017, the Supreme Court had agreed to hear the case. However, Phillips has lost much business as a result and no longer does wedding cakes.

While Main Street resists, big business has embraced the LGBTQ agenda in a very aggressive way. Corporate America filed an amicus brief on March 4, 2015, in support of same sex marriage advocates petitioning the US Supreme Court. It was signed by 379 large American corporations and urges the United States Supreme Court to impose same sex marriage on all Americans regardless of their religious or moral objections.[11]

---

10   Zahira Torres, "Civil rights commission says Lakewood baker discriminated against gay couple," *The Denver Post,* May 30, 2014, http://www.denverpost.com/news/ci_25865871/civil-rights-commission-says-lakewood-baker-discriminated-against.

11   Obergefell v. Hodges, 576 U.S. ___ (2015)(Nos. 14-556, 14-562, 14-574), http://sblog.s3.amazonaws.com/wp-content/uploads/2015/03/14-556tsac379EmployersandOrganizations.pdf. The following are some of those listed as Amici Curiae in support of petitioners: Aetna Inc., Alaska Airlines, Alcoa Inc., Amazon Services Inc., Amazon.com, American Airlines, American Apparel, American Express, Apple Inc. Aramark, AT&T, Bank of America, The Bank of New York Mellon Corporation, Barclays, Barnes & Noble, Bloomberg L.P., Bristol-Myers Squibb Company, Cablevision Systems, Capital One Financial, CBS Corporation, CIGNA Corporation, Cisco Systems, Inc., Citigroup Inc., The Coca-Cola Company, Colgate-Palmolive, Comcast, ConAgra Foods, Corning Inc., Cox Enterprises, Inc., Credit Suisse Securities (USA), CVS Health Corporation, Dana-Farber Cancer Institute, Delta Air Lines, Deutsche Bank AG, Dow Chemical Company, DuPont, eBay, Facebook, General Electric, General Mills, GlaxoSmithKline, Google, Hartford Financial Services, Hewlett-Packard, Intel, JPMorgan Chase, Johnson & Johnson, Kimberly-Clark, Levi Strauss, Marriott International,

Though that may surprise you, it should not, for many major US corporations regularly give monetary support to the Human Rights Campaign (HRC), which is the main homosexual lobbying organization behind the aggressive nationwide LGBTQ efforts for same-sex marriage and other initiatives. Such HRC litigation and outreach requires money, big money. Major corporate donors stumble over themselves to help HRC. Corporate supporters can be found at the website noted below[12] as can the corporate sponsors of the 2017 Human Right Campaign Los Angeles Gala Dinner.[13] Christians should know these names and prayerfully consider ways in which to make our displeasure known.

And there are ways. Recently, Target was and continues to be the object of a nationwide boycott led by the American Family Association over its bathroom policies related to the transgender issue. Boycotts are traditionally a tool of the Left, but it may be hoped that America's Christians will make their feelings known to corporate America in the only language it speaks, the language of the bottom line in dollars and cents.

Massachusetts Mutual Life Insurance, McGraw Hill Financial, Microsoft, Moody's, Morgan Stanley, The New England Patriots, New York Life, NIKE, Northrop Grumman, Oracle America, PepsiCo, Pfizer, Procter & Gamble, The San Francisco Giants, St. Jude Medical, Staples, Starbucks, Symantec, The Tampa Bay Rays, Target, Twitter, United Airlines, The Walt Disney Company, Wells Fargo & Co., Xerox, and others.

[12]   Corporate Partners, The Human Rights Campaign, http://www. hrc.org/the-hrc-story/corporate-partners.

[13]   Human Rights Campaign, 2017Dinner Gala, http://www. hrcladinner.com/confirmed-sponsors/.

When homosexual marriage is called the "Law of the Land" and pronounced a civil right, if you or a family member work for one of the companies demanding that the Supreme Court replace the laws of nature and nature's God with such a conception of "marriage," will you be able to keep your job if you express your views to your congressman, or write a letter to the editor, or call a talk show, or remove your child from LGBTQ agenda-driven family life sex-ed classes, or distribute a petition in opposition to the said agenda?

That the CEOs of these major companies fail to understand the relationship of personal morality to successful business is striking, but not surprising. Unlike trendy corporate CEOs, George Washington, in his 1789 first inaugural address, linked personal virtue to national happiness and security: "There is no truth more thoroughly established, than that there exists in the economy and course of nature, an indissoluble union between virtue and happiness. . . . The propitious smiles of Heaven, can never be expected on a nation that disregards the eternal rules of order and right, which Heaven itself has ordained."[14]

Washington also noted in his 1789 inaugural address that, "the destiny of the Republican model of Government, [is] . . . finally staked, on the experiment entrusted to the hands of the American people."[15] We the people are ultimately responsible for the government of our country, not

---

[14]   George Washington, "Washington's Inaugural Address of 1789," National Archives and Records Administration, http://www. archives.gov/exhibits/american_originals/inaugtxt.html.

[15]   Ibid.

our leaders, and not Congress.

Thomas Jefferson agreed with George Washington thirty-one years later. He said, "I know no safe depositary of the ultimate powers of the society but the people themselves."[16]

In a similar vein, the *Catechism of the Catholic Church* states, "It is not the role of the Pastors of the Church to intervene directly in the political structuring and organization of social life. This task is part of the vocation of the *lay faithful,* acting on their own initiative with their fellow citizens."[17]

Baltimore Sun newspaperman Frank R. Kent—Democratic Party historian, influential columnist, and New Deal critic—noted in 1923 how a political power elite takes charge. Kent wrote, "Any straight story of politics must show . . . that the power of political machines and political bosses is exactly equal to the tolerance of the people; that the extent of domination and control is accurately measured by the indifference and ignorance of the voters; that it is the enormous number of non-voters who make powerful political organizations possible."[18]

Kent saw the practical consequences of widespread ignorance of the workings of government. Jefferson asserted that if citizens are "not enlightened enough to exercise their control with a wholesome discretion, the remedy is . . . to inform their discretion by education. This is the true corrective of

---

[16]   *The Jeffersonian Cyclopedia*, ed. John P. Foley (New York: Funk & Wagnalls, 1900), no. 6566.

[17]   *Catechism of the Catholic Church* 2442.

[18]   Frank R. Kent, *The Great Game of Politics* (Buffalo, NY: Economics Books, Smith, Keynes and Marshall, 1959), p. viii.

abuses of constitutional power."[19]

And that is my goal in presenting *Reclaiming the Republic* to the reading public. This book shares the knowledge I have gleaned and acquired over the years through both practical experience and wide reading. My political education dates from the first time I volunteered in a political campaign in 1960 and extends through my taking part in high school political clubs and political demonstrations, teaching American history, organizing pro-life legislative efforts, reviewing grants in the executive office of the president, working for six years as a congressional aide (for one Democrat and two Republicans), analyzing public policy, and winning thirteen elections to the Virginia House of Delegates, the oldest continuously existing legislative body in the Western world.

The Founders of America, who measured their own actions and those of others by the laws of nature and of nature's God, set up our electoral system as a vehicle of self-government to secure the rights given to us by our Creator. This requires patriots and people of faith to have political and civic knowledge as well as the spirit and willingness to work for the common good. We need to know how laws are enacted and how elections are conducted, and we cannot be naïve. We must understand that a spirit alien to the Founders, to say nothing of Jesus Christ, now animates and guides many who are working within the institutions of government to undermine those laws of nature and of nature's God.

Longtime Democratic speaker of the house Tip O'Neill, from Massachusetts, once quipped, "All politics is local." In

---

[19]   *The Jeffersonian Cyclopedia*, ed. John P. Foley (New York: Funk & Wagnalls, 1900), no. 6566.

many ways, he was right. Restoring our Founders' vision for America starts in our neighborhoods where we cast our votes because we are most influential where we live. Increasingly today, as corporations have entered the culture wars, we can also exert great influence by where we shop and don't shop. Target Corporation is learning a difficult lesson as Christians across the country are taking their business elsewhere because of their stance taken with regards to the transgender bathroom issue.

If believers hesitate to shape the public arena now, it will be much harder to do so later as our opponents grow stronger in their determination and tighten their grip on the levers of power. Truly, we should have acted in concert and with dedication years ago. That said, we are not now in the circumstance of our fellow Christians in the Middle East who are daily confronted by heavily-armed, conscienceless terrorist groups with an overt agenda to destroy the Faith and those who profess it. Nevertheless, we are confronted by opponents who want to make us just as powerless and irrelevant through much more subtle means.

Everyone has gifts and can devote some amount of time to work to improve the common good, including children not old enough to vote. Every person can contribute something to this struggle. Recall the parable of the talents and the servant who hid his "small" gifts because he was afraid of his taskmaster's criticism. When the taskmaster returned, he demanded an accounting of the servant's inaction (see Mt 25:13–40).

Archbishop Charles Chaput emphasized that Jesus explained that loving God with your whole heart and your neighbor as yourself were the greatest commandments. He said, what "love means in practice can be found in the words Jesus used to describe his true disciples: *leaven in the world, salt of the earth, light of nations.* These are words of mission; a language not of good intentions, but of conscious *behavior.*"[20]

No matter the level of public civic involvement to which you can commit—whether it is trying to educate a neighbor, writing a letter to the editor, calling a talk show, attending a town hall public forum or candidate debate, going to a school parent-teacher conference, meeting with your elected officials, taking part in a corporate boycott, supporting a ballot question, donating to a campaign, calling voters or walking door-to-door on behalf of a candidate, running a precinct for a candidate, or becoming a candidate yourself— this book will convince you of the imperative for action and provide a blueprint to guide you in your efforts to reshape the culture to uphold the laws of nature and of nature's God.

In terms of the ballot, it is not necessary to convince a majority of all Americans, or even a majority of all those registered to vote, to change the direction of our country. Not all American citizens are registered to vote, and not all of those who are registered come out to vote in elections. We merely need to convince a small portion of voters to actively support candidates who support our values.

And don't forget that many voters will support a pro-marriage or pro-life candidate for reasons unrelated to these

---

[20]   Charles Chaput, *Render Unto Caesar: Serving the Nation by Living Our Catholic Beliefs in Political Life* (New York: Image Books, 2008), p. 50.

moral concerns, such as something very particular and local like a traffic issue. Their vote can count as much as yours toward restoring the moral foundation of American government.

Government "of, by, and for the people" does not run on autopilot. We can never have the attitude of despair that "one vote doesn't count" or "it's impossible to change the system!" Prayer and action can turn our country around! The Founders thought so. They appealed to heaven in the Declaration of Independence to the "Supreme Judge of the world for the rectitude of our intentions," and they petitioned God and sought "the protection of divine Providence." We should do no less!

Introduction

In the Declaration of Independence, Thomas Jefferson wrote of the "Laws of Nature and of Nature's God" that authorized the establishment of self-government for the American nation apart from Great Britain. Jefferson added, "We hold these truths to be self-evident, that all men are created equal, that they are endowed by their Creator with certain unalienable Rights, that among these are Life, Liberty and the pursuit of Happiness."

Jefferson, in the Declaration, wrote that the choice and the form of government may justly be decided by the citizens at large: "That to secure these rights, Governments are instituted among Men, deriving their just powers from the consent of the governed,—That whenever any Form of Government becomes destructive of these ends, it is the Right of the People to alter or to abolish it, and to institute new Government, laying its foundation on such principles and organizing its powers in such form, as to them shall seem most likely to effect their Safety and Happiness."

Similarly, Pope Pius XI, in 1931, wrote, "On the form of political government, . . . men are free to choose whatever form they please, provided that proper regard is had for the requirements of justice and of the common good."[1]

Leo XIII previously had stated:

> Those who may be placed over the State may in cer-
> tain cases be chosen by the will and decision of the
> multitude, without opposition to or impugning of the
> Catholic doctrine. And by this choice, in truth, the
> ruler is designated. . . .
>
> There is no question here respecting forms of gov-
> ernment, for there is no reason why the Church should
> not approve of the chief power being held by one man
> or by more, provided only it be just, and that it tend to
> the common advantage. Wherefore, so long as justice
> be respected, the people are not hindered from choos-
> ing for themselves that form of government which
> suits best either their own disposition, or the institu-
> tions and customs of their ancestors.[2]

Trust is the basis of respect between persons, and knowledge of how leaders act on behalf of their citizens is a necessary condition for government to function fairly. Pope John
Paul II explained this necessity as follows: "In the political
sphere, it must be noted that truthfulness in the relations
between those governing and those governed, openness in
public administration, impartiality in the service of the body
politic, respect for the rights of political adversaries . . . these
are principles which are primarily rooted in, and in fact
derive their singular urgency from, the transcendent value

---

[1]   Pope Pius XI, Encyclical *Quadragesimo Anno* (1931), no. 86.
[2]   Pope Leo XIII, Encyclical *Diuturnum* (1881), nos. 6, 7.

of the person and the objective moral demands of the functioning of States."[3]

At the foundation of the American Revolution and in the
formation of our national government, America's revolution-
ary leaders explained to the world why we were separating
from Great Britain. And in the establishment of our national
government at the Philadelphia Constitutional Convention
of 1787, opportunities for citizens to learn of the actions of
their elected officials were made part of the process of providing for accountability. Our Declaration of Independence
states, "When . . . it becomes necessary for one people to
dissolve the political bands which have connected them with
another, . . . a decent respect to the opinions of mankind
requires that they should declare the causes which impel
them to the separation. . . . Let Facts be submitted to a candid world."

Accountability to the citizens was woven into the original Constitution, which provided a way for citizens to learn
how their representatives voted on important matters. "Each
House shall keep a Journal of its Proceedings, and from time
to time publish the same, excepting such Parts as may in
their Judgment require Secrecy; and the Yeas and Nays of the
Members of either House on any question shall, at the Desire
of one fifth of those Present, be entered on the Journal."[4]

---

3   Pope John Paul II, Encyclical *Veritas Splendor* (1993), no. 101.
4   U.S. Const. art. I, § 5, cl. 3.

Unjust Laws Are Void

Contemporary legal positivists, who think that law is whatever a judge says it is, will be confounded by the proposition that unjust laws are void and should not be obeyed. American and British legal heritage from 1776 to the beginning of the twentieth century held that a "higher law" governed enactments of legislatures and decisions of courts. In 1790, British legal writer Sir William Blackstone was the most highly read commentator on the common law in America. His commentary stated, "This law of nature, being co-eval [same date of origin] with mankind and dictated by God himself, is of course superior in obligation to any other. It is binding over all the globe, in all countries, and at all times: no human laws are of any validity, if contrary to this; and such of them as are valid derive all their force, and all their authority, mediately or immediately, from this original."[5]

Virginia's George Mason, delegate to the 1787 Philadelphia Constitutional Convention and coauthor with James Madison of the Bill of Rights, elaborated on Blackstone's observations on the nullity of a law that violates the Creator's laws of nature. Mason made these points arguing against a pro-slave law in 1772 before the General Court of Virginia: "All acts of legislature apparently contrary to natural right and justice are, in our laws, and must be in the nature of things, considered as void. The laws of nature are the laws of God; Whose authority can be superseded by no power on earth. A legislature must not obstruct our obedience to

---

[5]   William Blackstone, *Commentaries on the Laws of England*, Introduction, § 2, Avalon Project, Yale University, http://avalon. law.yale.edu/18th_century/blackstone_intro.asp#1.

Him from whose punishments they cannot protect us. All human constitutions which contradict His laws, we are in conscience bound to disobey. Such have been the adjudications of our courts of Justice."[6]

While the united American colonies were still at war with Great Britain, Jefferson reflected on the presence of slavery in Virginia and in the United States. He feared the divine retribution that natural justice required for the moral error of man's laws allowing that another's liberty may be stolen through the legal institution of slavery in defiance of the divine law that all men are born free and are entitled to liberty as a rule of nature:

> Can the liberties of a nation be thought secure when we have removed their only firm basis, a conviction in the minds of the people that these liberties are of the gift of God? That they are not to be violated but with his wrath? Indeed, I tremble for my country when I reflect that God is just; that his justice cannot sleep forever; that considering numbers, nature and natural means only, a revolution of the wheel of fortune, an exchange of situation is among possible events; that it may become probable by supernatural interference! The Almighty has no attribute which can take side with us in such a contest.[7]

---

[6] Robin v. Hardaway, 2 VA (2 Jefferson) 109, 114, (1772), quoted in Charles Rice, *50 Questions on the Natural Law* (San Francisco: Ignatius Press, 1993), p. 34.

[7] Adrienne Koch and William Peden, eds., *The Life and Selected Writings of Thomas Jefferson: Including the Autobiography, the Declaration of Independence & His Public and Private Letters* (New York: Random House, 1944), pp. 278–79.

President George Washington, in what has become known
as his (September 1796) Farewell Address, echoed Jefferson's
sentiments regarding the link between personal and public
morality and resulting national happiness: "Can it be that
Providence has not connected the permanent felicity of a
nation with its virtue? The experiment, at least, is recom-
mended by every sentiment which ennobles human nature.
Alas! Is it rendered impossible by its vices?"[8]

While individuals experience judgment upon passage
from this life into eternal life, Jefferson and Washington
believed that nations reap their reward or punishment here
on earth. In a similar vein, the United States Conference
of Catholic Bishops commented on the prophet Zephaniah,
who was a contemporary of King Josiah (640–609 BC). The
Book of Zephaniah affirms that certain national calami-
ties resulted from the sins of the people and their leaders:
"Zephaniah's prophecy of judgment on Judah and Jerusalem emphasizes . . . the devastation and death that divine
judgment will bring. . . . a time of darkness, of anguish and
distress, of destruction and plunder of cities, and of threat to
all life, human and animal alike. The major sins motivating
this judgment are Judah's worship of other deities . . . and its
unjust and abusive leadership."[9]

Since actions have consequences, participation in intrin-
sically evil actions, even if permitted or required by civil
authority, must be resisted. Accordingly, Pope St. John Paul

---

[8]   George Washington, "Washington's Farewell Address 1796," The
       Avalon Project, Yale University, http://avalon.law.yale.edu/18th_
       century/washing.asp.
[9]   Zep Introduction (NABRE).

II reaffirmed this natural law right against collaboration with evil, especially when sanctioned or commanded by civil authorities:

> All people of good will, are called upon under grave obligation of conscience not to cooperate formally in practices which, even if permitted by civil legislation, are contrary to God's law. Indeed, from the moral standpoint, it is never licit to cooperate formally in evil. Such cooperation occurs when an action, either by its very nature or by the form it takes in a concrete situation, can be defined as a direct participation in an act against innocent human life or a sharing in the immoral intention of the person committing it. . . .
>
> To refuse to take part in committing an injustice is not only a moral duty; it is also a basic human right. . . . What is at stake therefore is an essential right which, precisely as such, should be acknowledged and protected by civil law. . . . Those who have recourse to conscientious objection must be protected not only from legal penalties but also from any negative effects on the legal, disciplinary, financial and professional plane.[10]

While there is no mention of original sin in the Declaration of Independence or the United States Constitution, man's propensity to violate the moral law is assumed and, in fact, becomes the basis for structuring governmental powers

---

[10]   Pope St. John Paul II, Encyclical *Evangelium Vitae* (1995), no. 74.

in a particular manner.

This assumption was articulated by James Madison in the *Federalist Papers*, portions of which essays would never pass the sensitivities of opinion page editors of our modern newspapers. Madison collaborated with Alexander Hamilton and John Jay in the project to secure approval of the Constitution:[11]

> But what is government itself, but the greatest of all reflections on human nature? If men were angels, no government would be necessary. If angels were to govern men, neither external nor internal controls on government would be necessary. In framing a government which is to be administered by men over men, the great difficulty lies in this: you must first enable the government to control the governed; and in the next place oblige it to control itself. A dependence on the people is, no doubt, the primary control on the government; but experience has taught mankind the necessity of auxiliary precautions.[12]

Madison's answer to providing some control over this human propensity is to divide power: "This policy of supplying, by opposite and rival interests, the defect of better

---

[11]   Alexander Hamilton, John Jay, and James Madison, *The Federalist*, ed. George W. Carey and James McClellan (Indianapolis: Liberty Fund, 2001), p. xlv. Madison is writing of angels in the sense of the good angels and the opposite of devils who are also angels but not good ones; nor is Madison challenging Aquinas's thinking concerning the ordering power or "government" among angels according to their functions and hierarchies.

[12]   Ibid., p. 269.

motives, might be traced through the whole system of human affairs, private as well as public. We see it particularly displayed in all the subordinate distributions of power, where the constant aim is to divide and arrange the several offices in such a manner as that each may be a check on the other that the private interest of every individual may be a sentinel over the public rights."[13]

Madison, in *The Federalist*, criticizes the accumulation of governmental powers: "The accumulation of all powers, legislative, executive, and judiciary, in the same hands, whether of one, a few, or many, and whether hereditary, self-appointed, or elective, may justly be pronounced the very definition of tyranny."[14]

Separation of Powers

The practical answer to this dilemma, according to James Madison—fourth president of the United States, delegate from Virginia to the federal Constitutional Convention, father of the Constitution and the Bill of Rights—was to divide the powers of government into different departments that could act as a check on each other: "The efficacy of various principles is now well understood. . . . The regular distribution of power into distinct departments; the introduction of legislative balances and checks; the institution of courts composed of judges holding their offices during good behavior; the representation of the people in the legislature by deputies of their own election. . . . They are means, and

---

[13]   Ibid.
[14]   Ibid., p. 249.

powerful means, by which the excellences of republican government may be retained and its imperfections lessened or avoided."[15]

Additionally, Madison wanted the principle of the division of powers to be structurally applied by the state governments as a check on abuses by the federal government.

> The powers delegated by the proposed Constitution to the federal government are few and defined. Those which are to remain in the State governments are numerous and indefinite. The former will be exercised principally on external objects, as war, peace, negotiation, and foreign commerce; with which last the power of taxation will, for the most part, be connected. The powers reserved to the several States will extend to all the objects which, in the ordinary course of affairs, concern the lives, liberties, and properties of the people, and the internal order, improvement, and prosperity of the State.[16]

Another Founding Father, Alexander Hamilton, went further than Madison, even suggesting that state governments would, by their natural competition with the national government, be guardians against federal encroachments even, if necessary, through the use of arms: "The State legislatures, who will always be not only vigilant but suspicious and jealous guardians of the rights of the citizens against encroachments from the federal government, will constantly have their attention awake to the conduct of the national rulers,

---

[15]   Ibid., p. 38.
[16]   Ibid., p. 241.

and will be ready enough, if any thing improper appears, to sound the alarm to the people, and not only to be the VOICE, but, if necessary, the ARM of their discontent."[17]

Perfection in Legislation

On September 17, 1789, the last day of the Philadelphia Convention, Benjamin Franklin, signer of the Declaration of Independence and delegate to the Constitutional Convention from Pennsylvania, urged his fellow delegates to support the final draft of the Constitution despite his serious reservations. Franklin, addressing the president of the Convention, George Washington, spoke from written notes:

> Mr. President, I confess that there are several parts of this constitution which I do not at present approve, but I am not sure I shall never approve them. . . . In these sentiments, Sir, I agree to this Constitution with all its faults, if they are such; because I think a general Government necessary for us. . . . I doubt too whether any other Convention we can obtain, may be able to make a better Constitution. For when you assemble a number of men to have the advantage of their joint wisdom, you inevitably assemble with those men, all their prejudices, their passions . . . and their selfish views. . . . It therefore astonishes me, Sir, to find this system approaching so near to perfection as it does. . . . Thus I consent, Sir, to this Constitution because I

---

[17]   Ibid., p. 130.

expect no better, and because I am not sure, that it is not the best.[18]

Pope St. John Paul II also addressed the question of deficiencies in legislation and the licitness, at times, of support for such proposals by lawmakers. He noted:

> A particular problem of conscience can arise in cases where a legislative vote would be decisive for the passage of a more restrictive law, aimed at limiting the number of authorized abortions, in place of a more permissive law already passed or ready to be voted on. Such cases are not infrequent. . . . When it is not possible to overturn or completely abrogate a pro-abortion law, an elected official, whose absolute personal opposition to procured abortion was well known, could licitly support proposals aimed at limiting the harm done by such a law and at lessening its negative consequences at the level of general opinion and public morality. This does not in fact represent an illicit cooperation with an unjust law, but rather a legitimate and proper attempt to limit its evil aspects.[19]

Caesar, God, and the Bill of Rights

On September 12, 1789, as the final version of the Constitution was being considered for submission to the Congress

---

[18]   James Madison, *Notes of Debates in the Federal Convention of 1787 Reported by James Madison* (New York: W. W. Norton, 1966), p. 653.

[19]   Pope St. John Paul II, Encyclical *Evangelium Vitae* (1995), 73.

for ratification by conventions in the states, Virginia's George Mason objected on the grounds that "he wished the plan had been prefaced with a Bill of Rights, & would second a Motion if made for the purpose. It would give great quiet to the people; and with the aid of the State declarations, a bill might be prepared in a few hours. Mr. GERRY concurred in the idea & moved for a Committee to prepare a Bill of Rights."[20]

Mason lost his motion on a vote of ten states voting no with one abstaining.[21] Shortly thereafter, on September 17, Mason announced he would not sign the Constitution.[22] On November 22, 1789, Mason's objections to the Constitution were published in the Virginia Journal at the request of George Washington's secretary, Tobias Lear, who wanted to publicly refute Mason.

Mason's first sentence read, "There is no Declaration of Rights, and the laws of the general government being paramount to the laws and constitution of the several States, the Declarations of Rights in the separate States are no security. Nor are the people secured even in the enjoyment of the benefit of the common law."[23]

Mason eventually won his point as it became apparent in state ratifying conventions that the Constitution as proposed would not be approved unless a Bill of Rights were

---

[20] Madison, *Notes of Debates in the Federal Convention of 1787*, p. 630.
[21] Ibid.
[22] Ibid., p. 631.
[23] George Mason, "George Mason's Objections to the Constitution," Gunston Hall, http://gunstonhall.org/library/archives/manuscripts/objections.html.

added to it.[24] When the first Congress sent what became the Bill of Rights to the states for ratification, the resolution was prefaced with the following words: "The Conventions of a number of States, having at the time of their adopting the Constitution, expressed a desire, in order to prevent misconstruction or abuse of its powers, that further declaratory and restrictive clauses should be added."[25]

The first ten amendments to the US Constitution are called the Bill of Rights. But what are these rights deemed so important to liberty by many of the Founders? The First, Ninth, and Tenth Amendments protect the rights of citizens and persons from excessive governmental actions: "Congress shall make no law respecting an establishment of religion, or prohibiting the free exercise thereof; or abridging the freedom of speech, or of the press; or the right of the people peaceably to assemble."[26] "The enumeration in the Constitution, of certain rights, shall not be construed to deny or disparage others retained by the people."[27] "The powers not delegated to the United States by the Constitution, nor prohibited by it to the States, are reserved to the States respectively, or to the people."[28]

---

[24] Michael Allen Gillespie and Michael Lienesch, eds., *Ratifying the Constitution* (Lawrence, KS: University of Kansas Press, 1989), pp. 10–15.

[25] Helen Veit, Kenneth Bowling, and Charlene Bickford, eds., *Creating the Bill of Rights: The Documentary Record from the First Federal Congress* (Baltimore: Johns Hopkins University Press, 1991), p. 3.

[26] U.S. Const. amend. I.

[27] U.S. Const. amend. IX.

[28] U.S. Const. amend. X.

Christ's words "Render to Caesar the things that are Caesar's, and to God the things that are God's"[29] assume that while men have obligations to the civil order, there are spheres of human life that are not any business of Caesar. Pope Leo XIII noted this point:

> The contention . . . that the civil government should . . . intrude into and exercise intimate control over the family and the household is a great and pernicious error. True . . . if within . . . the household there occur grave disturbance of mutual rights, public authority should intervene to force each party to yield to the other its proper due. . . . But the rulers of the commonwealth must go no further. . . . Paternal authority can be neither abolished nor absorbed by the State; for it has the same source as human life itself. . . . The socialists, therefore, in setting aside the parent and setting up a State supervision, act against natural justice, and destroy the structure of the home.[30]

Pope Leo XIII also affirmed the natural right of private organizations, clubs, or associations to exist within the state:

> These lesser societies and the larger society differ . . . , because their immediate purpose and aim are different. Civil society exists for the common good. . . . But societies which are formed in the bosom of the commonwealth are styled *private*. . . . "Now, a private society," says St. Thomas . . . , "is one which is formed for

---

29   Mk 12:17.
30   Pope Leo XIII, Encyclical *Rerum Novarum* (1891), no. 14.

the purpose of carrying out private objects; as when two or three enter into partnership with the view of trading in common." Private societies . . . cannot . . . be absolutely . . . prohibited by public authority. For, to enter into a "society" of this kind is the natural right of man; and the State has for its office to protect natural rights, not to destroy them.[31]

Pope Pius XI affirmed the long-held principal of subsidiarity, described in the following quotation. The principle applies in authorizing local governments, rather than a large central government, to address local concerns. And even before local civil government acts, private individuals and associations should be left to first address local situations. Pius XI noted:

As history abundantly proves, . . . many things which were done by small associations in former times cannot be done now save by large associations. Still, that most weighty principle, which cannot be set aside or changed, remains fixed and unshaken in social philosophy: Just as it is gravely wrong to take from individuals what they can accomplish by their own initiative and industry and give it to the community, so also it is an injustice and at the same time a grave evil and disturbance of right order to assign to a greater and higher association what lesser and subordinate organizations can do. . . .

The supreme authority of the State ought, therefore, to let subordinate groups handle matters and

---

[31]   Ibid., no. 51.

concerns of lesser importance, which would otherwise dissipate its efforts greatly.[32]

The signers of the Declaration of Independence were acutely aware of the necessity for divine assistance in the affairs of governments. The last sentence of that document reads, "And for the support of this Declaration, with a firm reliance on the protection of divine Providence, we mutually pledge to each other our Lives, our Fortunes and our sacred Honor."

James Madison, writing in Federalist 37, reflected on the many obstacles and opportunities for division and dissent among the delegates at the Philadelphia Convention. He believed the delegates were aided by Divine Providence and said so in attempting to convince fellow Americans to approve the new Constitution: "The real wonder is that so many difficulties should have been surmounted, and surmounted with unanimity almost as unprecedented as it must have been unexpected. It is impossible for any man of candor to reflect on this circumstance without partaking of the astonishment. It is impossible for the man of pious reflection not to perceive in it a finger of that Almighty hand which has been so frequently and signally extended to our relief in the critical stages of the revolution."[33]

---

[32] Pope Pius XI, Encyclical *Quadragesimo Anno* (1931), nos. 79, 80.

[33] Hamilton, Jay, and Madison, *The Federalist*, pp. 184–85.

PART ONE

Think Like the Founders

CHAPTER 1

Religious Liberty

*Congress shall make no law respecting an establishment of religion,
or prohibiting the free exercise thereof.*
First Amendment

An understanding of how the Founding Fathers arrived
at the religious liberty and conscience protections of
the First Amendment is necessary if we are to effectively
address the efforts of political progressives who would make
us complicit in calling good evil and evil good (see Is 5:20).
This history must be understood if we are to counter current
assumptions about the role of religion in public life now.

The road to what became the first ten amendments to
the Constitution, or the Bill of Rights, especially the First
Amendment with its protections for religious liberty, was
"paved" in many respects by the state of Virginia in general
and three Virginians in particular: George Mason, Thomas
Jefferson, and James Madison.

On January 16, 1786, the Virginia General Assembly
enacted the Statute for Religious Freedom, also a legislative
precursor to the First Amendment. The measure, which is
still part of the Code of Virginia, provides

that all men shall be free . . . in matters of Religion, and that the same shall in no wise diminish, enlarge or affect their civil capacities . . . and . . . therefore the proscribing any citizen as unworthy the public confidence by laying upon him an incapacity of being called to offices of trust and emolument, unless he profess or renounce this or that religious opinion, is depriving him injuriously of those privileges and advantages to which, in common with his fellow citizens, he has a natural right . . . and that if any act shall be hereafter passed to repeal the present, or to narrow its operation, such act will be an infringement of natural right.[1]

Later that same year, Mason's Declaration of Rights, approved on June 12 by the Virginia legislature while Americans were preparing to separate themselves from Great Britain, maintained: "That religion, or the duty which we owe to our Creator, and the manner of discharging it, can be directed only by reason and conviction . . . and therefore all men are equally entitled to the free exercise of religion, according to the dictates of conscience."[2]

Virginia, from 1776 to 1789 when the US Constitution went into effect, was an exception to the practice of state support for, or "establishment" by law of, particular Christian denominations or Christianity in general in the various colonies; such support also took the form of a religious test

---

[1]   Virginia Code 1919, § 57-1. http://law.lis.virginia.gov/vacode/title57/chapter1/section57-1/.

[2]   The Virginia Declaration of Rights, § 16. U.S. National Archives & Records Administration. https://www.archives.gov/founding-docs/virginia-declaration-of-rights.

regarding participation in public affairs by citizens of said colonies.

Establishment of religion had a precise meaning for the Founders. Thomas Cooley, one of two major commentators on the US Constitution of the nineteenth century and a member of the Michigan State Supreme Court, stated, "By establishment of religion is meant the setting up or recognition of a state church, or at least the conferring upon one church of special favors and advantages which are denied to others."[3]

In 1776, the constitutional provisions or religious establishment laws or practices of the original thirteen states were as follows: Virginia and Rhode Island provided for full freedom; New York allowed freedom of religion but required naturalized citizens to reject foreign allegiance in all civil and church matters; Delaware and Maryland required Christianity of all citizens; Pennsylvania, Delaware, North Carolina, and South Carolina required citizen support for the divine inspiration of the Bible; Pennsylvania and South Carolina also required a belief in heaven and hell; Delaware required acceptance of the Trinity; New Hampshire, Massachusetts, Connecticut, Maryland, and South Carolina required Protestant Christianity; New York, Maryland, and South Carolina excluded ministers from civil office.[4]

How could a national government accommodate such differences? A preliminary answer was adopted by Congress

---

[3]   Thomas M. Cooley, *The General Principles of Constitutional Law in the United States* (Bridgewater, VA: American Foundations Publications, ,2001), p. 205.

[4]   Anson Phelps Stokes and Leo Pfeffer, *Church and State in the United States* (New York: Harper and Row, 1964), p. 81.

on July 13, 1787, acting under the Articles of Confederation while delegates were meeting in Philadelphia forging a
new Constitution. On that date, a law known as the Northwest Ordinance, which detailed how western territories of
the United States would later be reorganized into six states
and governed, pointed to the solution. The Northwest Ordinance "contained five articles constituting nothing less than
a bill of rights for the inhabitants of the Territory. . . . These
articles were to have a strong influence on the Philadelphia
Convention and the amendments proposed by the First
Congress."[5]

The "bill of rights" in the Northwest Ordinance, besides
prohibiting slavery in these territories, stipulated: "Art. 1.
No person, demeaning himself in a peaceable and orderly
manner, shall ever be molested on account of his mode of
worship or religious sentiments, in the said territory. . . .
Art. 3. Religion, morality, and knowledge, being necessary
to good government and the happiness of mankind, schools
and the means of education shall forever be encouraged."[6]

Roughly six weeks later, on August 30, 1787, delegates to
the Philadelphia Constitutional Convention proposed and
adopted the same policy pursuant to a motion offered by
Mr. Pinkney (South Carolina), "but no religious test shall
ever be required as a qualification to any office or public
trust under the authority of the U. States."[7]

---

[5]   David Currie, "The Constitution in Congress: The Federalist
       Period, 1789-1801," *The University of Chicago Law Review* 61
       (Summer 1994): 843.
[6]   "Northwest Ordinance; July 13, 1787," The Avalon Project, Yale
       University, http://avalon.law.yale.edu/18th_century/nworder.asp.
[7]   Max Farrand, ed., *The Records of the Federal Convention of 1787*

In essentially following Virginia's example, the Northwest Ordinance held that no particular religious test would condition either citizenship or the holding of government office to residents or later citizens of these territories or the states formed out of the territories. The "no religious test" provision of the Constitution approved at Philadelphia neutered congressional ability to establish a national religious denomination. So the First Amendment became the flip side of the "no religious test" coin.

But on September 15, just two days before the convention was to end, Madison would learn that two of his fellow Virginia delegates would not endorse the final product of the convention. Edmund Randolph, governor of Virginia, wanted state conventions to consider the proposed constitution and be allowed to offer amendments to be ratified at a second constitutional convention. Without that, Randolph would not put his name to the Constitution.[8]

George Mason also said he would not sign the Constitution without a second convention.[9] Mason's objection and opening statement was that "there is no Declaration of Rights, and the laws of the general government being paramount to the laws and constitution of the several States, the Declaration of Rights in the separate States are no security."[10]

The absence of a bill of rights, notwithstanding, the Constitution was approved and forwarded to the congress

---

(New Haven: Yale University Press, 1966), 2:468. As voting in the convention was by state delegations, the measure was opposed only by North Carolina, and Maryland was divided.

8   Ibid., p. 631.
9   Ibid., p. 632.
10   Ibid., p. 637.

formed under the Articles of Confederation on September 17, 1789.

James Madison of Virginia, who originally opposed a bill of rights, saw from the experience of the state ratification debates on adopting the Constitution, especially in his own Virginia, that establishment of the Union would hinge on the adoption of a bill of rights to include, as part of its legislative intent, protections for individual conscience and religious liberty. On June 8, 1789, he noted in the House of Representatives that "a bill of rights has been the great object contended for. . . . The freedom of the press, and the rights of conscience . . . apprehensions had been entertained of their insecurity under the new Constitution; a bill of rights, therefore, to quiet the minds of the people upon these points, may be salutary."[11]

But Madison's initial offerings for a bill of rights would, in part, overshoot the mark. He noted, "I wish also, in revising the constitution, we may throw into that section, which interdicts the abuse of certain powers in the state legislatures, some other provisions . . . that no state shall violate the equal rights of conscience."[12]

Recall that most of the states had established some Christian doctrine or denomination as preferential or necessary to hold office. Rhode Island, which did not even bother to send delegates to the Constitutional Convention, had no established church or religious beliefs required to hold state office

11   Helen Veit, Kenneth Bowling, and Charlene Bickford, eds., *Creating the Bill of Rights: The Documentary Record from the First Federal Congress* (Baltimore: Johns Hopkins University Press, 1991), pp. 66–67.
12   Ibid., p. 85.

but had not ratified the Constitution, and so had no representatives in the first Congress at this point. North Carolina, which required acceptance of the divine inspiration of the Bible, also had not ratified the Constitution. Madison was proposing a "fix" to a perplexing question that only one state ratifying the Constitution subscribed to, namely, Virginia. That proposal would not and did not work.

Congressmen and senators from states with some form of "established" church would hardly vote to render their states powerless in such matters, especially in light of the recognition that a bill of rights was thought to be needed to place additional limits on the powers of the national government, not limits on state governments.

On August 15, 1789, the House of Representatives had under consideration the following wording, referring to national government, "No religion shall be established by law, nor shall the equal rights of conscience be infringed." Commenting on this language, Catholic congressman Daniel Carroll (Maryland), elected as a delegate to the Constitutional Convention and the Continental Congress, is recorded in the records of the debate as having noted: "As the rights of conscience are in their nature of particular delicacy, and will little bear the gentlest touch of the governmental hand; and as many sects have concurred in opinion that they are not well secured under the present constitution . . . he would not contend with the gentleman about the phraseology, his object was to secure the substance in such a manner as to satisfy the wishes of the honest part of the community."[13]

---

[13]   Ibid., p. 157.

On August 24, 1789, the House of Representatives, under the leadership of James Madison, proposed seventeen amendments to the Constitution. What became the First Amendment read at that time, "Congress shall make no law establishing religion or prohibiting the free exercise thereof, nor shall the rights of Conscience be infringed."[14]

On September 9, 1789, the Senate suggested removing the word *conscience* from the House-proposed constitutional amendment on religion.[15] The final wording of the First Amendment was approved by a House and Senate conference committee on September 24, 1789.[16]

The Constitution's bans on religious tests as a precondition for holding federal office and on congressional establishment of a national religion were enacted, in part, to ensure that citizens did not need to abandon their faith or right of conscience to serve as members of Congress or as federal judges or in executive agencies of the federal—that is, national—government. It was not thought of as a "firewall" to keep religion out of the public square. Associate Justice of the Supreme Court Joseph Story, a Madison appointee, wrote:

> The real object of the [first] amendment was, not to countenance, much less to advance Mahometanism, or Judaism, or infidelity, by prostrating Christianity;

---

14   Ibid., p. 38.
15   Ibid., p. 46. This could be done by striking the word "religion" and inserting "articles of faith or a mode of worship," and striking the words, "thereof, nor shall the rights of Conscience be infringed," and inserting "of Religion."
16   Ibid., pp. 48, 49.

but to exclude all rivalry among Christian sects, and
to prevent any national ecclesiastical establishment,
which should give to an hierarchy the exclusive
patronage of the national government. It thus cut off
the means of religious persecution, (the vice and pest
of former ages,) and of the subversion of the rights
of conscience in matters of religion, which had been
trampled upon almost from the days of the Apostles to
the present age.[17]

That first Congress included members of the 1787 Constitutional Convention. In 1789, these men, in addition to
proposing the First Amendment, reenacted the Northwest
Ordinance. Those actions contradict claims put forward
today by federal courts and modern progressives that the
First Amendment requires governmental indifference or
hostility to religious concerns. For as Justice William Rehnquist would note in 1985, dispersing public monies for religious schools and purposes in the Northwest Territories was
an accepted practice of the time, even as the debates over
religious liberty raged. Clearly, if it was thought contrary to
the letter or spirit of the amendments being discussed, that
practice would have been proscribed. Rehnquist wrote:

> The House of Representatives took up the Northwest
> Ordinance on the same day as Madison introduced
> his proposed amendments which became the Bill of
> Rights . . . it seems highly unlikely that the House of

---

[17]   Joseph Story, *Commentaries on the Constitution*, § 1871, quoted
in Philip Kurland and Ralph Lerner, eds., *The Founders' Constitution*, vol. 5 (Chicago: University of Chicago Press, 1987), p. 109.

Representatives would simultaneously consider proposed amendments to the Constitution and enact an important piece of territorial legislation which conflicted with the intent of those proposals. The Northwest Ordinance, 1 Stat. 50, reenacted the Northwest Ordinance of 1787 and provided that "[r]eligion, morality, and knowledge, being necessary to good government and the happiness of mankind, schools and the means of education shall forever be encouraged." . . . Land grants for schools in the Northwest Territory were not limited to public schools. It was not until 1845 that Congress limited land grants in the new States and Territories to nonsectarian schools. . . . Typical of these was Jefferson's treaty with the Kaskaskia Indians, which provided annual cash support for the Tribe's Roman Catholic priest and church. It was not until 1897, when aid to sectarian education . . . for Indians had reached $500,000 annually, that Congress decided thereafter to cease appropriating money for education in sectarian schools.[18]

The secular Left has been reading into the First Amendment their own hostility to the Judeo-Christian moral tradition, which originally animated and shaped American public life, by claiming the First Amendment requires indifference, if not outright opposition, to the moral claims on mankind of the Old and New Testaments in matters touching upon the government of the United States. The Reverend John Courtney Murray, SJ, more appropriately calls the religion

---

[18]   Wallace v. Jaffree, 472 U.S. 38 (1985), No. 83-812.

clauses of the First Amendment "Articles of Peace"—when dealing with the fact of American religious pluralism in securing the common good—and not a surrender or abandonment of moral principles.

Modern liberals claim Thomas Jefferson as one of their heroes in the Church/State debates. But is the constitutional line of church and state separation drawn by them the same as that drawn by Jefferson in his famous 1802 letter to Baptists from Danbury, Connecticut? Jefferson wrote, "Believing with you that religion is a matter which lies solely between Man & his God, . . . that the legitimate powers of government reach actions only, & not opinions, I contemplate with sovereign reverence that act of the whole American people which declared that their legislature should 'make no law respecting an establishment of religion, or prohibiting the free exercise thereof,' thus building a wall of separation between Church & State."[19]

Edward S. Corwin, the dean of constitutional commentators, suggests that Jefferson's letter was "not improbably motivated by an impish desire to heave a brick at the Congregationalists-Federalist hierarchy of Connecticut, whose leading members had denounced him two years before as an 'infidel' and an 'atheist.'"[20]

---

[19] Thomas Jefferson, "Jefferson's Letter to the Danbury Baptists," The Library of Congress, https://www.loc.gov/loc/lcib/9806/danpre.html.

[20] Edward S. Corwin, "The Court as National School Board," in *American Constitutional History, Essays by Edward S. Corwin*, ed. Alpheus Mason and Gerald Garvey, (Harper and Row, 1964), pp. 204–5.

A more complete view of Jefferson's policies on the link between government and religion can be found in his second inaugural address, given in 1805:

> In matters of religion, I have considered that its free exercise is placed by the constitution independent of the powers of the general government. I have therefore . . . left them, as the constitution found them, under the direction and discipline of state or church authorities acknowledged by the several religious societies. . . .
>
> I shall now enter on the duties to which my fellow citizens have again called me. . . . I shall need, . . . the favor of that Being in whose hands we are, who led our forefathers, as Israel of old, . . . who has covered our infancy with his providence, and our riper years with his wisdom and power; and to whose goodness I ask you to join with me in supplications, that he will so enlighten the minds of your servants, guide their councils, and prosper their measures, that whatsoever they do, shall result in your good.[21]

Additionally, when Jefferson was governor of Virginia, he did comply with the 1779 request of the Continental Congress to issue a formal and public call for a day of prayer and thanksgiving while America was still fighting for independence.[22]

---

21   Thomas Jefferson, "Thomas Jefferson Second Inaugural Address," The Avalon Project, Yale University, http://avalon.law.yale. edu/19th_century/jefinau2.asp.

22   "Whereas the Honourable the General Congress, impressed with a grateful sense of the goodness of Almighty God, in bless-

The modern secularists choose Jefferson as their model, but in doing so, they misrepresent the man; and, yet, even granting less religiosity to Jefferson himself, the general sense of America's Founders and her people was formed by Christian assumption. Justice Story wrote, "Probably at the time of the adoption of the Constitution, and of the amendment to it now under consideration [First Amendment], the general if not the universal sentiment in America was that Christianity ought to receive encouragement from the State so far as was not incompatible with the private rights of conscience and the freedom of religious worship. An attempt to

---

ing the greater part of this extensive continent with plentiful harvests, crowning our arms with repeated successes, conducting us hitherto safely through the perils with which we have been encompassed and manifesting in multiplied instances his divine care of these infant states, hath thought proper by their act of the 20th day of October last, to recommend to the several states that Thursday the 9th of December next be appointed a day of publick and solemn thanksgiving and prayer. . . .

"I do therefore by authority from the General Assembly issue this my proclamation, hereby appointing Thursday the 9th day of December next, a day of publick and solemn thanksgiving and prayer to Almighty God, earnestly recommending to all the good people of this commonwealth, to set apart the said day for those purposes, and to the several Ministers of religion to meet their respective societies thereon, to assist them in their prayers, edify them with their discourses, and generally to perform the sacred duties of their function, proper for the occasion.

"Given under my hand and the seal of the commonwealth, at Williamsburg, this 11th day of November, in the year of our Lord, 1779, and in the fourth of the commonwealth. THOMAS JEFFERSON." "Proclamation Appointing a Day of Thanksgiving and Prayer, 11 November 1779," *Founders Online*, National Archives, http://founders.archives.gov/documents/Jefferson/01-03-02-0187.

level all religions, and to make it a matter of state policy to hold all in utter indifference, would have created universal disapprobation, if not universal indignation."[23]

Story believed that the Judeo-Christian moral assumptions of Americans regarding government of the people were necessary to secure the common good: "It is impossible for those, who believe in the truth of Christianity, as a divine revelation, to doubt, that it is the especial duty of government to foster, and encourage it among all the citizens and subjects. This is a point wholly distinct from that of the right of private judgment in matters of religion, and of the freedom of public worship according to the dictates of one's conscience. The real difficulty lies in ascertaining the limits, to which government may rightfully go in fostering and encouraging religion."[24]

---

[23]   Joseph Story, *A Familiar Exposition of the Constitution of the United States* (Washington: Regnery Publishing, 1986), p. 316.

[24]   Ibid., pp. 314–15.

CHAPTER 2

Rolling Back Rule by Judges

Or

Just How "Supreme" Is the Supreme Court?

A nd so the Founders' vision and writings concerning religious liberty were a far cry from those of modern "progressives" or hard line secular liberals, which, in many cases, are animated by outright rejection of and hostility towards Judeo-Christian values. And yet, radical liberal secularists have made much headway in seeking to drive Judeo-Christian religious sensibilities and concerns from public life and law in our country. Sadly, the branch of government that has been used to most pernicious effect by those in favor of things such as abortion and homosexual marriage has been the judiciary. This usurpation and abuse of power, by the federal courts especially, would come as a surprise to many of the Founding Fathers as they viewed it as "the least dangerous" branch of government. And while called the Supreme Court and, yes, supreme in certain limited respects in terms of the law, it was never meant to be a tool by which self-government would be destroyed. This chapter will ask a series of "Did you know?" questions. Don't feel bad if you did *not* know . . . you are not alone.

Alexander Hamilton, a member of the 1787 Constitutional Convention from New York, wrote, "The judiciary, from the nature of its functions, will always be the least dangerous to the political rights of the Constitution; because it will be least in a capacity to annoy or injure them."[1]

Hamilton's conclusion assumed that the electorate would be knowledgeable about the powers of government and that Congress would exercise its own constitutional judgment and take primary responsibility for defending the rights of citizens. Little did he know that Americans of the twentieth and twenty-first centuries would forget that, with the exception of a limited category of cases enumerated in the Constitution, Congress has the authority to control whether judicial cases would even be heard in any federal court.

Did you know that the Constitutional Convention of 1787 rejected judges as lawmakers?

At the initiation of James Wilson (Pennsylvania) and James Madison (Virginia), both of whom feared the overriding power of the legislature, the Philadelphia Convention considered a measure to include the federal judiciary in a "Council of Revision," which would have allowed federal judges and the president to have a role in evaluating legislation for constitutionality before its enactment into law. In simple words, the judges would have been authorized

---

[1]   *Federalist*, no. 78.

to propound and propose the public policy of the United States. This was finally debated and rejected with four nays, three yeas, and two states divided.[2]

The measure—which was debated on at least three occasions, and with more than one variation—on giving judges negative power on legislation encountered the following objections as recorded by James Madison:

"Mr. Dickerson[3] . . . The Judges must interpret the Laws they ought not to be legislators."[4]

"Mr. Ghorum did not see the advantage of employing the Judges in this way. As Judges, they are not to be presumed to possess any peculiar knowledge of the mere policy of public measures. Nor can it be necessary as a security for their constitutional rights."[5]

"Mr. Gerry . . . The motion was liable to strong objections. . . . It was making Statesmen of the Judges; and setting them up as guardians of the Rights of the people. He relied . . . on the Representatives as the guardians of their Rights & interests."[6]

"Mr. L. Martin . . . A knowledge of mankind, and of Legislative affairs, cannot be presumed to belong in a

---

2   Max Farrand, ed., *The Records of the Federal Convention of 1787* (New Haven: Yale University Press, 1966), 2:80.
3   Dickerson was Madison's spelling of John Dickinson.
4   Farrand, *The Records of the Federal Convention*, 1:108.
5   Farrand, *The Records of the Federal Convention*, 2:73.
6   Ibid., p. 75.

higher degree to the Judges than to the Legislature. . . .
It is necessary that the Supreme Judiciary should have
the confidence of the people. This will soon be lost, if
they are employed in the task of remonstrating against
popular measures of the Legislature."[7]

"Mr. Rutledge thought the Judges of all men the most
unfit to be concerned in the revisionary council."[8]

"Mr. Pinkney opposed the interference of the Judges
in the Legislative business; it will involve them in parties, and give a previous tincture to their opinions."

"Mr. Mercer . . . disapproved of the Doctrine that the
Judges as expositors of the Constitution should have
the authority to declare a law void."[9]

"Mr. Dickinson was strongly impressed with the
remark of Mr. Mercer as to the power of the Judges to
set aside the law. He thought no such power ought to
exist. He was, at the same time, at a loss what expedient
to substitute. The Justiciary of Arragon, he observed,
became by degrees the lawgiver."[10]

That last comment of Mr. Dickinson recorded by Madison was prophetic as to our own situation. For who can
deny that in the United States today, at least in the cultural

---

[7]   Ibid., p. 77.
[8]   Ibid., p. 80.
[9]   Ibid., p. 298.
[10]   Ibid.

sphere, the justiciary has become the lawgiver. We need not understand his reference to Arragon; we need but look at the recent history of so-called homosexual marriage. Defeated everywhere at the ballot box, it has become the law of the land through the unconstitutional lawmaking by judges across the country. We can't say we were not warned.

Did you know that the Supreme Court does not have the exclusive right to interpret the Constitution?

James Madison, who is called the Father of the Constitution and was a member of the Federal Convention, took notes that are considered the authoritative record of that event. He held that appointed judges could never be superior in power and authority to elected representatives.

Madison was also a member of the first Congress. In a debate on presidential powers, he stated:

> But the great objection . . . is, that the legislature itself has no right to expound the Constitution; that wherever its meaning is doubtful . . . the judiciary is called upon to declare its meaning. I acknowledge, in the ordinary course of government, that the exposition of the laws and Constitution devolves upon the judicial; but I beg to know upon what principle it can be contended that any one department draws from the Constitution greater powers than another, in marking out the limits of the powers of the several departments.[11]

---

[11]   James Madison, "Speech in Congress Proposing Constitutional Amendments, On Presidential Removal Power, June 17, 1789," in Jack Rakove, ed., *James Madison, Writings* (New York: Library of America, 1999), p. 464.

Madison previously observed, "In the State Constitutions & indeed in the Fedl. one also, no provision is made for the case of a disagreement in expounding them; and as the Courts are generally the last in making their decision, it results to them, by refusing or not refusing to execute a law, to stamp it with its final character. This makes the Judiciary Dept paramount in fact to the Legislature, which was never intended, and can never be proper."[12]

Madison did hold that it was a proper function of judges to resist every executive and legislative "encroachment upon rights expressly stipulated for in the Constitution by the declaration of rights."[13] Judges, however, were not appointed to "fill in voids or cracks" in the Constitution.

Thomas Jefferson also inveighed against judicial supremacy. As president, he wrote to Mrs. John Adams, "But the opinion which gives to the judges the right to decide what laws are constitutional, and what not, not only for themselves in their own sphere of action, but for the Legislature and Executive also, in their spheres, would make the judiciary a despotic branch."[14]

Writing to a Virginia judge, Spencer Roane, Jefferson noted, "In denying the right they [the Supreme Court] usurp of exclusively explaining the Constitution, I go further than you . . . our Constitution . . . My construction of

---

[12]   James Madison, "Observations on Jefferson's Draft of a Constitution for Virginia, 15 Oct. 1788," in Jack Rakove, ed., *James Madison, Writings*, (New York: Library of America, 1999), p. 417.

[13]   Madison, "Speech in Congress Proposing Constitutional Amendments," in Rakove, *James Madison, Writings,* p. 449.

[14]   *The Jeffersonian Cyclopedia*, ed. John P. Foley (New York: Funk & Wagnalls, 1900), p. 796.

the Constitution is . . . that each department is truly independent of the others, and has an equal right to decide for itself what is the meaning of the Constitution in the cases submitted to its action; and especially to act ultimately and without appeal."[15]

Jefferson also told William Jarvis, "It is a very dangerous doctrine to consider the judges as the ultimate arbiters of all constitutional questions. It is one which would place us under the despotism of an oligarchy. . . . The Constitution has erected no such single tribunal, knowing that to whatever hands confided, with the corruptions of time and party, its members would become mere despots. It has more wisely made all the departments coequal and cosovereign within themselves."[16]

In other words, Jefferson did not dispute that the court could decide a case in controversy. But he rejected the notion that the court could decide with finality the question of whether the judges themselves were the makers of public policy arising out of the occasion of a case decided by the court. And he did not accept the idea that the court was the only and final authority in deciding what the Constitution meant. He held that the legislature was only bound by its own understanding of the Constitution.

President Andrew Jackson, in his 1832 veto message of the National Banking Bill followed Jefferson's reasoning in affirming departmental equality in defining the meaning of the Constitution:

---

[15]   Ibid., p. 190.
[16]   Ibid., p. 845.

> Each public officer who takes an oath to support the Constitution swears that he will support it as he understands it, and not as it is understood by others. It is as much the duty of the House of Representatives, of the Senate, and of the President to decide upon the constitutionality of any bill or resolution which may be presented to them for passage or approval as it is of the supreme judges when it may be brought before them for judicial decision. . . . The authority of the Supreme Court must not, therefore, be permitted to control the Congress or the Executive when acting in their legislative capacities.[17]

Abraham Lincoln, in his first inaugural address given on the eve of the Civil War against the background of the Dred Scott slavery decision challenged judicial supremacy: "The candid citizen must confess that if the policy of the Government upon vital questions affecting the whole people is to be irrevocably fixed by decisions of the Supreme Court, the instant they are made in ordinary litigation between parties in personal actions the people will have ceased to be their own rulers, having to that extent practically resigned their Government into the hands of that eminent tribunal."[18]

The Congress has not always accepted the finality of Supreme Court decisions. For example, in June 1862 the

---

[17]   Andrew Jackson, "President Jackson's Veto Message Regarding the Bank of the United States; July 10, 1832," The Avalon Project, Yale Law School, http://avalon.law.yale.edu/19th_century/ajveto01.asp.

[18]   Abraham Lincoln, "First Inaugural Address of Abraham Lincoln," The Avalon Project, Yale Law School, http://avalon.law.yale.edu/19th_century/lincoln1.asp.

Congress passed a statute signed by President Lincoln that abolished slavery in all then existing and future territories that may be acquired by the United States.[19] But, you may ask, what of the 1856 Dred Scott vs. Sanford Supreme Court decision declaring, among other points, that Congress lacked the constitutional authority to prohibit slavery in any part of the territories as was done in the Missouri Compromise of 1820 splitting the Louisiana Territory into areas for free populations and areas for slave populations?[20] Well, what of it? Congress and the president simply ignored it.

Did you know that Congress controls the types of cases the Supreme Court hears?

In what will certainly be news to most people, the Supreme Court actually receives from Congress the power that they have so abused in cases involving both abortion and the homosexual agenda in recent decades. That power, or jurisdiction, may be removed if the Congress so desires.

Jurisdiction, or the power to hear and rule on a particular case, is either *original* or *appellate*. Original jurisdiction means the parties go directly to a court to hear or settle a

---

[19]   "Be it enacted by the Senate and House of Representatives of the United States of America in Congress assembled, That from and after the passage of this act there shall be neither slavery nor involuntary servitude in any of the Territories of the United States now existing, or which may at any time hereafter be formed or acquired by the United States, otherwise than in punishment of crimes whereof the party shall have been duly convicted." "Law Enacting Emancipation in the Federal Territories," Freedmen & Southern Society Project, http://www.freedmen.umd.edu/freeterr.htm.

[20]   Dred Scott v. Sanford, 60 U.S. 393 (1856).

case. Appellate jurisdiction means cases are heard by a particular court only after they have been heard in a lower court.

According to the Constitution, the Supreme Court's original jurisdiction is limited to "all cases affecting ambassadors, other public ministers and counsels, and those in which a State shall be a party."[21] Very few cases have reached the Supreme Court under its original jurisdiction. The Constitution continues: "In all the other Cases before mentioned, the Supreme Court shall have appellate Jurisdiction, both as to Law and Fact, *with such Exceptions, and under such Regulations as the Congress shall make.*"[22]

This means that Congress has broad powers to limit, modify, or even abolish the appellate jurisdiction of all federal courts, including the Supreme Court. In 1799, Justice Chase ruled that the power of federal courts, including the Supreme Court, to hear certain cases is conferred by Congress:

> If Congress has given the power to this Court, we possess it, not otherwise: and if Congress has not given the power to us, or to any other Court, it still remains at the legislative disposal. Besides, Congress is not bound, and it would, perhaps, be inexpedient, to enlarge the jurisdiction of the federal courts, to every subject, in every form, which the constitution might warrant.[23]

---

[21]   U.S. Const. art. III, § 2.
[22]   Ibid., emphasis added.
[23]   Turner v. Bank of North America, 4 U.S. 8 (1799).

Here is a justice of the Supreme Court acknowledging, within ten years of the implementation of the Constitution, that Congress has unfettered power to limit and regulate the kinds of cases federal courts, including the Supreme Court, may hear. It may, in fact, go so far as to abolish the Court's appellate jurisdiction altogether. Remember, the Constitution only required the existence of a single court—that is, the Supreme Court. The very existence of all other federal courts is optional. The Constitution provides, "The Congress shall have Power to . . . constitute Tribunals inferior to the Supreme Court."[24]

In 1979, the late Democrat senator from West Virginia Robert Byrd amended a bill that took jurisdiction away from the lower federal courts and the US Supreme Court to "review any case arising out of state laws relating to voluntary prayers in public schools and public buildings."[25]

Edward S. Corwin notes that considerable, and even absolute, congressional control can be exercised over decisions of all federal courts:

> [Because of] . . . Congress' . . . control over the Court's appellate jurisdiction, as well as of the total jurisdiction of the lower federal courts . . . . Congress is in the position to restrict the actual exercise of judicial review at times, or even to frustrate it altogether. Thus, in 1869 it prevented the Court from passing on the constitutionality of the Reconstruction Acts by repealing the latter's jurisdiction over a case which had already

---

[24]   U.S. Const., art. I, § 8, cl. 9.
[25]   Comm. on the Judiciary, Marriage Protection Act of 2004, H.R. Rep. No. 108-614, at 10 (2004).

been argued and was ready for decision, and in World War II it confirmed the right to challenge the validity of provisions of the Emergency Price Control Act and of orders of the OPA [Office of Price Administration] under it to a single emergency court of Appeals and the Supreme Court of Appeals and to the Supreme Court upon review of that court's judgments and orders.[26]

Members of Congress are without excuse if they plead ignorance of their authority over courts. In the annotated Constitution prepared for members of Congress by the Library of Congress, congressional power over federal courts' appellate jurisdiction is described in sweeping terms:

> See . . . Justice Frankfurter's remarks in *National Mutual Ins. Co. v. Tidewater Transfer Co.* . . . (1948) "Congress need not give this Court any appellate power; it may withdraw appellate jurisdiction once conferred and it may do so even while a case is sub judice [before the court and not yet decided]." In *The Francis Wright* . . . (1882), upholding Congress's power to confine Supreme Court review in admiralty cases to questions of law, the Court said: "[W]hile the appellate power of this court under the Constitution extends to all cases within the judicial power of the United States, actual jurisdiction under the power is confined within such limits as Congress sees fit to prescribe. . . . Not only may whole classes of cases be kept out of the jurisdiction altogether, but particular classes of questions may

---

[26]   Edward S. Corwin, *The Constitution and What it Means Today* (Princeton: Princeton University Press, 1974), pp. 178–79.

be subjected to reexamination and review, while others
are not."[27]

In 2004, the House of Representatives, in a vote of 233
to 194, passed H.R. 3313, The Marriage Protection Act
of 2004, introduced by Congressman John N. Hostettler
(R-IN), which eliminated the ability of federal courts to hear
or decide legal challenges to the Defense of Marriage Act
(DOMA). President Clinton had signed the DOMA law in
1997, which provided that no state shall be required to "recognize" any "marriage" between persons of the same sex that
was recognized or entered into under the laws of any other
state.

The House Judiciary Report spelled out the purpose of
Representative Hostettler's bill:

> H.R. 3313 would prevent unelected, lifetime-ap-
> pointed Federal judges from striking down the pro-
> tection for states Congress passed in the Defense of
> Marriage Act ("DOMA")—by the overwhelming
> margin of 342–67 in the House and 85–14 in the
> Senate—that provides that no state shall be required
> to accept same sex marriage licenses granted in other
> states.
>
> H.R. 3313 does not attempt to dictate results: it
> only places final authority over whether states must
> accept same-sex marriage licenses granted in other
> states in the hands of the states themselves. H.R. 3313
> stands for the proposition that lifetime-appointed

---

[27]   S. Doc. No. 112-9, at 843–44 (2014).

Federal judges must not be allowed to rewrite marriage policy for the states.[28]

Amazingly, or perhaps not so, when the Hostettler bill was debated in the House of Representatives on July 22, 2004, a member opposed to the bill produced a memo from the Library of Congress that asserted, "We are not aware of any precedent for a law that would deny the inferior federal courts original jurisdiction or the Supreme Court of appellate jurisdiction to review the constitutionality of a law of Congress."[29] The Library of Congress Research Division would soon be eating crow for its attempt to undermine the authority of Congress through such a transparently preposterous fabrication of feigned ignorance regarding the exercise of congressional powers to control court jurisdiction.

Hostettler's bill passed, despite the Library of Congress memo. But to correct the public record, Phil Kiko, chief of staff to the Judiciary Committee chairman, Congressman James Sensenbrenner, sent a letter to the Library of Congress official who had impugned Hostettler's bill. Kiko pointed out that starting in 1789, and many times thereafter, Congress had removed constitutional review both from lower federal courts as well as the Supreme Court.[30] The official at the

---

28   Comm. on the Judiciary, Marriage Protection Act of 2004, H.R. Rep. No. 108-614, at 2 (2004).

29   150 Cong Rec. E1604 (daily ed. Sept. 13, 2004) (statement of Rep. Sensenbrenner).

30   "Under the Judiciary Act of 1789, if the highest state courts upheld a federal law as constitutional and decided in favor of a right under such federal statute (and there was no coincidental federal diversity jurisdiction), no appeal claiming such federal law was unconstitutional was allowed to any federal court, including the

Library of Congress eventually did acknowledge the error, admitting, "Our earlier memorandum was incorrect."[31]

The Marriage Protection Act was referred to the Senate, and although Republican George Bush was president and Republicans had a 51 to 49 majority in the Senate, no further action was taken. The lesson here is that, absent pressure from alert and interested citizens, a Republican majority guarantees nothing, even though fine words are in the Republican platform affirming real marriage and the protection of human beings before birth! Tradition-minded Christians must take an active interest in electoral affairs to ensure that our representatives truly represent our views, most especially in resisting the relentless assault on Judeo-Christian values of recent decades.

Supreme Court. The Judiciary Act of 1789, therefore, denied the inferior federal courts original jurisdiction and the Supreme Court appellate jurisdiction to review the constitutionality of literally thousands of laws of Congress in the many and various circumstances meeting the criteria just mentioned. Congress did not grant a more general federal question authority to the lower federal courts until after the Civil War . . . and Congress did not grant the Supreme Court the authority to review state court rulings upholding a claim of federal right until 1914." 150 Cong Rec. E1604 (daily ed. Sept. 13, 2004).

31 "We do acknowledge that the cited provisions of the first Judiciary Act do in some respects prevent federal judicial review of the constitutionality of some acts of Congress. . . . That the effect of § 25 might only infrequently result in the constitutionality of a federal statute being insulated from review does not alter the fact that as written and construed the section did operate to preclude any federal court from deciding the validity of a federal statute from 1789 to 1875. Accordingly, our earlier memorandum was incorrect." 150 Cong. Rec. E1605 (daily ed. Sept. 13, 2004).

Not only must we elect true social conservatives as our representatives, we must educate them if need be. Take what you have learned in the preceding pages and contact your political representatives to share that knowledge with them. The Congress clearly has the power to prevent all federal courts, including the Supreme Court, from exercising jurisdiction over laws passed by Congress or state legislatures. This power can and should be a tool that our elected officials use to protect the laws they pass protecting children from abortion and upholding the true nature and integrity of marriage. Exercising that power is a question of will, not authority. Does your representative have the requisite will to be a true force for good? If not, vote him or her out!

Did you know that it is possible to remove federal court jurisdiction over social issues?

The attack against marriage and the attack against legal protection of children before birth has been conducted through the federal courts since the mid-1960s by bypassing state legislatures that, since 1789, had the legal responsibility to maintain civil order and protect the health and general welfare of persons in their states. The efforts to legalize abortion for rape, incest, and fetal handicap were slowing down as state right to life groups began to organize and fight back in state legislatures. It was the US Supreme Court's 1973 *Roe* and *Doe* decisions that rescued the faltering abortion liberalization efforts by invalidating all state laws that protected children from the abortionists' scalpels and suction devices.

Similarly, the initial "victories" which same-sex "marriage" advocates achieved came only after state courts invalidated state constitutions or statutes defining natural marriage. For example, in May 2008, California's high court declared unconstitutional a statute and an earlier referendum identifying marriage as only between one man and one woman.[32] This California Supreme Court decision was later reversed in November 2008, by a largely democratic electorate, when the Proposition 8 referendum passed, defining marriage, again, as a union of one man and one woman.[33]

That referendum was later undone by an LGBTQ legal challenge in the federal courts. The August 2010 decision overturning Proposition 8 came from Federal District Judge Vaughn Walker, a homosexual who lived with his physician "partner." Walker later "went public with his orientation in April 2011, more than two months after his retirement."[34]

Walker should have recused himself. Federal law provides that "any justice, judge, or magistrate judge of the United States shall disqualify himself in any proceeding in which his impartiality might reasonably be questioned."[35] The Federal Judicial Center, which was created by Congress in 1967 as a research and education center for the federal judiciary, has published a manual to provide guidance on such

---

[32]   In re Marriage Cases, 43 Cal. 4th 757 (2008).

[33]   "California Proposition 8, the 'Eliminates Right of Same-Sex Couples to Marry' Initiative (2008)," Ballotpedia, http://ballotpedia.org/California_Proposition_8,_the_%22Eliminates_Right_of_Same-Sex_Couples_to_Marry%22_Initiative_(2008).

[34]   Bob Egelko, "Judge Vaughn Walker tells his side of Prop. 8 trial," SFGate, April 20, 2014, http://www.sfgate.com/lgbt/article/Judge-Vaughn-Walker-tells-his-side-of-Prop-8-5416851.php.

[35]   28 U.S.C. § 455 (2012).

questions.[36] It states, "A judge contemplating disqualification under § 455(a), then, should not ask whether he or she believes he or she is capable of impartially presiding over the case. Rather, the question is whether a judge's impartiality might be questioned from the perspective of a reasonable person, and every circuit has adopted some version of the 'reasonable person' standard to answer this question."[37]

Could any reasonable person who knew that Judge Walker was living with his "partner" for ten years and that Walker and his "committed other" stood to benefit at least socially, and perhaps legally, from his ruling question whether he could be impartial? Of course! Recall that the standard is would any reasonable person "question"; one need not decide one way or the other. Certainly one could question in such a case. Was Walker formally chastised or criticized by his judicial peers for making his decision? No!

With such a judicial stacking of the deck, many on both sides of the marriage and life issues think that only the passage of constitutional amendments, which require the concurrence of two-thirds of the US House and Senate and the approval of three-fourths of the state legislatures or conventions called for that purpose, can reverse this situation. They are mistaken.

Another remedy, much easier to achieve, is to use the powers in the Constitution established by the Founders to exclude federal courts, including the Supreme Court, from

---

[36]   Federal Judicial Center, Home Page, http://www.fjc.gov/.

[37]   Charles Gardner Geyh, *Judicial Disqualification: An Analysis of Federal Law*, 2nd ed. (Federal Judicial Center, 2010), https://www.fjc.gov/sites/default/files/2012/JudicialDQ.pdf, p. 18.

making any decisions at all on such matters. Such an effort would prevent any federal court from overturning state or federal laws affirming traditional marriage and the protection of children in the womb. How could that be done without a constitutional amendment? Any federal or state laws protecting pre-born children and real marriage enacted after passage by Congress of legislation removing all appellate jurisdiction from federal courts could not be declared unconstitutional by federal judges. They would be prevented from doing so because the prior legislation would have prevented them from having jurisdiction over those particular cases. But first, let us consider objections to this approach.

Is there a constitutional right to a Supreme Court hearing?

Objections against removing federal court jurisdiction in matters of marriage and abortion were addressed by John Roberts, now the chief justice of the Supreme Court, in a memo written when he was a Justice Department special assistant to the US attorney general in the early years of President Reagan's first term.

Excerpts from Roberts's memo clearly show that removing federal court jurisdiction in these areas is constitutional. Referring to article III, section 2, clause 2, Roberts underlined the words in his memo, and he noted that the specific

> language stands as a plenary grant of power to Congress to make exceptions to the appellate jurisdiction of the Supreme Court. The exceptions clause by its terms contains no limit; the power to make exceptions

to the Court's appellate jurisdiction exists by virtue of
the express language of the clause over questions of
both law and fact.

. . . The clause does <u>not</u> say that Congress may
make such exceptions as do not impair the essential
functions of the Supreme Court. . . .

Throughout the 19th Century, the Supreme Court
also interpreted the Judiciary Act of 1789 as withholding authority to review state court decisions upholding the validity of a federal statute. . . . This created
a situation in which federal laws could be upheld in
some jurisdictions, although struck down in others.
. . . There was no suggestion that prior interpretation
was unconstitutional. . . .

As Frankfurter and Landis put it: "For a full hundred years there was no right of appeal to the Supreme
Court in criminal cases. Until 1889 even issues of life
and death could reach the Court only upon certifica-
tion of division of opinion. . . ." Here again there was
no suggestion that the lack of Supreme Court appellate review somehow unconstitutionally interfered
with the essential functions of the Supreme Court.[38]

Removing lower federal and Supreme Court review of
state or congressional statutes affirming traditional marriage
and the protection of children does not impair the essential
functions of the federal courts.

---

[38]   John Roberts, memorandum, "Proposals to Divest the Supreme
Court of Appellate Jurisdiction: An Analysis in Light of Recent
Developments," National Archives and Records Administration,
https://www.archives.gov/files/news/john-roberts/accession-60-
89-0172/006-Box5-Folder1522.pdf, pp. 2, 17–18.

**Did you know that the Constitution does
not give the role of final arbiter of its
interpretation to the Supreme Court?**

It is argued, however, that divesting the Supreme
Court of jurisdiction over a particular class of cases
would undermine the constitutional role of the Court
as the ultimate arbiter of constitutional questions. The
Constitution, however, does not accord such a role to
the Court. . . .

. . . If Congress were to divest the Supreme Court
of appellate jurisdiction, . . . it would not undermine
the entire system of judicial review. Rather, it would
simply be exercising its "ample authority to make such
exceptions" as are necessary to remove the "partial
inconveniences" which have developed in the system.
Hamilton, Federalist No. 80.[39]

The role of the Supreme Court as provided for by the
Founders was to decide cases; it was not authorized to
finally decide and impose a uniformity of public policy and
non-appealable, judge-made law that defies the consent of
the governed and transgresses the natural moral law. Roberts
points out that for 125 years the court could not review certain state court actions:

From the Judiciary Act of 1789 until the Act of
December 23, 1914, 38 Stat. 790, the Supreme Court
had no appellate jurisdiction of any kind over state
court decisions interpreting the Federal Constitution

---

[39] Ibid., pp. 20–21.

and striking down state laws on the basis of the Federal Constitution. Thus, an interpretation of the Federal Constitution by a state Supreme Court, even if considered erroneous by the United States Supreme Court, and even if in direct conflict with prior decisions of the highest courts of other states (or, for that matter, a prior decision of the United States Supreme Court), could not be reviewed.[40]

Eliminating federal court jurisdiction over marriage and abortion does not deny fundamental due process rights of "having your day in court." Roberts states:

> The pending proposals to divest the Supreme Court of appellate jurisdiction . . . all provide for at least some judicial forum, either the lower federal courts or state courts, to hear any claims. Due process does not require judicial review in a federal court of final review by the Supreme Court. . . .
>
> Any proper application of fundamental rights equal protection analysis would have to be based on an asserted fundamental right of access to federal court, rather than any fundamental right to an abortion or exercise of First Amendment freedoms. . . . Access to federal court, however, has never been identified as a fundamental right. The fundamental right involved in this area is the right to due process, and that right can be satisfied by access to state courts.[41]

---

[40] Ibid., pp. 16–17.
[41] Ibid., pp. 23, 25.

The "exceptions and regulations" clause of article III, section 2, clause 2 is not the only source of congressional power to restrict or eliminate federal court review of congressional acts. Congress passed the Fourteenth Amendment amidst great hostility from a Supreme Court that had produced the Dred Scott decision. Members of Congress suspected, with much evidence, that the court was ready to attack congressional reconstruction legislation. Roberts explains:

> Congress may derive additional authority in regulating Supreme Court appellate jurisdiction over Fourteenth Amendment cases by virtue of §5 of that Amendment. . . . It is certainly within the broad scope of §5 for Congress to determine that in certain cases, such as abortion and school desegregation cases, the guarantees of due process and equal protection are more appropriately enforced by state courts. . . .
>
> It should be noted that §5 of the Fourteenth Amendment can be considered to give Congress the power to divest the Supreme Court of appellate jurisdiction over Fourteenth Amendment claims even if Congress is considered to lack this power under Article III. . . . *The Framers of the Fourteenth Amendment intended it to be enforced primarily by Congress, and not the federal courts.*[42]

---

[42]   Ibid., pp. 25, 27 (emphasis added).

CHAPTER 3

Judges Are Human Too

Or

Bigotry From the Bench

One step, if not the first step, in developing a proper, that is to say properly limited, respect for the judicial branch and judges in general is to consider briefly how their own biases have affected their judgment in a couple of famous cases. They are not demigods ruling impartially from on high. They are men and women who bring their own biases to their jobs; some succeed in not letting those biases influence their decisions, and some fail.

For example, a New Jersey law allowed local school boards to make rules and enter into contracts for transporting children to and from non-profit private schools, rules and contracts which would require the local government to reimburse parents for such costs. A school district taxpayer challenged this law in the case *Everson v. Board of Education of the Township of Ewing*.

While the court upheld the New Jersey law, the decision, written by Justice Black, claimed that the provision of the First Amendment that prohibited Congress from passing a "law respecting an establishment of religion" would also apply to states because the Fourteenth Amendment would prohibit states from passing a "law respecting an establishment of religion."

Black noted, "The First Amendment has erected a wall between church and state. That wall must be kept high and impregnable. We could not approve the slightest breach. New Jersey has not breached it here."[1]

So, while parents of children subject to compulsory education laws were reimbursed for transportation to school, the language of Black's decision would serve to ultimately eliminate parental influence in the moral sphere in public education to the point that Ten Commandment ethics would be subordinated to the demands of the LGBTQ agenda in future court decisions.

Historian Daniel Driesbach noted that the *wall* that Justice Black built was far different from Jefferson's: "Black's wall . . . separates religion and all civil government. . . . Jefferson's 'wall' separated church and federal government only. . . . Black's wall separates religion and civil government at all levels—federal, state and local. . . . Black turned the First Amendment . . . on its head."[2]

Driesbach astoundingly points out that "Hugo Black's biographer reported that the justice did not peruse the proceedings of the First Congress, which debated the provision now known as the First Amendment, until '[a]fter Everson

---

1   Everson v. Board of Education of the Township of Ewing, 330 U.S. 1 (1947).

2   Daniel Driesbach, *Thomas Jefferson and the Wall of Separation between Church and State* (New York: New York University Press, 2002), pp. 125–26.

was decided.'"[3]

Legal historian and religious liberty specialist John Witte Jr. pointed out the dubious legal pedigree of Black's wall of separation: "In Everson, the disestablishment standard that the Court chose was the strong separationist standard already in place in some state constitutions and initially proposed in the Defeated Blaine Amendment of 1875."[4]

The Blaine Amendment, named for Representative James G. Blaine of Maine, was introduced in the House of Representatives in 1875. The proposed amendment provided, "No State shall make any law respecting an establishment of religion, or prohibiting the free exercise thereof; and no money raised by taxation in any State for the support of public schools, or derived from any public fund therefor, nor any public lands devoted thereto, shall ever be under the control of any religious sect; nor shall any money so raised or lands so devoted be divided between religious sects or denominations."[5]

This amendment passed the House of Representatives in 1875 on a vote of 180 to 7. It failed of two-thirds passage in the Senate on a vote of 28 in favor to 16 against.[6] In other words, Justice Black took an amendment proposed to the US Constitution in 1875 that was never submitted to the states for ratification and claimed that the policy contained therein

---

3   Ibid., p. 124.
4   John Witte, Jr., *Religion and the American Constitutional Experiment: Essential Rights and Liberties*, 2nd ed. (Boulder, CO: Westview Press, 2004), p. 138.
5   44 Cong. Rec. __ (December 14, 1875).
6   Philip Hamburger, *Separation of Church and State* (Cambridge, MA: Harvard University Press, 2002), p. 298.

was the real and authentic meaning of the Constitution!

How can a Supreme Court justice run so far afield of the historical record and precedent? Justice Hugo Black's personal and political background offers an explanation. Black, a US senator from Alabama, owed his political success to his 1921 legal defense of an Alabama Klansman—the Reverend Edwin Stephenson, a Methodist preacher accused of the murder of Father James Coyle, a Birmingham, Alabama Catholic priest—and his eventual membership in Alabama's Ku Klux Klan.

Reverend Stephenson, upon learning that his daughter had married a Catholic from Puerto Rico, went to St. Paul's Catholic Church where he found Father Coyle on the rectory porch. Father Coyle acknowledged to Reverend Stephenson that he had presided at the wedding of Stephenson's daughter, Ruth, to a Catholic Puerto Rican, Pedro Gussman earlier that day. A struggle ensued with the result that Stephenson shot Coyle dead. Stephenson's parental discipline of his adult daughter, Ruth, earlier in 1921 had included tying Ruth to her bed for three days, nailing the windows of her room shut, and whipping her.[7]

Black was retained by the head of the Alabama Klan, Grand Dragon Jim Esdale, to defend Stephenson. Black suspected that the dark-skinned Gussman had "negro ancestry" and managed to have the lights of the courtroom lowered to make Gussman's skin look dark. Black asked the jury to

---

[7]   Glenn Feldman, *Politics, Society, and the Klan in Alabama, 1915-1949* (Tuscaloosa: University of Alabama Press, 1999), quoted in Philip Hamburger, *Separation of Church and State* (Cambridge, MA: Harvard University Press, 2002), pp. 424, 426.

look at Gussman's skin, hair, and eyes but did not ask him any questions.[8] He didn't have to. Black's argument strongly suggested that Father Coyle had duped Ruth into marrying Gussman. Black noted, "Because a man becomes a priest does not mean that he is divine. . . . Who believes that Ruth Stephenson has not been proselytized? A child of a Methodist does not suddenly depart from her religion unless someone has planted in her mind the seeds of influence. When you find a girl who has been reared well persuaded from her parents by some cause or person, that cause or person is wrong."[9] Black even used a secret Klan hand signal in the courtroom. Yes, Stephenson was acquitted.

In 1923 Black joined the Richard E. Lee Klan chapter and was appointed kladd of the klavern, an officer who initiates members into the Klan by an oath about white supremacy and the necessity to separate church and state. Black's name eventually was put on the Klan stationary. When he ran for the US Senate in 1926, Black spoke to most of the 148 Klan chapters across Alabama about the menace of Catholicism.[10]

That Black wrote what he did in *Everson* should not be a surprise. And that Black could command a majority of the Supreme Court who would simply make up their own amendments to the Constitution shows a profound hostility to government by the people on the part of the justices. And why not? What did they have to fear from the people's timid

8   Feldman, *Politics, Society, and the Klan in Alabama, 1915-1949*, quoted in Hamburger, *Separation of Church and State*, p. 425.

9   Roger K. Newman, *Hugo Black: A Biography* (New York: Pantheon, 1994), pp. 83, 86, quoted in Hamburger, *Separation of Church and State*, pp. 425, 426.

10   Hamburger, *Separation of Church and State*, pp., 426, 427.

representatives? The record is unambiguous. For decades, a clear majority of members of Congress have been content to do nothing more than issue press releases in response to the erosion of government by the people according to the "Laws of Nature and of Nature's God." It is our hope that this book will serve to provide legislative tools to the representatives of the people who need those and some backbone to the ones who need that.

Homosexual "Marriage" and Religious Liberty

Black's "judicial amendment" of the religious liberty clause of the First Amendment in *Everson* reached its logical conclusion with the *Obergefell* same-sex "marriage" decision in which the majority justices fabricated moral laws and devised tortured meanings for the Constitution.

Justice Roberts pointed out that the *Obergefell* decision

> creates serious questions about religious liberty. Many good and decent people oppose same-sex marriage as a tenet of faith, and their freedom to exercise religion is—unlike the right imagined by the majority—actually spelled out in the Constitution. Amdt. 1.
>
> Respect for sincere religious conviction has led voters and legislators in every State that has adopted same-sex marriage democratically to include accommodations for religious practice. The majority's decision imposing same-sex marriage cannot, of course, create any such accommodations. The majority graciously suggests that religious believers may continue to "advocate" and "teach" their views of marriage. . . .

The First Amendment guarantees, however, the freedom to "exercise" religion. Ominously, that is not a
word the majority uses.

Hard questions arise when . . . a religious college
provides married student housing only to opposite-sex
married couples, or a religious adoption agency
declines to place children with same-sex married couples. Indeed, the Solicitor General candidly acknowledged that the tax exemptions of some religious
institutions would be in question if they opposed
same-sex marriage. . . . Unfortunately, people of faith
can take no comfort in the treatment they receive from
the majority today.[11]

And Justice Thomas pointed out:

Numerous amici—even some not supporting the
States—have cautioned the Court that its decision
here will "have unavoidable and wide-ranging impli-
cations for religious liberty." . . . The two will come
into conflict, particularly as individuals and churches
are confronted with demands to participate in and
endorse civil marriages between same-sex couples.

The majority appears unmoved by that inevitabil-
ity. . . . Religious liberty is about freedom of action in
matters of religion generally, and the scope of that liberty is directly correlated to the civil restraints placed
upon religious practice.[12]

---

[11]   Obergefell v. Hodges, 576 U.S. ___ (2015).
[12]   Ibid.

The administration of justice is too important to be left to judges. Regarding the issue of where the real responsibility for governance resides in America, Justice Warren said it was not with the judiciary: "In our democracy it is still the Legislature and the elected Executive who have the primary responsibility for fashioning and executing policy consistent with the Constitution. . . . But the day-to-day job of upholding the Constitution really lies elsewhere. It rests, realistically, on the shoulders of every citizen."[13]

Let's do our job; let's carry the cross; let's take back our country . . . inch by legislative inch if we have to.

[13]   Earl Warren, "The Bill of Rights and the Military," *Air Force Law Review* 60, p. 26.

Chapter 4

A Note About Tolerance

Or

The Stick With Which They Beat Us

Intolerance is the alleged "sin" of the modern age. Successfully labeling an individual as "intolerant" isolates and dismisses that person from serious consideration in public policy questions. But let us examine what tolerance is and some of its characteristics. First, it involves a type of restraint from acting.

Thomas Jefferson gave us this example of tolerance in the Declaration of Independence: "Prudence, indeed, will dictate that Governments long established should not be changed for light and transient causes; and accordingly all experience hath shewn, that mankind are more disposed to suffer, while evils are sufferable, than to right themselves by abolishing the forms to which they are accustomed."

So tolerance involves refraining from action in the face of a real or perceived evil. Secondly, tolerance requires the acceptance of certain standards, truths, or propositions held to be true. In fact, the only people who can truly be tolerant are those with firm unwavering standards or principles.

Persons who think all truths are relative or shifting cannot be tolerant by definition. They have no firm moral principles that can be violated in such a way as to require their "tolerance" of said violations. (Of course, most people aren't that consistent and display very little in the way of toleration of the expression of traditional religious views in the public square. The way in which the term "hate speech" is so loosely employed today is an example of their intolerance of opposing views.)

French Catholic philosopher Etienne Gilson explained tolerance this way:

> It is only when we are certain that what somebody says or does is wrong, that we can judge it advisable to tolerate it. . . . Tolerance does not consist in accepting all philosophical statements as more or less probable, but, being absolutely certain that one of them is true and the others false. . . . Thomas Aquinas taught that the Jews should be allowed to worship in their own way. . . . As a Christian, he knew for sure that the Jews were wrong, and this was precisely the reason why, from his own point of view, they had to be tolerated. Nearer to home, the Quebec Act of 1774 was a true act of tolerance, because the effect was that, in Canada, Popery would henceforward be tolerated by men who were absolutely sure that Popery was wrong. . . .
>
> Tolerance is a moral and a political virtue, not an intellectual one. . . . Our only duty towards ideas is to be right. . . . What we really mean by saying that we tolerate certain ideas is that we tolerate the existence of

certain men who hold those ideas and that we respect
their freedom of speech . . . because, even though we
know that their ideas are wrong, these men are our fellow countrymen with whom we have to live in peace.
. . . Tolerance is nothing else than a particular application to the needs of political life, of the moral virtue
of friendship.[1]

Political liberals in general and advocates for homosexual
causes in particular have made significant progress in their
political and social demands by claiming they only seek
equal treatment of persons. But, in fact, these advocates seek
social approval or legal acceptance of particular behaviors.
Their demands are constantly cloaked in terms of "accepting
persons" when, in fact, it is the homosexual, transgender, or
other aberrant behavior for which they seek social and legal
acceptance.

The effort to legitimize perverse behavior manifests itself
in LGBTQ efforts to establish "safe spaces" or to be "wel-
coming" to LGBTQ students; this is a mask for the real
goal of securing legal acceptance or recognition of the sexual
behavior. But the homosexual lobby will not stop at that
level of acceptance that they have, by and large, achieved;
they will not stop until everyone must "approve" under penalty of law. We Christians must be firm in balancing our love
for our neighbors with our fidelity to God's law. Equality of
persons is not equality of behavior. Vice is *not* virtue. Self-
restraint is not the equal of self-indulgence.

---

[1]   Etienne Gilson, "Dogmatism and Tolerance," *International Journal* 8, no. 1 (1953): pp. 12, 13.

Christ taught us to love the sinner but hate the sin. But homosexual advocates have merged *person* and *behavior*. And because many homosexuals equate their behavior with their identity, and because the law is a teacher, to gain any legal recognition and acceptance of homosexual practice in the civil law is to establish the licitness of their behavior.

And as the homosexual lobby movement has made such progress in its quest for "tolerance," people who hold to traditional moral values are, not surprisingly, increasingly treated with intolerance. In the minds of many today, Christians and others who would deny "equality" do not really deserve to be "tolerated" in the civil order. And they are not.

Justice Roberts noted the persistent name-calling by same sex marriage proponents:

> Perhaps the most discouraging aspect of today's decision is the extent to which the majority feels compelled to sully those on the other side of the debate. The majority offers a cursory assurance that it does not intend to disparage people who, as a matter of conscience, cannot accept same-sex marriage. . . . That disclaimer is hard to square with the very next sentence, in which the majority explains that "the necessary consequence" of laws codifying the traditional definition of marriage is to "demea[n]or stigmatiz[e]" same-sex couples. . . . The majority reiterates such characterizations over and over. By the majority's account, Americans who did nothing more than follow the understanding of marriage that has existed for our entire history—in particular, the tens of millions

of people who voted to reaffirm their States' enduring definition of marriage—have acted to "lock . . . out," "disparage," "disrespect and subordinate," and inflict "[d]ignitary wounds" upon their gay and lesbian neighbors. . . . These apparent assaults on the character of fair minded people will have an effect, in society and in court. . . . Moreover, they are entirely gratuitous. It is one thing for the majority to conclude that the Constitution protects a right to same-sex marriage; it is something else to portray everyone who does not share the majority's "better informed understanding" as bigoted.[2]

In 2013, Justice Kennedy, in striking down the federal Defense of Marriage Act, which allowed states to reject recognizing same-sex marriage laws of other states, had this to say about the moral character of same-sex "marriage" opponents:

> DOMA's principal effect is to identify a subset of state sanctioned marriages and make them unequal. The principal purpose is to impose inequality, not for other reasons like governmental efficiency. . . . [DOMA] places same-sex couples in an unstable position of being in a second-tier marriage. The differentiation demeans the couple, whose moral and sexual choices the Constitution protects. . . . It humiliates tens of thousands of children now being raised by same-sex couples. . . .

---

[2]   Obergefell v. Hodges, 576 U.S. ___ (2015).

DOMA also brings financial harm to children of
same sex couples. . . .

. . . The principal purpose and the necessary effect
of this law are to demean those persons who are in a
lawful same-sex marriage.[3]

Kennedy, who does not appear to have claimed in public
that he is clairvoyant, nevertheless gets away with his gratuitous and abusive highbrow moral denunciations of real
marriage supporters because of his status as a justice. His
statements and those of others similarly situated provide
social cover for editorial and political denunciations at the
community level of LGBTQ opponents and those who publicly adhere to sexual morality based on the Old and New
Testaments.

So, while we arrange our arguments in logical order,
adduce proofs, or cite peer review social science studies
showing the individual and social damage from homosexual behavior, our opponents respond with invective-laced
denunciations of our so-called "homophobic" efforts, and
the liberal media is content to sweep the truth out of the
public arena because opposition to the LGBTQ agenda
makes us intolerant bigots and places us on the wrong side
of history and progress. At least that is the hope of our opponents, who need an unthinking, uncritical, and amoral public to secure their "victories."

Bishop Fulton Sheen explained it this way: "Tolerance
is an attitude of reasoned patience towards evil, and a for-
bearance that restrains us from showing anger or inflicting

---

[3]   United States v. Windsor, 570 U.S. ___ (2013).

punishment. But what is more important than the definition is the field of its application. The important thing here
is this: Tolerance applies only to persons, but never to truth.
Intolerance applies only to truth, but never to persons. Tolerance applies to the erring. Intolerance to the error."[4]

Advocates of the homosexual agenda rely upon confusing,
in the minds of American citizens, the social purpose of the
civil necessity for social tolerance with the rigorous application of intellectual reason in maintaining moral truths. Political liberals need to sow this particular confusion in order
to disarm public resistance to their radical and fundamental
opposition to the "Laws of Nature and of Nature's God" as
they implement their program for homosexuality, abortion,
religion, the family, and the role of an omnipotent state.

We who are marked with the sign of Faith must not let
this confusion proceed any further if we are to successfully
affect public policy to secure the common good.

---

[4]   George Marlin, Richard Rabatin, and John Swan, eds., *The
Quotable Fulton Sheen: A Topical Compilation of the Wit, Wisdom,
and Satire of Archbishop Fulton J. Sheen* (New York: Doubleday,
1989), p. 321.

CHAPTER 5

The Intolerance of Those
Advocating "Tolerance"

Or

Religious Freedom Slipping Away

The regime of "tolerance" that homosexual advocates want to impose on America was exposed during the Spring 2015 fight in the Indiana legislature between conservatives and LGBTQ believers; the homosexual lobby's view of tolerance was outlined by a prominent homosexual advocate in the *New York Times*:

> Homosexuality and Christianity don't have to be in conflict in any church. . . . The continued view of gays, lesbians and bisexuals as sinners is a decision. . . . Our debate about religious freedom should include a conversation about freeing religions and religious people from prejudices. . . . Religion is . . . the final holdout . . . for homophobia. It will give license to discrimination. It will cause gay and lesbian teenagers in fundamentalist households to agonize . . . : Am I broken? Am I damned? . . .

. . . Mitchell Gold, a prominent . . . gay philanthro-
pist, . . . told me that church leaders must be made
"to take homosexuality off the sin list." His commandment is . . . warranted. All of us . . . should know better
than to tell gay people that they're an offense.[1]

Looking Through Their "Playbook" Decades Later

The success of the LGBTQ agenda in recent years has largely
depended on identifying the homosexual movement as a
modern version of the civil rights struggle. This is, of course,
nonsense. There never were heterosexual-only water foun-
tains in any Southern state. Separate sexually segregated elementary or secondary schools were not built for LGBTQ
children. Homosexuals and lesbians could sit anywhere on
buses, trains, and other public transportation. Homosexuals were never enslaved as a class or brought to America in
chains. Homosexuals never were forbidden from marrying
heterosexuals. A number, in fact, did. Homosexuals did not
have to engage in nationwide "sit ins" at restaurant lunch
counters to be served a meal. Lesbians did not have to take
literacy tests as a condition for voting.

But the fact of it being nonsense has not stopped the
homosexual lobby from striving mightily to convince the
American public that gay rights follow naturally upon the
legitimate civil rights movement of the 1960s. Their stun-
ning success attests to the genius, if you can call it that, of

[1]   Frank Bruni, "Bigotry, the Bible and the Lessons of Indiana," *New York Times*, April 3, 2015, http://www.nytimes.
com/2015/04/05/opinion/sunday/frank-bruni-same-sex-sinners.
html?_r=0.

their tactics. Marshall Kirk and Hunter Madsen described with remarkable prescience and candor the way in which homosexual advocates would gain political and social ascendency. In their 1989 book *After the Ball*, they laid out the Madison Avenue public relations tactics, which have been tremendously successful, aided as they have been by the prevailing politically correct atmosphere and the ever-increasing intolerance of and hostility towards traditional Christian views. They were off in the timing but correct in their judgment of the efficacy of their tactics:

> We mean conversion of the average American's emotions, mind and will, through a planned psychological attack, in the form of propaganda fed to the nation via the media. . . .
>
> Conversion makes use of Associative Conditioning . . . to include really adorable, athletic teenagers, kindly grandmothers, avuncular policemen, ad infinitum. . . . The objection will be raised . . . that we are exchanging one false stereotype for another equally false . . . it makes no difference that the ads are lies . . . because we're using them to ethically good effects. . . .
>
> . . . We seek desensitization *and nothing more.* . . . forget about trying . . . to persuade folks that homosexuality is a *good* thing. But if you can get them to think it is just *another* thing—meriting no more than a shrug of the shoulders—then your battle for legal and social rights is virtually won. . . .
>
> . . . The public should not be shocked and repelled by premature exposure to homosexual behavior itself.

... The imagery of sex per se should be downplayed and the issue of gay rights reduced . . . to an abstract social question . . . to emphasize the civil rights/discrimination side of things. . . .

. . . Gays must be portrayed as victims in need of protection. . . . The purpose of victim imagery is to make straights feel very uncomfortable . . . with shame. . . .

. . . Gays should be portrayed as victims of *circumstance* . . . they no more chose their sexual orientation than they did . . . their height. . . . To suggest in public that homosexuality might be *chosen* is to open up a can of worms labeled "moral choice and sin." . . . Straights must be taught that it is . . . natural for some persons to be homosexual . . . wickedness and seduction have nothing to do with it. . . . *Since no choice is involved, gayness can be no more blameworthy, than straightness.* . . . Gays should be portrayed as *victims of prejudice.*[2]

If Americans who still hold traditional values are honest with ourselves, we can only marvel at how successful they have been. This was truly a campaign aided and abetted by the cultural "elites" at major news outlets, entertainment companies, corporate America and many "Christian" churches. It was a campaign that adhered to its "playbook" and achieved the desired result. And the result has been and will be disastrous to the religious freedoms of Christians as the below examples illustrate.

---

[2]   Marshall Kirk and Hunter Madsen, *After the Ball: How America Will Conquer its Fear and Hatred of Gays in the 90s* (New York: Penguin Books, 1989), pp. 153, 154, 177, 178, 183, 184.

Sexual Orientation and "Discrimination"

Most states are "employment at will" states. This means that an employer does *not* need good cause to terminate your job, unless an employee has special contractual rights spelled out in an employment contract. Exceptions to being fired at will are:

> *State Human Rights Act*: A person may not be fired on the basis of Race, Color, National Origin, Religion, Sex (including pregnancy, childbirth, and related medical conditions), physical or mental Disability, Age, Genetic information, or Marital status); *Federal Civil Rights Acts of 1964 & 1968*: A person may not be fired on the basis of Race, Color, National origin, Religion, Sex (including pregnancy, childbirth, and related medical conditions), Disability, Age (40 and older), Citizenship status or Genetic information.

The homosexual advocacy group the Human Rights Campaign states that as of this writing, nineteen states and the District of Columbia prohibit "discrimination" based on sexual preference or gender identity. An additional three states prohibit "discrimination" based on sexual orientation.[3]

Thus, the class of persons who seek legal standing or special protection because of their sexual orientation or their subjective and shifting preference for "gender identity" different from their biological identity are not, at this writing, part of most state or federal civil rights laws. Even during the Obama administration, when Democrats controlled both

---

[3]   "The Need for Full Federal LGBT Equality," Human Rights Campaign, http://www.hrc.org/fullfederalequality/.

Houses of Congress, neither sexual orientation nor "gender identity" were added to the federal civil rights laws.

LGBTQ hiring and firing can work in two directions. The Apple Computer Company hired former Alabama state representative Republican Jay Love (2003–13), who served as chairman of the Alabama House of Representatives Taxing Committee, to lobby for Apple in Alabama. But Apple, operating under the rubric of the "new tolerance," fired Love when they discovered that one of his past sins was his opposition to same-sex "marriage."[4]

The firing or non-hiring of individuals for their support of natural marriage is a habit with homosexual leaders and their sympathizers. Brendan Eich, founder of Mozilla (the Firefox Internet browser), was fired as CEO of Mozilla after he was "outed" for the crime of supporting California's Proposition 8 campaign to protect authentic marriage. As reported in Slate, "Brendan Eich is gone. The creator of JavaScript and co-founder of mozilla.org has quit as Mozilla's CEO, forced out by the uproar over a donation he made six years ago to a ballot measure against gay marriage. There's no record of Eich discriminating against gay employees—'I never saw any kind of behavior or attitude from him that was not in line with Mozilla's values of inclusiveness,' says the company's chairwoman, Mitchell Baker."[5]

---

4   Amanda Terkel, "Apple Breaks Ties with Anti-Gay Alabama Lobbyist," *The Huffington Post*, February 19, 2015, http://www. huffingtonpost.com/2015/02/17/_n_6699054.html.

5   William Saletan, "Purge the Bigots," *Slate*, April 4, 2014, http://www.slate.com/articles/news_and_politics/frame_ game/2014/04/brendan_eich_quits_mozilla_let_s_purge_all_ the_antigay_donors_to_prop_8.html.

The author of the article thought Eich got what he deserved.[6]

In another case, science fiction writer and Southern Virginia University professor Orson Scott Card (a Mormon and past board member of the National Organization for Marriage) was eased out of the DC Comics Superman project for his opposition to same-sex marriage and was kept at a respectable distance from promoting the film adaption of his own novel, Ender's Game, featuring Harrison Ford, Asa Butterfield, and Abigail Breslin (2013).[7] When DC Comics hired Card in 2013 to write for their *Adventures of Superman*, homosexual advocates expressed their opposition, eventually threatening a boycott of DC Comics if Card was still retained by DC Comics to work on the project "because he is opposed to gay marriage."[8]

Former ESPN and CBS broadcaster and former Southern Methodist University and NFL football star tailback Craig James was fired by Fox Sports Southwest. In 2012, James lost a four-way Republican primary in Texas for the US Senate, which Ted Cruz won. He made comments against same sex marriage. He specifically criticized former Dallas mayor Tom Leppert for his participation in a homosexual rights

---

[6]   Ibid.

[7]   Andy Lewis and Borys Kit, "'Ender's Game' Author's Anti-Gay Views Pose Risks for Film," *The Hollywood Reporter*, February 20, 2013, http://www.hollywoodreporter.com/heat-vision/enders-games-orson-scott-cards-422456.

[8]   Todd Starnes, "DC Comics Faces Boycott Over Anti-Gay Superman Writer," *Fox News*, February 13, 2013, http://nation.foxnews.com/anti-gay-comics/2013/02/12/dc-comics-faces-boycott-over-anti-gay-superman-writer.

parade, saying he would never do such a thing.[9]

The *New York Daily News* reported, "James had yet to sign a contract and made only one appearance on the show before Fox Sports cut ties with him. . . . The alleged root of the problem was James' controversial comments on gays, such as claiming during a failed 2012 U.S. Senate run that they would 'have to answer to the Lord for their actions.' A Fox spokesperson implied that . . . by saying, 'We just asked ourselves how Craig's statements would play in our human resources department. He couldn't say those things here.'"[10]

As one would expect, advocates of the new tolerance are, of course, targeting Catholic schools. A homosexual teacher at the Catholic Mount de Sales Academy in Macon, Georgia, filed a lawsuit in 2014 against the school, which did not renew his contract as a band teacher after the school discovered his plans to "marry" a man. The school, which had posted its hiring policy on the Internet, indicated a willingness to hire individuals regardless of their sexual orientation, gender identity, gender expression, or any other characteristic protected by federal, state, or local law.[11] Neither Georgia

---

9   Tod Robberson, "Is anyone really trampling on Craig James'
        religious freedom?," *The Dallas Morning News*, August 4, 2015,
        http://dallasmorningviewsblog.dallasnews.com/2015/08/is
        -anyone-really-trampling-on-craig-james-religious-freedom.html/.

10   Jamie Uribarri, "Fox Sports Southwest charged with discrimi-
        nation over Craig James firing," *New York Daily News*, March 6,
        2014, http://www.nydailynews.com/sports/college/fox-sports
        -charged-discrimination-craig-james-firing-article-1.1713059.

11   "EEOC Backs Mount de Sales band director in discrimination
        case," 13WMAZ, March 30, 2015, http://www.13wmaz.com/
        story/news/local/macon/2015/03/30/eeoc-backs-mount-de-sales-
        band-director-in-discrimination-case/70680918/.

nor the federal government designate sexual orientation as a protected class. So the teacher filed a complaint with the federal Equal Employment Opportunity Commission, which issued a letter on January 30, 2015, that found "there is reasonable cause to conclude that he 'was discriminated against because of his sex (sexual stereotyping) in violation of Title VII of the Civil Rights Act of 1964, as amended.'"[12]

Abolishing the First Amendment

"Equality acts" are legislative proposals that seek to provide legal protections to individuals based on homosexual behavior or gender identity confusion by adding sexual orientation and gender identity into state or federal civil rights laws. These proposals have expansive definitions encompassing public accommodations going far beyond hotels, restaurants, movie theaters, or other places of business where racial minorities were barred.

Equality acts expand the definition to include any establishment that provides a good, service, or program. This broad definition can refer to a store, shopping center, online retailer or service provider, salon, bank, gas station, food bank, service or care center, shelter, travel agency, or funeral parlor, or establishment that provides health care, accounting, or legal services. Private schools are establishments that provide a "service," that is, education. Significantly, equality acts exclude religious beliefs as a valid reason not to comply with government demands that individuals, businesses, or organizations affirm, comply, or facilitate homosexual or

---

[12]   Ibid.

transgender status, behavior, celebrations, or relationships.

If state or federal "civil rights" acts are amended in this fashion, the First Amendment's freedom to practice religion will have been abolished. Federal regulations or guidelines affirming the agenda of equality acts have been applied by federal executive agencies and are being litigated in states now. Failure of Congress to clamp down on backdoor bureaucratic alterations in federal civil rights laws litigated through the liberal federal court system will produce the same effect as congressional passage of equality acts.

PART TWO

The Playbook:
Terms, Strategy, and Tactics

Thus far you have read of the Founding Fathers' thoughts concerning religious freedom and how they are similar in certain respects to those of the popes and other churchmen, but very different from those of modern radical secularists who would drive all traces of religious expression from the public square. You have learned some little-known facts concerning the respective powers of the judicial and legislative branches of the federal government. And you have seen in print that which has unfolded before our very eyes over the last few decades: the progress made by the abortion and homosexual lobbies in imposing their agendas against the wishes of the American people, and, more importantly, you have learned something of their tactics in doing so. Now it is time to do something with that knowledge. It is time to take action.

Chapter 6

Strategy and Tactics for Legislators

Or

How to Protect Ourselves Through the "Power of the Purse"

When it comes to determining the direction public policy takes, James Madison wrote, "This power over the purse may, in fact, be regarded as the most complete and effectual weapon with which any constitution can arm the immediate representatives of the people, for obtaining a redress of every grievance, and for carrying into effect every just and salutary measure."[1]

Limiting types of spending can be done in state legislatures on budgets, or in Congress on various appropriations bills. Control of the purse is an essential function of legislatures. Courts have no business ordering money to be spent, unless it is to comply with payments required in a valid contract.

---

[1]   *Federalist*, no. 58.

Congressional Power of the Purse

Both liberals and conservatives have successfully used appropriations amendments to change and otherwise affect and influence public policy over the past fifty years. Every appropriations bill consists of page after page of limitations, conditions, or prohibitions limiting how federal tax dollars may be spent, if spent at all. The history of such prohibitions includes:

- Cutting off military funding for American support of the Vietnam war, which led to the fall of Saigon in 1975.
- Prohibiting Medicaid funding of abortion on demand via the Hyde Amendment in 1976.
- Prohibiting funds to assist anti-communists to overthrow the Communist government in Angola in 1975–76.
- Prohibiting federal monies from paying for abortion in the District of Columbia and the military in the late 1970s (Rep. Dornan).
- Blocking the implementation of a published IRS regulation preventing President Jimmy Carter from compelling private, predominantly Christian schools to prove they were not discriminating on the basis of race in order to keep their tax-exempt status in 1979.
- Banning the use of tax funds to assist Contra rebel groups from overthrowing the Nicaraguan government in 1982.

Even though the *Obergefell* decision has been made, the LGBTQ remaking of society is not complete. LGBTQ forces have to eliminate any vestige of one man/one woman marriage in social structures by withholding federal funds, tax exemptions, licensing, contracts, or benefits allowed to private institutions which do not accept same-sex marriage or policy corollaries like imposing transgender requirements on schools, businesses, private non-profit organizations, churches, etcetera.

So, offering appropriations amendments to bills funding federal agencies will be an important vehicle by which to stop LGBTQ efforts in courts and federal or state executive agencies from coercing Christian institutions and individual consciences into compliance with their agenda.

Using history as a guide, a Hyde Amendment approach will be most effective.

History as a Guide

The first congressional responses to the pro-abortion *Roe v. Wade* court decision were conscience or taxpayer protections. Thus, in 1973, the initial response to *Roe v. Wade* in the US Senate was a vote of ninety to one in favor of an amendment to the Hill Burton Act offered by Senator Frank Church (D-ID), which provided that receipt of funding through three federal programs could not be used as a basis to compel a hospital or individual to participate in abortion or sterilization procedures if the hospital or individual had moral or religious objections to those practices.

The first vote in the House of Representatives post-*Roe* came in June 1973 with a floor amendment preventing the Legal Services Corporation (LSC) from litigating abortion cases or challenges. [As a grant reviewer at the Office of Economic Activity, which superintended the Legal Services Corporation, I furnished information to congressional offices detailing the LSC spending on abortion litigation in support of the *Roe* and *Doe* abortion decisions that led to a floor amendment cutting off tax funds for abortion litigation by the LSC.]

And in 1976, a friend and I devised a rough draft of what would become the original Hyde Amendment curtailing the use of Medicaid funds for abortion. The justification for such an amendment was documentation, obtained by my friend through a Freedom of Information request, that specified that roughly 280,000 abortions had been paid for by federal tax money. I gave the rough draft of the amendment and the document demonstrating the federal funding of abortion to Representative Bob Bauman (R-MD) outside the floor of the House of Representatives. I urged that an amendment be offered on the floor of the House of Representatives to the Labor and Health, Education and Welfare Appropriations bill cutting all funding of abortion. Rep. Bauman, in turn, presented the proposal to Congressman Henry Hyde, then a freshman Republican legislator from Illinois. The result was the Hyde Amendment, which passed and is still federal law.

A similar approach by real marriage supporters to limit applications of the *Obergefell* decision would produce various "Hyde amendments for marriage" because of the public familiarity with the Hyde abortion funding ban. Current conscience legislation in state and federal laws relating to abortion, performance of sterilization, distribution of birth control or abortion pills by pharmacists, exemptions from genetic counseling requirements, and reciting the Pledge of Allegiance in public schools all make the acceptance of conscience protection exemptions for compliance with *Obergefell* an increased likelihood.

Had Indiana legislators in the spring of 2015 approached their religious liberty legislation as part of the tradition of already enacted conscience laws, a different outcome may have resulted from their failed State of Indiana Religious Freedom Restoration Act effort. Planned Parenthood notes that forty-five states expressly allow some health care providers to refuse to do abortions, and all of those states allow health care workers to refuse to take part in abortions.[2]

Since 2005, the Weldon Amendment has been part of the Health and Human Services appropriations legislation. It provides that, "None of the funds made available in this Act [HHS Appropriations] may be made available to a Federal agency or program, or to a state or local government, if such agency, program, or government subjects any institutional or individual health care entity to discrimination on the basis that the health care entity does not provide, pay for, provide coverage of, or refer for abortions."[3]

The public fight that will ensue in Congress with record votes to prevent compulsory acceptance and compliance

---

[2]   "Refusing to Provide Health Services," Guttmacher Institute, September 1, 2017, https://www.guttmacher.org/state-policy/ explore/refusing-provide-health-services.

[3]   Weldon Amendment, Consolidated Appropriations Act, Pub. L. No. 111-117, 123 Stat. 3034 (2009).

with the LGBTQ agenda by "Hyde"-type marriage, transgender, or anti-LGBTQ spending amendments will ensure
that voters understand which members of Congress will protect them from such compulsion and which will not. Even a
loss on an amendment curbing applications of *Obergefell* is
not a loss in the long run because the bottom line is to secure
a record vote of who supported and who opposed real marriage. We need a public marker so we can decide which representatives to support for re-election and which to oppose.

House Marriage Appropriations Amendments to Blunt LGBT "Marriage"

The following are appropriations bills that could properly
be amended to confront the implementation of the *Obergefell* decision.

Labor, Health and Human Services bills, which include
appropriations for:

(1) The Department of Education, which would include
scholarships, student aid awarded to students who go to religious college.

(2) Office of Civil Rights: Elementary School Family Life
Education courses could be insulated from being required to
teach the licitness of same-sex "marriage" or imposing transgender demands on the use of traditional single-sex facilities,
etcetera.

Defense Appropriations bills can be amended to protect chaplains from being compelled to perform same-sex
marriages.

The **Commerce Appropriations bill** funds the Justice Department, and a Hyde marriage amendment could prevent:

- US Marshals from delivering court orders to comply with *Obergefell* and its LGBTQ progeny;
- the Civil Rights Commission from establishing compliance with *Obergefell* and its LGBTQ progeny;
- the Equal Employment Opportunity Commission from hearing cases from aggrieved homosexuals who were discharged or not rehired because they "married" their partners in violation of the religious teaching of such schools on marriage or privacy and safety protections in providing single-sex facilities.

Financial Services and General Government bills, which includes:

- Treasury Department for 501c (3) standing of churches, schools, colleges, and hospitals.
- Federal Judiciary (hearing further cases applying extensions of *Obergefell*).
- Small Business Administration (denying grants or contracts unless the small business accepts and applies benefits to same-sex married couples, or transgendered).
- Executive Office of the President (executive orders mandating compliance with any aspect of *Obergefell*).

If congressmen or senators tell citizens that Hyde marriage amendments may not properly be added to various appropriations bills, they are either inexcusably ignorant or they

are not telling the truth. The House Appropriations Committee Financial Services and General Government Report
for the 2016 appropriations bill explains that the appropriations bill does the following:

- Prohibits the White House from ordering the IRS to
  determine the tax-exempt status of an organization.
- Checks the expansion of Executive Branch authorities
  by: prohibiting funding for signing statements that
  abrogate existing law; prohibiting funds for Executive
  Orders that contravene existing law; requiring cost
  estimates to be included for new Executive Orders and
  Presidential Memorandums; prohibits funding for
  so-called "czars"; and prohibiting changes in agency
  spending without the enactment of appropriations
  bills.[4]

And the actual 2016 House Financial Services Appropriations Bill curbs the federal judiciary as follows: "For expenses
necessary for the operation of the Supreme Court, as
required by law, excluding care of the building and grounds,
including hire of passenger motor vehicles . . . not to exceed
$10,000 for official reception and representation expenses."[5]
So federal judges are already curbed and limited by congressional appropriations amendments regarding both the
amount and purpose for which federal monies may be

---

[4]   Comm. on Appropriations, Financial Services and General Gov-
        ernment Appropriations Bill, 2016, H.R. Rep. No. 114-194, at
        4, 6 (2015).
[5]   Financial Services and General Government Appropriations Act,
        2016, H.R. 2995, 114th Cong. (2015).

spent. Congress, because it has the exclusive power over the national purse, can and does restrict how money may be spent, including restricting or prohibiting whether any money may be spent litigating legal cases.

Missed Amendment Opportunities

Both the House and Senate, and their appropriations committees, can put restrictions on appropriations bills. So, if an opportunity is missed in the House, spending limitation amendments maybe added in the Senate Appropriations Committee or on the Senate floor.

And because Congress has developed a habit of not passing individual agency appropriations bills—instead passing one single bill near the end of the year called an Omnibus that funds all federal agencies—that Omnibus bill can be amended on the floor of the House of Representatives if a "Rule" is approved by the entire House allowing Hyde-type marriage amendments. This has been done.

The semi-exception or procedural complication to adding amendments in the full Senate is the Senate practice of filibuster, or prolonged debate for the purpose of avoiding up or down votes on measures before the entire Senate. Cutting off debate is called "cloture" and must be supported by a certain number of elected senators.

Appropriations bills have been "talked to death" in the Senate without ever taking a final up or down vote.[6] In 1917, the Senate, under severe criticism for becoming an

---

6   *Congressional Quarterly's Guide to the Congress of the United States: Origins, History and Procedure* (Washington: Congressional Quarterly, 1971), p. 80.

obstructionist legislative body, adopted Rule 22 limiting debate if two thirds of the Senate so voted.[7] At present, Senate Rule 22 now provides that debate on legislation can be curtailed by a vote of "three fifths of the Senators duly chosen and sworn," or sixty senators.[8]

There are direct and indirect ways around the Senate filibuster. First, an amendment limiting some aspect of the LGBTQ agenda can be added to an appropriations bill in the Senate Appropriations Committee. Bills in the Senate Appropriations Committee (or any Senate committee) are not subject to a requirement that three-fifths of committee members must agree to cut off debate. So, if any LGBTQ limiting amendments were added in the Senate Appropriations Committee, the burden would be on LGBTQ partisans to remove the provision(s) from the appropriations bill on the Senate floor. Or they could disguise their real objection to the anti-LGBTQ to procedural opposition to even considering the measure. The risk, however, is that such objectors can be tagged with refusing to fund the federal government for a narrow reason.

As long as record votes are secured on retaining or removing pro-family amendments, no effort is wasted. (As of this writing, the authorities I have consulted are divided whether the budget reconciliation process, under which parts of the Obama health insurance were enacted, could be used to enact specific limitations on the use of appropriated money for LGBTQ purposes.)

---

7   Ibid., p. 81.
8   Senate Cloture Rule, S. Prt. No. 112–31 (2001).

"Hyde" Marriage Amendments Need
to Address Specific Actions

The appropriations amendments, to be effective, would have to blunt the effect of the Supreme Court decision mandating recognition or implementation of homosexual "marriage" and must prohibit the use of monies or fees from being used to compel unwilling organizations or individuals to comply with any aspect or extended application of the ruling in *Obergefell v. Hodges*.

At a minimum, "Hyde" marriage protection amendments should prohibit the use of funds to:

- Remove the tax-exempt status of any church, institution, university, school, or non-profit entity declining to facilitate or participate in same-sex "marriage";
- Require any federal contractor or grantee to accommodate same-sex "marriage";
- Discipline military chaplains who decline to perform or participate in a same-sex "marriage";
- Require federal employees to undergo sexual attitude restructuring education;
- Withhold any federal grant or contract to any state which declines to implement same-sex "marriage";
- Prohibit free speech of those who advocate for one-man, one-woman marriage by federal agencies;
- Coerce state or local governments or private organizations, businesses, or individuals to comply with *Obergefell*;
- Allow federal courts to hear challenges to state or federal laws enacted after *Obergefell v. Hodges* that affirm

one-man, one-woman marriage and decline to recognize same-sex marriage;

- Bar the use of federal monies from being used to implement transgender policies at elementary, secondary schools, or colleges. Or prohibit any federal education monies from going to any state education department, program, or subsidiary of such, or local school districts from receiving *any* federal education monies if the school has policies implementing aspects of the transgender agenda.

The following Hyde marriage protection amendment language is suggested: *Provided that no funds under this Act, or any provision of the law, may be used to require individuals or organizations to provide services, contract for, support, facilitate, or participate in services or ceremonies related to same-sex marriage, pursuant to Obergefell v. Hodges, and/or its associated cases. Nor may any funds in this Act be denied to individuals or organizations, which decline to provide employment or employment benefits for persons in same-sex unions, or which fail to provide for separate facilities based on sexual orientation or gender identity.*

To preclude implementation of *Obergefell*, and also to provide support for states that did not seek to repeal any of their marriage statutes or constitutional provisions regarding marriage, language similar to the following could be offered to the Financial Services Appropriations Bill both in the House and the Senate: "None of the funds appropriated in this Act may be used to issue any precept of enforcement regarding the judgment of the United States Supreme Court in the case of *Obergefell et al. v. Hodges, Director, Ohio Department of Health, et al.*, decided June 26, 2015."

If Congress or a state passed a one-man, one-woman marriage law even after *Obergefell,* federal courts could be prevented from striking down these new measures if appropriations amendments were passed prohibiting the use of funds by federal courts to rule in the arena of marriage. Such budget amendments would have the practical effect of restricting federal courts' Article III appellate jurisdiction. As we saw in an earlier chapter, in the early 1980s, John Roberts, then special assistant to the attorney general and now chief justice, wrote a detailed memo asserting that the limiting of federal courts' Article III appellate jurisdiction by Congress is constitutional and does not deny any due process rights.[9]

Language to eliminate federal courts from hearing any new state or federal law recognizing only one-man, one-woman marriage could read as follows: *No funds may be expended by any court created by Act of Congress or the Supreme Court in appellate jurisdiction to hear or decide any question pertaining to any of the United States' marriage statutes or their constitutional provisions related to marriage limited by sex.*

Congress doing nothing affirms the legitimacy of the court's *Obergefell* decision. The silence of Congress would be an affirmation of the greatest voter suppression scheme accomplished under color of authority in American history in which

---

[9]   John Roberts, memorandum, "Proposals to Divest the Supreme Court of Appellate Jurisdiction: An Analysis in Light of Recent Developments," National Archives and Records Administration, https://www.archives.gov/files/news/john-roberts/accession-60-89-0172/006-Box5-Folder1522.pdf.

the votes of more than fifty million Americans who supported marriage amendments in referenda were summarily dismissed. Five unelected, appointed judges have, in effect and based on unsubstantiated hearsay, ruled that not only is representative government irrelevant but also unconstitutional!

The Hyde Amendment approach is necessary *now* to clearly identify for the public the totalitarian goals of same-sex marriage proponents who tolerate no First Amendment religious liberty protections for persons who adhere to the teachings of Jesus Christ or Moses, or who respect the "Laws of Nature and of Nature's God."

Because appropriations bills are necessary to keep the government functioning, they must be considered and passed yearly. Other bills can be buried in committees. Appropriations bills cannot be ignored.

Call to Action

Hyde-like marriage protection amendments can be lifeboats for individual and institutional religious liberty. A fight must be waged to blunt implementation of same-sex "marriage" every year during consideration of appropriations bills in Congress. State budgets should also become instruments for public policy implementation in defense of life and marriage.

Citizens have a right to know where their federal and state representatives stand on the question of marriage. The risk of permanent damage to individuals, our institutions, and our country are too great to allow those who represent "We the People" to duck accountability at this juncture or refuse to defend marriage by not using the appropriate constitutional tools at their disposal. We who support real marriage, as understood and practiced for millennia, should not be penalized in our persons, churches, schools, businesses, or families.

A few weeks after the *Obergefell* travesty, Catholic churches throughout the nation were sent a nationwide bulletin insert.[10] On Sunday, July 5, 2015, in my own parish the pastor read his statement on *Obergefell*, calling it an "unjust decision" and explaining that Catholics needed to be ready for persecution. At the end of his homily, the congregation heartily applauded.

The implementation of *Obergefell* does not depend on the Justice Department, the sitting president, or the Supreme Court. It does depend on the steadfastness of Americans of goodwill in demanding prudential action from their elected officials.

10   "One Man, One Woman, for Life," United States Conference of Catholic Bishops, http://www.usccb.org/issues-and-action/ marriage-and-family/marriage/promotion-and-defense-of- marriage/upload/Marriage-Redefinition-Lead-Messages-5-6-13. pdf; "Marriage and the Supreme Court," United States Conference of Catholic Bishops, 2015, http://www.usccb.org/issues- and-action/marriage-and-family/marriage/promotion-and- defense-of-marriage/upload/Bulletin-AFTER-Scotus-brown.pdf.

CHAPTER 7

Legislation and the
Art of the Possible

Or

A To-Do List for Legislators

Politics has been described as "the art of the possible." In other words, politicians should not scorn to do whatever good they can even if their entire program is not politically possible at any given time. The legislative process has also been described in more colorful language. Nineteenth-century Prussian chancellor Otto von Bismarck is reputed to have remarked that no one should watch how sausage and laws are made. Thus, the question arises how can one successfully navigate the legislative arena relying on Christian principles without losing one's wits or soul?

As we have seen, Pope St. John Paul II recognized that murky moral situations arise with frequency in the legislative arena, especially in cases where attempts are made to limit grave evils that have previously been recognized in the civil law. It is worth reviewing his teaching in this context: "When it is not possible to overturn or completely abrogate a pro-abortion law, an elected official, whose absolute personal opposition to procured abortion was well known, could licitly support proposals aimed at limiting the harm done by such a law and at lessening its negative consequences at the level of general opinion and public morality. This does not in fact represent an illicit cooperation with an unjust law, but rather a legitimate and proper attempt to limit its evil aspects."[1]

While some legislative efforts should directly address outlawing grave moral evils such as abortion or so-called homosexual marriage, in a society that has reached such a level of moral disorder, restricting, impeding, or even partially outlawing such behavior will present serious practical difficulties. The following are some measures, however, that would achieve a good end and are politically feasible.

Exposure of Abortionists to Civil Liability: Abortionists claim two things: abortion is safer for women than childbirth, and they are defending women's rights. Both claims are false. By applying the premise that women should be compensated for injuries they suffer, bills that would extend the time for filing tort claims for injury from legal abortion would cut into abortion profits and compensate injured women. A woman should be allowed two years from the time the injury is discovered, not from the time of the abortion, to file a tort claim. This is reasonable, as a woman may only discover later in life that she has difficulty carrying a "wanted" baby to term. Legislation to allow a delayed claim to be filed against the abortionist and the clinic or facility

---

[1]   Pope St. John Paul II, Encyclical *Evangelium Vitae* (1995), no. 73.

where the abortion was performed could help women and save lives.

Prohibit Abortion for Sex Selection: Techniques for discovering the sex of children long before birth are now widely available. Simply amending a state human rights or civil rights law to prevent the abortion of a child of the "wrong" sex would allow pro-life forces to piggyback on public sentiment against sex discrimination.

Collect Abortion Complication Data: For years the US Centers for Disease Control (CDC) perpetrated fraud on the public in their claims about abortion safety. For example, the CDC asked abortionists to only report abortion complications to public health authorities that the abortionists discover while the woman is on the operating table.

In the late 1980s, a public health professor and I wrote to hospital emergency room and Ob/Gyn doctors in Virginia asking whether they treated standard complications identified by the CDC on women who aborted in the previous year. The number of complications reported to us was about 650 percent greater than those Virginia authorities reported for the same time period. An abortion complication reporting law should require a state health department to collect and analyze data on complications resulting from any abortion procedure by a physician who treats the complication within sixty days of an abortion, in addition to those complications noted by the abortionist. Such a law would at least capture short-term complications from legal abortion.

Ban Forced or Coerced Abortion: Any person who forces or coerces a pregnant female of any age to have an abortion against her will should be subject to criminal sanctions of varying severity. An enhanced penalty should apply if the coerced female is younger than eighteen. Because of lessened maturity, a coerced female under age eighteen should be allowed to bring a civil action against the person who forced or coerced her to have an abortion within one year of her eighteenth birthday or, if the female is more than eighteen years of age at the time of the abortion, within one year of the date of the abortion. An action for the wrongful death of the unborn child against the person who forced or coerced her to have an abortion should also be allowed.

Ban Tax Money for Abortion: The Hyde Amendment banning Medicaid expenditures from being used to pay for abortion resulted in a legal challenge to its constitutionality. The US Supreme Court, in 1980, concluded, "Regardless of whether the freedom of a woman to choose to terminate her pregnancy for health reasons lies at the core or the periphery of the due process liberty recognized in *Wade,* it simply does not follow that a woman's freedom of choice carries with it a constitutional entitlement to the financial resources to avail herself of the full range of protected choices."[2]

Unless the provisions of a state constitution require tax payments for abortion, every state should engage in budget battles to stop tax-funded abortions. If state court decisions ruled that for some reason abortion funding is a constitutional right, a campaign should be mounted for an amendment to that state's constitution. No civil right under the US Constitution is abridged or taken away simply because abortions are not tax-paid.

---

[2]   Harris v. McRae, 448 U.S. 297 (1980).

Ban Tax Funds for Groups That Perform Abortions: In 1988, President Ronald Reagan's Department of Health and Human Services issued regulations governing the conditions under which money available under Title X of the Public Health Service Act, which paid for birth control services, could be spent. To use a parallel example, a federal grant would not be given to the Ku Klux Klan for urban renewal in inner cities with the proviso that no money could be spent by the KKK for racial discriminatory purposes because the prohibition would be of no effect in prohibiting racial discrimination by an organization formed for that purpose.

Reagan's regulations provided that a "Title X project may not provide counseling concerning the use of abortion as a method of family planning or provide referral for abortion as a method of family planning;" and a Title X project was prohibited from referring a pregnant woman to an abortion provider, even if she requested it. The Title X program, since its inception in 1970, had a provision providing that federal funds could not be used in programs "where abortion is a method of family planning." The Supreme Court sustained the Reagan regulations and said they were not prohibited by either the First or Fifth Amendments.[3] Because of this decision, states are not constitutionally required to fund programs that include abortion.

Marriage and Life: Even if a state legislature or the Congress doesn't support the right to life, or real one-man, one-woman marriage, securing record votes on raising the issues or life or marriage will identify for the public which legislators are for or against a proposal. Having benchmark votes

---

[3]   Rust v. Sullivan, 500 U.S. 173 (1991).

will help to restore legal protections for preborn children and reestablish real marriage as part of the civil law because such votes will make it clear who wants to accommodate the destruction of real marriage and who wants to protect it, and then, armed with that knowledge, social conservative voters can elect the right people to office in future elections.

Prohibit the Death Penalty for Pregnant Women: A way to secure a vote that affirms the humanity of the preborn child in civil law is to prohibit the execution of a pregnant woman. This is a "soft" vote on the humanity of the preborn child. Nevertheless, it allows pro-life groups to emphasize in the public arena that the innocent should not be put to death for the crimes of the guilty.

Provisional Reversal of Roe v. Wade (at State the Level): Such a statute would provide that if the United States Supreme Court decisions in *Roe v. Wade* and/or *Doe v. Bolton*[4] are overturned, states would once again be allowed to protect preborn children according to the provisions of their state law which were in effect as of January 1973 or another date if more comprehensive legal protections were recognized in an earlier version of that state's criminal abortion law. A state official would be charged with giving public notice of the Supreme Court's reversal. Such announcement would trigger a set date for the state's previous abortion law to become effective without additional action by the legislature. (In order to secure the strongest protection for preborn children, a date earlier than January 1973 may have to be designated in states that enacted so-called abortion "reform" legislation

---

4   Roe v. Wade, 410 U.S. 113 (1973); Doe v. Bolton, 410 U.S. 179 (1973).

between 1965 and 1972.)

Direct Challenge to Roe v. Wade: Supreme Court justice Harry Blackmun noted in *Roe v. Wade*: "The appellee and certain amici argue that the fetus is a 'person' within the language and meaning of the Fourteenth Amendment. In support of this, they outline at length and in detail the well-known facts of fetal development. If this suggestion of personhood is established, the appellant's case, of course, collapses, for the fetus' right to life would then be guaranteed specifically by the [Fourteenth] Amendment."[5]

A finding of fact affirmed by a state legislature, and/or the Congress, that individual human life commences at conception or fertilization would, in the words of the pro-abortion *Roe* and *Doe* court, provide the legal foundation for standing in court to seek legal protection for the lives of children before birth. The gist of the Human Life Bill introduced in the 1980s by Representative Henry Hyde, Senator Helms, Congressman Bob Dornan, and others included findings affirming the humanity of the child *in utero* as a "person" under the Fourteenth Amendment. None of these measures became law.

State legislatures could formally assert that scientific information affirms the humanity of the child in the womb for purposes of the state constitution, or Congress could define the term *person* in the Fourteenth Amendment, to set up a challenge to *Roe* and *Doe* in federal or state courts. Both houses of a state legislature (Nebraska has only one chamber), would affirm the conclusions of various medical, scientific, or other authorities as legislative findings that human

---

5   Roe v. Wade, 410 U.S. 113 (1973).

rights pertain and apply fully to all human beings or persons before birth because human life begins at conception or fertilization. The joint resolution would end with a statement to the effect that: "RESOLVED, the House of Representatives and Senate of the state (commonwealth) of _____ recognize and find that the life of the human person commences at conception, also known as fertilization, and that the United States Supreme Court 1973 *Roe* and *Doe* decisions striking down state laws criminalizing abortion, which protected preborn children, are based on false science."

Retaining State Marriage Laws and Amendments: In 1923, the US Supreme Court held the District of Columbia minimum wage law to be unconstitutional.[6] Thirteen years later, the Supreme Court reversed itself and held laws banning child labor to be constitutional.[7] The attorney general of the United States advised President Franklin Roosevelt that Congress, which has jurisdiction over the District of Columbia (Washington, DC), did not have to reenact the DC minimum wage law because the earlier court decision merely suspended enforcement and did not abrogate the law itself.

So removing pro-life or pro-real marriage language from state constitutions or statutes would require that we re-pass such laws in the future if the court reversed itself. This plays into the hands of our secular opponents. They should be left on the books.

Efforts to Remove "One-man, One-woman" Marriage Laws from State Code Books or Repealing "One-man, One-woman" Constitutional Amendments Need to Be Strongly Resisted: To

---

6   Adkins v. Children's Hospital, 261 U.S. 525 (1923).
7   West Coast Hotel v. Parrish, 300 U.S. 379 (1937).

allow such removal or rescission is to acknowledge the legitimacy of the Supreme Court *Obergefell* decision. (Remember that the Supreme Court undermined its own legal and moral legitimacy by ruling in *Dred Scott v. Sanford* that runaway slave Dred Scott was "property" and not a person.) Again, securing record votes on removal or reversal of marriage law or amendments will show the public who still supports real marriage.

Efforts to Add Same-sex Marriage or Transgender Components to "Family Life" Courses in Schools Should Be Opposed: A way to block such efforts would be to insist that the medical pathologies associated with homosexual behavior should be made part of any such curriculum. LGBTQ proponents do not want the truth regarding the multiple psychiatric and medical problems associated with homosexual behavior to become a topic of public discussion, and they may prefer to drop their effort rather than address such thorny issues.

Federal Marriage Amendments: Marriage amendments to the US Constitution can either allow states to reenact state laws or enact state constitutional amendments defining marriage as a relationship between one man and one woman, or an amendment to the US Constitution could actually define marriage as only a relationship between one man and one woman.

Asking your member of Congress to support a marriage amendment can keep the marriage issue alive. But placing all our legislative efforts for the restoration of real marriage into the passage of constitutional amendments affirming real marriage is an approach our opponents did not take because of its inherent difficulty. Remember, since 1789, only four

US Supreme Court decisions have been reversed by constitutional amendments.

The above are simply a few suggestions to legally protect family, human life, and marriage.

CHAPTER 8

Special Tactics for Legislators in the Individual States

While the Constitution states, "All legislative Powers herein granted shall be vested in a Congress of the United States,"[1] and the "Constitution, and the Laws of the United States . . . made in Pursuance thereof . . . shall be the supreme Law of the Land."[2] Congress, nevertheless, is without any authority to compel states to carry out federal laws, unless the states agree, as we shall see below in court cases going back to the mid-nineteenth century.

And since many federal programs depend for their success on state cooperation, state refusal to assist the implementation of federal programs is an effective and constitutional way to practically suspend the operation of a federal law within those states. A state that refuses to participate in a federal program is said to be exercising its anti-commandeering powers.

---

[1]   U.S. Const. art. I, § 1.
[2]   U.S. Const. art. VI, cl. 2.

Supreme Court opinions dating back to 1842 explain this legal doctrine, which affirms that a state has exclusive sovereignty in certain instances against the federal government and such powers are not limited to a refusal to spend state money. Justice Joseph Story, for the court, held that the federal government could not force states to implement or carry out the Fugitive Slave Act of 1793: "The States cannot, therefore, be compelled to . . . carry into effect the duties of the National Government, nowhere delegated or entrusted to them by the Constitution. On the contrary, the natural, if not the necessary, conclusion is, that the National Government, in the absence of all positive provisions to the contrary, is bound, through its own proper departments, legislative, judicial, or executive, as the case may require, to carry into effect all the rights and duties imposed upon it by the Constitution."[3]

A second relevant case arose from a lawsuit by the state of New York objecting to provisions of a 1985 federal law dealing with state obligation to handle nuclear waste. The court, in 1992, decided that:

> Congress may not simply "commandee[r] the legislative processes of the States by directly compelling them to enact and enforce a federal regulatory program." . . . "States are not compelled to enforce the steep slope standards, to expend any state funds, or to participate in the federal regulatory program in any manner whatsoever. If a State does not wish to submit a proposed permanent program that complies with the

---

[3]   Prigg v. Pennsylvania, 41 U.S. 16 Pet. 539 (1842).

Act and implementing regulations, the full regulatory burden will be borne by the Federal Government."

. . . "The Act commandeers the legislative processes of the States by directly compelling them to enact and enforce a federal regulatory program."[4]

More recently, in the 2012 challenge to Obamacare, the Supreme Court held that Congress could not compel states to accept changes to the Medicaid program: "As for the Medicaid expansion, that portion of the Affordable Care Act violates the Constitution by threatening existing Medicaid funding. Congress has no authority to order the States to regulate according to its instructions. Congress may offer the States grants and require the States to comply with accompanying conditions, but the States must have a genuine choice whether to accept the offer. The States are given no such choice in this case: They must either accept a basic change in the nature of Medicaid, or risk losing all Medicaid funding."[5]

The Power of State Anti-Commandeering Laws

Just what effect on public policy can state passage of anti-commandeering or non-compliance laws have? A refresher on these points of history, law, and the Constitution is important for social conservatives, especially because state defiance of congressional enactments occurred over the issue of slavery.

---

[4]   New York v. United States (91-543), 488 U.S. 1041 (1992).
[5]   National Federation of Independent Business v. Sebelius, 567 U.S. __ (2012).

In December 1860, the legislature of South Carolina referred to the anti-commandeering laws as the reason for secession from the Union: "The States of Maine, New Hampshire, Vermont, Massachusetts, Connecticut, Rhode Island, New York, Pennsylvania, Illinois, Indiana, Michigan, Wisconsin and Iowa, have enacted laws which either nullify the Acts of Congress or render useless any attempt to execute them. . . . In none of them has the State Government complied with the stipulation made in the Constitution.[6]

The Fugitive Slave Act of 1850, among other things, allowed federal commissioners to give a claimant the authority to remove a fugitive slave from a free state back to his slave state of origin including through forcible means. It penalized anyone obstructing a slave captor as well as any US Marshal up to $1,000 for not assisting fugitive slave captors and required them to issue warrants to assist runaway slave claimants by providing that "all good citizens are hereby commanded to aid and assist in the prompt and efficient execution of this law whenever their services may be required . . . anywhere in the state where they are issued.[7]

Northern states responded by passing personal liberty laws:

> These laws generally prohibited the use of the State's
> jails for detaining fugitives; provided State officers

---

[6] *The Annals of America*, vol. 9, *1858-1865: The Crisis of the Union* (Chicago: Encyclopedia Britannica, 1968), s.v. "South Carolina Declarations, December 24, 1860."

[7] *The Annals of America*, vol. 8, *1850-1957: A House Dividing* (Chicago: Encyclopedia Britannica, 1968), s.v. "The Compromise of 1850."

under various names throughout the State to act as counsel for persons alleged to be fugitives; secured to all such persons the benefits of *habeas corpus* and trial by jury; required the identity of the fugitive to be proved by two witnesses; forbade State judges and officers to issue writs or give assistance to the claimant, and imposed a heavy fine or imprisonment for the crime of forcibly seizing or representing as a slave any free person with intent to reduce him to slavery.[8]

The Massachusetts legislature went out of their way to twit Congress with a host of defiant provisions starting with an express reference to the Fugitive Slave Law of 1850 as the reason for establishing draconian obstacles to removing fugitive slaves from Massachusetts: the writ of habeas corpus would apply to fugitives; jury trials were required; a slave claimant had to specify his charge in writing and claimants were barred from appearing in trial court; alleged facts had to be proved by two witnesses; removal from Massachusetts of an individual pursuant to a false claim merited a fine of $1,000–5,000 and a jail sentence of one to five years; a Massachusetts official who authorized removal of an individual pursuant to the Fugitive Slave Act was deemed to have resigned any state government office and was forever ineligible for future office; any attorney assisting slave removal was barred from practicing law; sheriffs, police, jailers, or member of the volunteer militia who assisted the recovery of slaves could be fined from $1,000–2,000 and jailed from

---

8   Marion M. Miller, ed., *Great Debates in American History,* vol. 4 (New York: Current Literature Publishing Company, 1913), p. 230.

one to two years. No jail or prison could be used to detain or imprison anyone guilty of violating the Fugitive Slave Act.[9]

In Wisconsin, the controversy over the Fugitive Slave Law led the state judiciary in 1858 to defy the US Supreme Court.[10] The bottom line or lesson learned is that the states

---

[9]   *The Annals of America*, vol. 8, *1850-1957: A House Dividing* (Chicago: Encyclopedia Britannica, 1968), s.v. "Massachusetts Personal Liberty Act of 1855."

[10] "It will be seen, from the foregoing statement of facts, that a judge of the Supreme Court of the State of Wisconsin in the first of these cases, claimed and exercised the right to supervise and annul the proceedings of a commissioner of the United States, and to discharge a prisoner, who had been committed by the commissioner for an offense against the laws of this Government, and that this exercise of power by the judge was afterwards sanctioned and affirmed by the Supreme Court of the State.

"In the second case, the State court has gone a step further, and claimed and exercised jurisdiction over the proceedings and judgment of a District Court of the United States, and upon a summary and collateral proceeding, by habeas corpus, has set aside and annulled its judgment, and discharged a prisoner who had been tried and found guilty of an offense against the laws of the United States, and sentenced to imprisonment by the District Court.

"And it further appears that the State court have not only claimed and exercised this jurisdiction, but have also determined that their decision is final and conclusive upon all the courts of the United States, and ordered their clerk to disregard and refuse obedience to the writ of error issued by this court, pursuant to the act of Congress of 1789, to bring here for examination and revision the judgment of the State court. . . .

"The judges of the Supreme Court of Wisconsin do not distinctly state from what source they suppose they have derived this judicial power. . . . It certainly has not been conferred on them by the United States; and it is equally clear it was not in the power of the State to confer it, even if it had attempted to do so; for no State can authorize one of its judges or courts to exercise judicial power, by habeas corpus or otherwise, within the juris-

do not have to act as doormats for federal programs, especially, for example, when a president such as Barack Obama places his sexual progressives in federal agencies who then devise novel applications for civil rights laws such as claiming that the failure of public schools to provide bathroom or locker room accommodations to a biological male who identifies as a female constitutes sex discrimination forbidden by the Civil Rights Act of 1964 or 1968, this even though Congress never debated or approved such applications or meanings for the law.

This approach has the added advantage of putting political liberals on the defensive because this state non-cooperation tactic was used by northern states to thwart the recapture of runaway slaves, and to prevent the enslavement of free African-Americans who could be falsely singled out by southern slavers and their agents and who were also forbidden from testifying in their own defense by the federal Fugitive Slave Law. Some commentators refer to anti-commandeering laws as "nullification" laws. While such statutes can certainly have the effect of making a particular federal law of no effect in that state, it does not technically "nullify" it, but it does render it inoperative in that state.

The pedigree of non-cooperation is impeccable. James Madison, the Father of the Constitution, pointed to state

---

diction of another and independent Government. And although the State of Wisconsin is sovereign within its territorial limits to a certain extent, yet that sovereignty is limited and restricted by the Constitution of the United States. . . .

"The judgment of the Supreme Court of Wisconsin must therefore be reversed in each of the cases now before the court." Ableman v. Booth, 62 U.S. 506 (1858).

non-cooperation with the federal government as the most effective means to neutralize federal policies: "Should an unwarrantable measure of the federal government be unpopular in particular States . . . or even a warrantable measure be so . . . The disquietude of the people; their repugnance and, perhaps, refusal to co-operate with the officers of the Union; the frowns of the executive magistracy of the State; the embarrassments created by legislative devices . . . would oppose, in any State, difficulties not to be despised."[11]

---

[11]   *Federalist*, no. 46.

Chapter 9

Tactics for Citizens

The Boycott as a Tool to Tame Corporate America's Promotion of Anti-Christian Values

The goal of this book is to both educate and inspire legislators and citizens to take action in the noble effort to "roll back" the gains made by the radical Left in recent decades. Legislative tactics have already been outlined, and the nuts and bolts of becoming an active citizen on the local level will follow. But here I'd like to make brief mention of a tactic that has often been considered one of the Left, but which is a tool everyday citizens can use to make their voices heard in the only language that some powerful forces in our country understand: that of the bottom line. It has the added benefit of being easy as it actually involves doing nothing; to be precise, it involves not shopping somewhere and letting the company you are boycotting know that you are doing so and why you are doing so.

Corporate America has been no friend to conservative values. Just look back to the introduction of this book at the list of companies that have played an active role in subverting Christian values and strong-arming their employees, host cities, and other entities to accept homosexual marriage and the transgender agenda. But this last controversy over who may use which bathrooms may have been a bridge too far even for the American public, which has proved itself all too pliable in these matters. Has the silent majority been awoken? Happily, so-called, misguided tolerance has its limits, even for many liberal Americans, and those limits seem to have been reached where the safety of their children is concerned.

It is long past time that Christians made our voices heard in the boardrooms of corporate America by the exercise of boycotts. The American Family Association (AFA), under the direction of Tim Wildmon, called for and is leading the most successful pro-traditional values boycott in our nation's history against Target Corporation, a boycott that currently has more than 1.5 million signatories. Here is the relevant text from the AFA website, www.afa.net:

> The American Family Association is calling for a boycott of Target after the retail giant said it would allow men to use the women's restrooms and dressing rooms in their stores.
>
> On its web site, Target announced, "[W]e welcome transgender team members and guests to use the restroom or fitting room facility that corresponds with their gender identity. . . . Everyone deserves to feel like they belong."

This means a man can simply say he "feels like a woman today" and enter the women's restroom . . . even if young girls or women are already in there. Target's policy is exactly how sexual predators get access to their victims. And with Target publicly boasting that men can enter women's bathrooms, where do you think predators are going to go?

Clearly, Target's dangerous new policy poses a danger to wives and daughters. Over 1 million people agree with us and pledged to boycott Target stores until protecting women and children is a priority.

One solution is a common-sense approach and a reasonable solution to the issue of transgendered customers: a unisex bathroom. Target should keep separate facilities for men and women, but for the trans community and for those who simply like using the bathroom alone, a single occupancy unisex option should be provided.

The AFA is to be commended for spearheading this effort. And while this book deals principally with political knowledge, engagement, and action, the boycott is a form, and a very effective and underutilized form at that, of action directed at those who would run roughshod over the rights and sensibilities of Americans holding conservative values.

Is it having an effect?

Target's stock price had declined 30 percent by late February 2017 from April 2016 when it announced it would accommodate transgendered individuals in the bathroom of their chosen gender, rather than their biological sex.[1] Business Insider reported that "1.4 million people signed a pledge to stop shopping at Target unless it reversed the policy. Sales fell nearly 6% in the three quarters after the post compared with the same period last year, and same-store sales have dropped every quarter since the post."[2]

Clearly, going forward, the boycott can be a tool increasingly used by Christians to voice their displeasure with corporate America's assault on their values.

---

[1]   Warner Todd Huston, "Target Retailer Hits $15 Billion Loss Since Pro-Transgender Announcement," Brietbart, February 28, 2017, http://www.breitbart.com/big-government/2017/02/28/target-down-30-percent-since-transgender-boycott-began/.

[2]   Hayley Peterson, "The Target boycott cost more than anyone expected — and the CEO was blindsided," Business Insider, April 6, 2017, http://www.businessinsider.com/target-ceo-blindsided-by-boycott-2017-4.

CHAPTER 10

You Must Understand How Things Work in Order to Work Effectively for Change

Or

Civics 101

Congress shall make no law . . . abridging the right of the people . . .
to petition the Government for a redress of grievances.
First Amendment

Elected officials do not know everything. If they did, they would be television commentators or editorial writers for newspapers! Members of Congress, state legislators, county or city council members, while vested with authority to make decisions for the common good, largely depend upon others for information to make those decisions.

All elected officials represent the American people and are employed and fired by "we the people." You and I pay their salaries, their office rent, their travel and legislative expenses. Elected officials should be approached as public servants of the people, not as demi-gods. We must respect their authority but understand that it comes with limits that are delineated in our national and state constitutions. According to the Declaration of Independence, the people are sovereign, not the elected representatives, and certainly not appointed officials.

Federal Representatives

Every US citizen is represented in Washington, DC, in the national legislature or United States Congress by two US senators, regardless of the population of a state, and by one congressman who represents a "congressional district." Or, in the case of smaller states, one US congressman represents an entire state. The "Congress" refers to both the House and Senate together, even though members of the House of Representatives are called "congressmen." All told, there are 100 US senators and 435 congressmen from the fifty states (plus "delegates" from territorial possessions of the United States who may casts votes on legislation in House of Representatives committees, but not on final passage of measures).

Contact information for your congressman can be found online at *house.gov*. By filling in your nine-digit zip code, you can learn who represents you. If you do not know your nine-digit zip code, look at a bulk mail label on advertising mail or bills you receive.

Contact information for your two senators is found at *senate.gov*. Click "senators" to select individuals by last name or by state. Phone numbers for the Washington, DC, office and district offices will be shown.

You can also call the US capitol's main switchboard phone number, 202-225-3121, to be connected by the operator to your political representatives.

When you contact your senators or congressmen, you will most likely speak with an aide. Make sure you also tell him/her where you vote, and give the precinct name if you know it. This information lets your representative know you are better informed about public affairs than the average citizen.

If you belong to a civic group, church, or have joined a homeowners or neighborhood association, mention its name and number of members. If you take part in community, school, civic, service, or sports organizations, tell him which ones and how many other people participate. The goal is to make the aides understand you know many others either who think like you or with whom you regularly share information. If you hold a leadership position in any of these groups, mention this.

State Representatives

In state capitols, with the exception of Nebraska which has a single chamber legislative body, citizens are represented by state senators and state representatives (also called "assemblymen" or "delegates" depending on the state). They run for office in "state election districts," which are different in size and geographic boundaries from congressional districts. Citizens pay the salaries and office expenses of these men and women who pass laws in our state legislatures. These legislatures meet at the state capitol to pass laws and vote on state budgets, and most have offices or meeting space, also located at the state capitol, during legislative sessions, if not year-round.

Some state officials keep offices in their home districts as well, but even if they do not, you can ask to meet your state senator or state representative anywhere, even at a fast food restaurant. Get to know your state legislators and let them hear your concerns, or they will only hear from lobbyists or our opponents. Be courteous and to the point. If you are visiting a legislator's office, always leave your contact information with a summary of your views and specific questions. Ask for the name of the staff aide who handles the particular issue for the legislator.

Local Representatives

Some people erroneously think that Congress is the only governmental institution that affects them. Depending upon where you live, your local lawmakers may be called councilmen, supervisors, or aldermen. Actions and policies supported by local town, city, or county government officials can have profound consequences, even if local officials are less visible or less well known than state or federal officials. Local elected officials directly affect your livelihood. They set rates for commercial and residential real property, personal property, and sales taxes, as well as various local license and business fees. They implement public school policies, make land use and zoning decisions, build and operate public schools, to name a few of their duties. *Whether or not an abortion clinic comes to your area will depend on zoning ordinances.*

Very few people vote in local elections, which means that those who do vote have much greater influence over public policy. Recall that it was not Congress, but the local government of New London, Connecticut, that condemned and turned over nine acres of homeowners' private property to developers for "economic development."

This resulted in the 5-4 *Kelo v. New London*[1] US Supreme Court decision in 2005, which held that local town, city, county, or parish governments can condemn your home for a "public purpose" such as increasing tax revenue for your locality. There is a big difference between "public purpose" such as economic development and "public use," such as a park, road, etcetera. This Supreme Court decision means that private property can be taken by governmental bodies (or state regulated utilities) for a so-called good reason, a practice our Founders would find atrocious. Imagine that was your home. Do you still think local political action does not matter?

Importance of Communicating With Lawmakers

I cannot emphasize enough the benefit of citizens sharing their concerns with their elected representatives at least by phone, emails, or regular letters. If officials have public "Town Halls," you can multiply your power and influence with lawmakers in a public meeting and ask questions to educate your neighbors. Some local governing bodies have "citizens time" at the beginning of their public meetings where anyone may bring up local concerns for two or three minutes.

---

[1]   Kelo v. New London, 545 U.S. 469 (2005).

Effective Communication

Legislators measure a citizen's depth of concern on an issue in part by the degree of trouble it took the constituent to make the contact. A personal visit to a lawmaker arranged by a group of constituents, which may involve traveling a distance, is always a very effective form of contact. Phone, email, or letter contact is also very useful, but cannot replace a personal meeting. Handwritten or personally typed letters show that a constituent went through additional time and trouble to communicate, but emails (not form emails) also grab attention.

Petitions sent to state legislators or congressmen, unless they contain hundreds of names, generally are on the low end of influencing a legislator, and petitions without addresses, phone numbers, emails, or other means of contacting the signer are of little value. However, individuals who sign petitions can be a resource for future lobby efforts. It is easier to convince a petition signer to take an additional step than trying to convince someone who will not even sign their name. Keep copies of all petitions before turning them over to a legislator. Petition signers could become the backbone of your civic group.

If a lawmaker is contacted by the leader of an organized group, he or she takes extra notice because community leaders influence other voters. In the mind of a lawmaker, a pastor of a church speaks for the church's members, which a legislator knows translates into many potential votes for or against him.

Most people do not understand just how powerful even a small number of people can be in the mind of a legislator.

I recall an instance about ten years ago when a colleague with some seniority in the Virginia General Assembly came to me puzzled because he had received five letters, all hand-written, from different constituents in his district about the same topic. He wanted to know what the ruckus was about! So few citizens actually take the time to contact their legislators, especially at the state level, that those who do, can exert much influence.

A legislator understands that you or others in your group may campaign for or against him in the next election depending upon how he votes. Your presence reminds the legislator of this reality.

When writing, research both sides of the argument and try to include responses to anticipated objections to your position. Go over your letter or email more than once. Make sure you write what you want to say before your press "send" for an email. Don't write anything in a letter you would not want to see in a newspaper or on the Internet. Keep copies of all correspondence, which will come in handy especially at election time!

If you have prior public statements from your legislator from older newspapers, campaign brochures, or websites that do not match your legislator's current views or votes, ask why his position changed. Do not assume ill will. Some factor could have changed to explain a switched position or vote. Keep friends informed about what you learn.

Do not simply express views. When expressing your concerns, always ask questions. If your legislator does not answer your questions or sends you a form letter response, write again and ask the questions again. At some point you can share the lack of response to your inquiries with neighbors or local papers. The lack of candor could become a campaign issue. Lack of transparency could convince other voters it's time to elect a new representative.

Members of the US House of Representatives and US Senate have web forms for constituents to send emails. These systems reject emails sent from outside the member's district or state. You can only really influence persons who directly represent you because you hire and fire them with your vote. You have little hold over representatives from other districts unless you donate to their campaigns, or the legislator is seeking another office that would allow you to vote for them.

Legislator's First Principles

I asked a congressman at a 2009 public meeting whether he had read President Obama's economic stimulus bill before he voted for it. He did not answer "yes" or "no," but asked me if it was a trick question! He then explained how many reports he had read and groups he had consulted. He danced well but never directly answered my question. Any office holder has a minimal duty to at least understand a bill before voting for or against it.

What an Oath of Office Requires

The US Constitution provides that "the Senators and Representatives before mentioned, and the Members of the several State Legislatures, and all executive and judicial Officers, both of the United States and of the several States, shall be bound by Oath or Affirmation, to support this Constitution."[2]

The present Oath of Office, which all US congressmen and senators take, reads as follows: "I, NAME, do solemnly swear (or affirm) that I will support and defend the Constitution of the United States against all enemies, foreign and domestic; that I will bear true faith and allegiance to the same; that I take this obligation freely, without any mental reservation or purpose of evasion; and that I will well and faithfully discharge the duties of the office on which I am about to enter. So help me God."[3]

I had a ten-minute conversation with a US senator in the fall of 2009 at a college football game. I explained that a very sound legal case could be made that the Obamacare individual insurance mandate was unconstitutional. The senator responded that I was probably right, but his main concern was health care costs! Did this senator put his oath first, or some other consideration?

An oath is a swearing before God to do or not do certain things. An oath to "support and defend the Constitution" binds one to use only the means and goals authorized by the Constitution to secure the common good. The US Constitution is the fundamental social compact between American citizens and their elected officials. Actions of our national and state governments are to be judged by this standard. State legislators take an additional oath to also support their respective state constitutions. An oath to the Constitution is also required of the president.[4]

---

2   U.S. Const. art. VI, cl. 3.
3   Oath of Office, Pub. L. No. 89–554, 80 Stat. 424 (1966).
4   U.S. Const. art. II, § 1, cl. 8.

Unless lawmakers read bills before they vote on them, they cannot possibly know if the measures agree or conflict with either the federal or state constitutions, or if what they are voting for or against comports with the common good.

The Founders wanted to ensure that office holders would have an allegiance to the American Republic, not to a dictatorship or to a leader.

William Shirer, a 1930s correspondent for CBS, Hearst syndicate Universal News Service, the New York Herald, and the Chicago Tribune, pointed out the frightening difference between the two types of oaths of allegiance:

> To leave no loopholes Hitler exacted from all officers and men of the armed forces an oath of allegiance— not to Germany, not to the constitution, which he had violated by not calling for the election of Hindenberg's successor, but to himself. It read: "I swear by God this sacred oath, that I will render unconditional obedience to Adolph Hitler, the Fuehrer of the German Reich and people, Supreme Commander of the Armed Forces, and will be ready as a brave soldier to risk my life at any time for this oath."[5]

Adherence and loyalty to the US Constitution is a moral and legal necessity for all legislators. If current lawmakers cannot demonstrate that proposals they vote on are constitutional under the United States or respective state constitutions, then we need to find new legislators.

---

[5]   William L. Shirer, *The Rise and Fall of the Third Reich: A History of Nazi Germany* (New York: Simon and Schuster, 1959), pp. 226–27.

The Path of Legislation

Bills

Congress and state legislatures suggest changes, repeals of, or additions to the current law in bills, which are numbered, such as H.B. 10—indicating that it was the tenth bill introduced; *H* identifies the legislative body (House) into which the measure was introduced. The date of introduction, the committee to which the bill is assigned, the names of sponsors, patrons, or co-patrons of the measure, a bill Title, and the text of the suggested language changes are also indicated in the bill.

In Congress, a bill stays "alive" for the two-year length of the particular Congress in which the bill was introduced. If bills do not pass during that time period, they must be re-introduced in the following Congress. State legislatures also have session time limits before legislation expires.

Omnibus Bills

An omnibus bill is legislation that contains many different, unrelated topics. When such bills are voted up or down, it is often difficult to determine a legislator's real view on an issue because the vote was taken on many disparate topics. Passing bills containing many separate provisions that would have little to no chance of passing if offered as single bills is called logrolling.

Omnibus bills are still part of the legislative process and can offer opportunities to raise issues by offering particular "amendments" that isolate specific concerns. Depending on the conditions governing the offering of amendments, such bills may provide opportunities. But if a lawmaker votes for or against an omnibus bill, it is not clear what specific reason prompted the vote. So it has a tendency to diminish public accountability.

Resolutions

The other form of legislation is called a resolution. Except for constitutional amendments, resolutions are used to express a formal position on a public policy matter without passing a law that would change the legal code. A measure introduced in the House is called a House resolution, and if introduced in the Senate is called a senate resolution. If the measure is considered by both the House and the Senate, it is called a joint resolution. Resolutions are numbered. Concurrent resolutions are also used when both legislative bodies will consider the identical matter.

Resolutions were used extensively and quite successfully by the colonial legislatures to press American demands on Parliament and also to organize resistance to Great Britain. For example, Patrick Henry's "Resolves" affirming taxation only with representation were approved in 1765 by the Virginia House of Burgesses. In March of 1773, the Virginia legislature passed a resolve to establish a Virginia Committee of Correspondence to monitor British usurpations of power and to urge other colonial legislatures to do the same.

In 1798, James Madison, credited as the father of the Constitution, drafted the Virginia Resolves (or Resolutions) which severely criticized the Federalist-controlled Congress and President John Adams for passage of the Alien and Sedition Acts. These acts resulted in fining and jailing

Jeffersonian Republicans and newspaper editors for sympa-
thizing with the French Revolution.

Jefferson and his supporters believed they would lose a
challenge of these acts in federal court because of the many
Federalist-leaning judges, so they supported passage of
resolutions by the Kentucky and Virginia legislatures that
declared the Alien and Sedition Acts unconstitutional and
urged similar resolutions in other states. The resulting controversy produced a Jefferson victory for president over
incumbent John Adams and his Federalist congressional
supporters, as well as repeal of the Alien and Sedition Acts.

Constitutional amendments to federal or state constitutions are introduced as joint resolutions. Another type of
resolution, called a simple resolution, governs the operation
of one chamber of a legislative body. These simple resolutions are not considered by the other legislative body. Congress sometimes uses a joint resolution to enact a public law
for a limited or temporary purpose.

Bill Sponsors or Patrons

To sponsor or patron a bill means that the lawmaker is proposing the legislation, or wants the public to know they
favor the measure. Legislators can add their name to a bill
introduced by another member and become a co-sponsor or
co-patron. Any member of the legislative body may become
a co-sponsor of a bill. Legislators make their positions known
publicly by sponsoring or co-sponsoring particular measures.

The more co-patrons a bill receives, the more support it
garners to pass. When both conservative and liberal legislators co-sponsor the same bill, this strongly suggests the bill

has broad, bipartisan support.

Legislators often introduce similar bills. Some state legislatures allow similar bills to be merged into one main bill enabling each member who was a sponsor or co-sponsor to gain credit for introducing it.

Legislative Committees

A committee is a sub branch of a legislative body organized to evaluate particular classes of legislation. All legislation passes through committees. Committees with large numbers of bills or resolutions assigned to them are often organized into sub-committees.

Committees permanently established to handle legislation are called standing committees. A special kind of temporary committee, called a conference committee, consists of a few members from the House and the Senate appointed to iron out differences between each chamber's versions of a bill. Conference committees are necessary because a bill must be approved in identical form by both the House and the Senate. The resulting conference report will later be accepted or rejected in its entirety by each body by votes in each legislative chamber.

Legislation is first debated in committee and can only be "reported" to the full House or Senate for a vote by a majority of committee members, provided a quorum (the minimum number necessary to conduct business) is present. Leaders of the political party with the majority of legislators usually choose who will serve on the various committees. If both political parties have the same number of legislators, the leaders of each work together to assign committee members equally.

The selection of committee members by the party leaders in power will ensure that certain bills will or will not be considered. Killing bills in committee virtually ensures the measure will not have a chance to pass on the floor, thus avoiding a vote by all legislators.

Usually members from "safe" seats, or districts that were won by a large percentage of voters, are assigned to certain committees by the leadership for the sole purpose of killing particular bills. The leadership can also form "ad hoc" committees to kill controversial measures. Watching bills in committee is very important because, unless a bill survives committee action, there will never be a vote by the full body on the "floor" of the House or Senate (whether at the state or federal level), and there is no chance the proposal will become law. By choosing members from "safe" seats to serve on committees that handle controversial legislation, other members who have closer elections can avoid having to vote on certain controversial measures.

The only measure to minimize this is to get your member to be the chief sponsor of a bill, or to be a co-sponsor of a bill you favor. That puts them on record so even if the bill is never voted on, that member has expressed support for the bill. But if a member introduces "by request," it simply means that it was introduced as a courtesy to a constituent. Budget bills may be introduced at the request of a governor and include provisions the money committee may disagree with. Such bills do not necessarily indicate support for certain provisions. You have to wait until final passage to make such determinations.

Chairmen of Committees Have More Clout

The chairman of a legislative committee controls the agenda of the committee by deciding which bills will be heard by it, which bills will be put on a fast track for passage, and which will be slated for defeat. Often, preferred members, usually committee chairmen, will be selected by party leaders to patron a bill even if other members originally introduced the measure. These decisions are not made in public, but ahead of time in consultation with the leaders of the political party with a majority of elected representatives.

But party leaders can be influenced if many citizens request meetings, make phone calls, and send emails or letters in favor of particular bills. If the legislator who represents you happens to chair a committee or is in a leadership position, he or she will be better positioned to pass or defeat bills. But any legislator who is confident on his feet, even a newly elected member who is backed by the people, can be effective in passing or defeating legislation if enough "pressure" in the form of calls, emails, letters, and personal meetings come from the grass roots.

Legislative Motions

Bills are reported out of committee by a committee member who makes a "motion to report." If a quorum is present to do business, and a majority of members vote to report the measure, the bill or resolution is sent to the "floor" of the full House or Senate for a vote. Motions to report must be seconded by another committee member or the bill or resolution dies.

A bill can also be reported or sent to another legislative committee for further consideration, debate, or quiet demise. This is why it is important for a citizen to attend or monitor committee meetings and report back to others as to how their legislators voted in committee. Some state legislatures give very little public notice of when a bill is coming up for a hearing or a vote. Some states broadcast committee meetings or sessions of each chamber via the Internet.

In some state legislative bodies, committees permit voting by proxy, which allows a legislator who is present at the committee meeting to vote on behalf of a committee member who is absent. A legislator who says he will support a bill must do so at all levels of passage, including attending legislative committee meetings that consider the bill you are interested in. Ducking a meeting so colleagues can kill a bill on a voice vote or for failure to make a motion or "second" to report is a coy way to kill a bill. Agreeing to vote for or sponsor a measure is important, but a dedicated legislator must do more to secure passage of important legislation.

A legislator must be willing to cast a proxy vote if this is allowed, usually only in committees. (Proxy votes are not allowed in the US Congress.) Your representative must also be willing to "second" a motion to report a bill out of committee and to use all parliamentary means to secure passage. Of course, this means having the courage to challenge the will of the party leadership if the leadership had decided the bill should be killed. That kind of leadership is rare. When candidates present themselves to you in your district, try to take their measure as best you can to see if they possess that rarest of qualities . . . political courage.

Getting Around Committee
Roadblocks by Discharge Petition

Even if a bill you favor is not reported out of a committee, or the chairman never calls it up for a hearing or a vote, a parliamentary motion can "discharge" a bill from committee directly to the floor of the legislative body for a vote. Rarely used, discharging a committee of legislation—that is, removing consideration of the bill from that committee and moving it to the full legislative body—can be achieved by a simple motion to do so. The second way to discharge a committee, which is done in the House of Representatives, requires a certain number of members to sign a petition to secure the discharge of the measure to the entire body.

In states that allow for a discharge motion, a legislator secures recognition from the speaker of the House or the presiding officer of the Senate and moves to discharge committee "X" of bill "Y." Members vote on that motion. If the motion to discharge passes, then the measure is placed on a legislative calendar and scheduled for an up or down vote on the bill by the full House or Senate according to the regular schedule for consideration.

Congress and some state legislatures allow for a discharge petition procedure whereby members sign a petition usually kept by the clerk of the legislative body to bypass normal committee consideration. If enough members sign the petition (usually a majority), the bill is placed on the legislative calendar and is scheduled to receive an up or down vote.

Discharge measures, although rarely successful, are meant to be used when a committee refuses to report or even take up consideration of a bill. Even if the discharge motion fails, the vote that is taken on the motion to discharge, if it is a record vote, can let voters know the positions of their legislators on the underlying issue.

Those who strongly favor the bill are inclined to discharge the committee and bring the bill to a vote; those who oppose the measure will more often vote against the motion. Some members might oppose discharge petitions because they do not want to circumvent the regular committee process, even if the regular process has been less than responsive to the will of the people.

A motion to discharge a committee is a threat to the party leadership that normally controls the legislative agenda because discharging the bill prevents the leadership from burying it in committee without a hearing or vote. Sometimes a motion to discharge can succeed in bringing a bill out of committee to be considered even if the discharge effort itself falls short because the publicity surrounding the effort brings attention to the bill. The leadership might become nervous about stifling the will of the people and decide to consider the bill in the normal committee process.

To shepherd a bill on to eventual passage via this discharge petition process is, however, exceedingly rare. In Congress, from 1909 through 1971, only twenty bills passed the US House of Representatives as a result of 835 discharge petitions filed to bypass unresponsive legislative committees.[6] The proposed Equal Rights Amendment to the Constitution, which failed to gain the support of ¾ of the states, was

---

6   *Congressional Quarterly's Guide to the Congress of the United States: Origins, History and Procedure* (Washington: Congressional Quarterly, 1971), p. 114.

reported from the House Judiciary by a discharge petition filed by Congresswoman Martha Griffiths in August 1970.[7] On September 30, 2015, Representative Stephen Fincher filed a petition to discharge the Committee on Rules, which had refused to take up House Resolution 450 providing for the House to take up H.R. 597, a bill that reauthorized the Export-Import Bank of the United States. The petition garnered 218 signatures on October 9, and H.R. 597 was later considered by the entire House of Representatives.[8]

Types of Legislative Votes

Legislators vote in different ways. There are voice, division, and record, (or roll call) votes. A voice vote is initiated by the presiding officer of the committee or legislative body with a request that those in favor of a motion so indicate by saying yes (or aye) and those opposed say no (or nay). This is the simplest and fastest way of voting. But it also leaves the public completely in the dark as to how their representative voted, because no list of representatives and how they voted is kept. The loudest side wins the vote.

A division vote counts the number of members for and against a measure. A division may be called for when the shouts of "ayes" and "nays" on a voice vote are too close to call. A division vote is obtained by a show of hands for and against a proposal. Again, the public would not know how a legislator voted unless someone happened to be in the gallery

---

7   "The Equal Rights Amendment," History, Art & Archives, US House of Representatives, http://history.house.gov/Historical-Highlights/1951-2000/The-Equal-Rights-Amendment/.

8   Discharge Petition No. 114-2 (2015).

watching who raised their hands and who didn't. A division vote records the number of legislators for and against a motion, but not the names of the members.

A record (or roll call) vote records the names of those who voted for and against a measure. Such a vote informs the public how a legislator voted. Securing roll call votes on controversial bills requires grassroots effort and coordination. Many, if not most, legislators prefer to hide their positions on controversial issues rather than expose themselves to complaints of voters who disagree with them. To find the results of record votes you may have to research legislative websites for records of votes in committee.

This is the dark hole of legislation, killing bills in committee by either not allowing a motion to report or approving a motion to "lay the bill on the table," which is a way to kill a bill without a direct "yes" or "no" vote. Sometimes members will duck votes in this manner. This is a way to keep the status quo without going on record, and thus being exposed, as desiring to preserve the status quo. When you inspect committee records and fail to see any motions to report, or you see such actions referenced, you should contact your legislator to find out what is going on.

The Importance of Record Votes

A legislator willing to call for or "demand" a record vote must first find someone willing to second his or her motion. Without a second, a record vote is not possible. Most legislatures have a rule requiring that one-fifth of the members must second a demand for a record vote when a bill is before the entire House or Senate, and one-fifth of the members must indicate their support for a record vote. Convincing one-fifth of a legislative body to act against the wishes of the party leaders is difficult but not impossible.

Obtaining a record vote is often a struggle that takes place out of public view. In the 2007 assembly session, I introduced HB 2757, which recognized that human life begins at fertilization and is entitled to protection under the Constitution of Virginia. We require all third graders in Virginia to learn the simple scientific fact that human life begins at the union of sperm and egg, yet my bill caused the Republican leadership of the Virginia House of Delegates to go into full lockdown mode to avoid a record vote.

I eventually obtained a record vote after I secured the support of the pro-abortion democratic minority leader, who agreed to have his caucus raise their hands for a record vote even though they would overwhelmingly vote against my bill on final passage. The end result was a record vote for the first time on the direct question of protecting all children from abortion since the *Roe* and *Doe* decisions of 1973. Although we lost, by just a few votes, the vote showed where legislators really stood. (The Republicans who did not want to go on record on this question were not pleased with me.)

Budget Amendments and Public Policy
Average citizens are not able to be part of closed-door agreements in the legislative process to move major legislation. With so many complex bills and so many opportunities for lawmakers to bury bills, dodge votes, and hide their true intentions, how can citizens find out their representatives' true positions on a particular issue?

The most concrete way to pinpoint your legislator's position is to secure a record vote about a particular issue on an amendment to the budget bills that fund the government. Budget amendments can usually be offered on the floor of the House or Senate whether in Congress or state legislatures.

The entire budget bill must pass or the government will shut down because it cannot operate without money. Amendments to the budget cannot be ignored, and because they do not go through the normal committee process, they are easier to pass or defeat.

I offered such an amendment to the financial year 2015-16 Virginia state budget prohibiting the governor (who was supported by Planned Parenthood) from using any money in the $96 billion state budget to alter comprehensive abortion clinic regulations enacted the summer before he was elected. My amendment passed the House of Delegates on February 12, 2015, despite the Republican leadership's usually successful efforts to "bury" all "social or moral issue" bills in committees. Had the measure stayed in the budget, it would have resulted in the law being applied under the earlier and tighter abortion restrictions. Again, this is the power of the purse restricting how public money may be spent. My amendments ultimately failed in the conference committee because not enough pro-life lawmakers were appointed to the conference committee.

Obtaining Record Votes in Congress

In the early 1980s, I worked as a legislative aide to former congressman Bob Dornan (R-CA). I was charged with finding parliamentary ways to obtain record votes on social policy issues. I found that adding amendments to appropriations bills was the easiest and most effective way to obtain these record votes.

Our efforts to amend bills and obtain record votes became so successful that former Democrat house speaker Tip O'Neill changed the Rules of the House of Representatives to increase from twenty to twenty-five the number of legislators needed to call for a record vote. When we succeeded in finding twenty-five legislators, the speaker changed another rule to make record votes even harder to achieve.

His new rule applied when the 435-member House of Representatives resolved itself into a 100-member "Committee of the Whole House" for consideration of appropriations bills. If a member offered a floor amendment limiting how federal dollars may be used, a motion could be made for the committee to "rise" and report the bill back to the House of Representatives without ever having to even debate or vote on the proposed amendment. This shrewd tactic allowed members to avoid a record vote on a controversial issue. Only if the motion to rise failed, could the budget amendment be offered. As noted above, O'Neill's most famous quip was that "all politics is local." Sadly, in this case he applied that adage in such a way as to prevent citizens from around the country from knowing exactly where their legislators stood on the most pressing issues of the day. Knowing that "all politics is local," O'Neill could not run the risk of letting people back home know how their representatives in Congress voted as it might have cost a lot of O'Neill's fellow Democrats their elections!

Hyde Amendment to the Federal Budget

In the spring of 1976, a friend gave me documentation from a Freedom of Information (FOI) request he had made that the US Department of Health, Education and Welfare (HEW, now Health and Human Services) had been paying for elective abortions in the very programs that were purportedly set up to prevent the so-called need for abortion. HEW had paid for roughly three hundred thousand abortions with our tax money up to that date.

I gave this information to Congressman Bob Bauman (R-MD) by asking a page to call the congressman off the floor of the House of Representatives for a moment. (Representative Bauman and I had both been active in the Young Americans for Freedom group many years earlier.) I showed him the FOI documents and suggested an amendment to the Health, Education and Welfare Appropriations Act prohibiting the use of federal tax money for abortion. He said he knew a freshman congressman who might offer the amendment.

The first-term member of Congress turned out to be Representative Henry Hyde (R-IL). The original successful Hyde Amendment cut off federal funding of Medicaid tax-paid abortions except to preserve the life of the mother, with the rape and incest reasons added in later versions of the Hyde Amendment.[9]

Roll call votes on budget amendments that barred abortion funding quickly made legislators who supported abortion funding vulnerable in their elections, while at the same time promoting good public policy.

---

[9]   Harris v. McRae, 448 U.S. 297 (1980).

Congress and the Power of the Purse

As noted above, only the Congress has the power to appropriate money. Neither the president nor the courts have either this duty or power under our US Constitution. Federal courts need money from Congress to pay the salaries of judges, clerks, building overhead, and maintenance of the federal courthouses. Likewise, all executive departments ask Congress for funding. While the president can veto an entire appropriations bill, he cannot veto a portion or a part of an appropriations act.

In April 1980, the US Supreme Court upheld the constitutionality of the Hyde Amendment banning tax-paid abortions in *Harris v. McRae*. In 1981, liberal New York Democrat congressman Charlie Rangel, who supported abortion and abortion funding, engaged Congressman Bob Dornan and myself in a discussion on the Hyde Amendment. In so many words he told us that Congress could never give up the "power of the purse." He said in roughly these words, "You know, we differ on abortion. But if the Supreme Court had said that they were going to tell us how to spend our (i.e., taxpayer) money, I would have put in court-stripping bills faster than you could!" (Congressman Rangel was referring to Congressman Bob Dornan.)

Searching Federal & State Legislation

Congressional legislation can be searched from your home computer. Just go to https://www.congress.gov/legislation/about to search for all bills and resolutions introduced since 1973 and for amendments since 1981. Searches can be made by the name of the House or Senate member who introduced or co-sponsored bills, by bill subject, bill number, or the list of bills sent to a particular committee.

If you prefer to do hard-copy research, ask your local library if they subscribe to *Congressional Quarterly Weekly Report*, a private publication that reports on the legislative actions of Congress and includes articles and record votes taken in the full House and Senate.

State legislatures have websites of varying quality identifying legislation introduced. Some are more complete in posting legislative actions and outcomes on bills, as well as finding introduced legislation. If your state legislature does not provide citizens with the ability to track bills, you need to ask your state representatives for greater transparency. Legiscan.com is a research tool that searches and tracks legislation by state, bill number, or subject matter.

Presidents and Governors—Executive Orders

Both state governors and US presidents have inherent powers to issue executive orders, which are formal regulations or directions issued by the executive for carrying out public policy as contained in the federal or state constitutions or statutes. The authority to issue executive orders comes from two sources: powers granted in the respective state or federal constitutions or acts of legislatures. Executive orders, if valid, have the force of law and courts treat and enforce them as such.

An executive order is not supposed to contradict or change a law or the Constitution. Like statutes, executive orders may be revoked by a subsequent executive order, a new law passed by the legislature, or a court decision declaring the executive order unconstitutional.

When executive orders lack statutory or constitutional authority, they are properly challenged by plaintiffs and stricken down by federal courts, as occurred when President Obama sought to provide legal status to classes or persons which the Congress had previously considered but had refused to do.

Vast powers have been claimed and exercised using executive orders. For example, on February 19, 1942, President Roosevelt issued the infamous Japanese Internment Order, which provided that the:

> Secretary of War, and the Military Commanders . . . prescribe military areas in such places and of such extent . . . from which any or all persons may be excluded, and with respect to which, the right of any person to enter, remain in, or leave shall be subject to whatever restrictions the Secretary of War . . . may impose in his discretion. The Secretary of War is hereby authorized to provide for residents of any such area who are excluded therefrom, such transportation, food, shelter, and other accommodations as may be necessary . . . to accomplish the purpose of this order.
>
> . . .
>
> . . . Including the furnishing of medical aid, hospitalization, food, clothing, transportation, use of land, shelter, and other supplies, equipment, utilities, facilities, and services.[10]

---

[10]   Exec. Order No. 9066 (1942).

This order was later challenged by "Fred" T. Korematsu, an American-born citizen of Japanese heritage whose parents were born in Japan. Korematsu declined to leave San Leandro to report to a Civil Control Station required by the order for relocation and was convicted in federal court in September 1942. The US Supreme Court, in a sharply divided 6–3 decision, upheld Korematsu's conviction in late 1944, thereby upholding the forced "relocation" of Japanese Americans.[11]

An interesting point given current concerns about the use of information collected by federal agencies is that the US Army roundup of 120,000 Japanese Americans in California was, in part, facilitated by the US Census Bureau, which is supposed to ensure the privacy of census records. Researchers at Fordham University and the University of Wisconsin disclosed how the Census Bureau assisted the December 9, 1942 report, issued two days after Pearl Harbor, of the Japanese population living in the United States, and its possessions and territories.[12]

---

[11]   Korematsu v. United States, 323 U.S. 214 (1944).

[12]   Stephen Holmes, "Report Says Census Bureau Helped Relocate Japanese," *New York Times*, March 17, 2000, http://www.nytimes.com/2000/03/17/us/report-says-census-bureau-helped-relocate-japanese.html.

CHAPTER 11

Stick to Your Principles
and Get Involved

Or

Reagan Proved That
Conservatives Can Win

No free country has ever been without parties, which are a natural
offspring of Freedom.
James Madison, 1787 Constitutional Convention

Political Parties

While political parties are nowhere mentioned in the US Constitution, they have been a fact of American political life since at least 1787. There have always been two major political parties in America regardless of their formal names: the "Ins" and the "Outs."

Since the end of the Civil War, every American political movement that has surfaced has been absorbed into either the Democratic or Republican Parties. While a 2015 Gallup survey found that 44 percent of voters identify as

Independents, 27 percent as Republicans, and 28 percent as Democrats, when "pushed" by pollsters to name the political party the voter "leans to," the results shift to 44 percent Republican and 42 percent Democrat.[1]

What voters tell pollsters is not always reflected at the ballot box. In 2015, Republicans had control of thirty state legislatures, Democrats controlled eleven legislatures, and power was split between Democrats and Republicans in eight legislatures. Members of Nebraska's unicameral legislature run as "non-partisan" candidates and are overwhelmingly conservative.

Party membership of the state legislators in February 2015 broke down as follows: House members at the state level: 2342 Democrats, 3024 Republicans; Senate members at the state level: 821 Democrats, 1087 Republicans (with 57 Independents, 49 of whom are from Nebraska and vote like conservative Republicans).[2]

As you can see, the number of registered Independents in state legislatures is miniscule. Even individuals who previously had been elected as a Democrat or a Republican find it very difficult to run as an Independent later. For example, Teddy Roosevelt had been president from 1901–1908, assistant secretary of the Navy from 1897–1898, the Rough

---

[1]   "Party Affiliation," Gallup News, results for March 6-9, 2015,
        http://www.gallup.com/poll/15370/party-affiliation.aspx.
[2]   "2015 State and Legislative Partisan Composition," National
        Conference of State Legislatures, February 4, 2015, http://www.
        ncsl.org/Portals/1/Documents/Elections/Legis_Control_2015_
        Feb4_11am.pdf. Nebraska is not really Independent; it is conservative. It is illegal to run for the state senate as either a Democrat
        or Republican.

Rider hero of the Spanish-American War in 1898, governor of New York from 1898–1900, and vice president under President William McKinley, who had been assassinated. In 1900 Roosevelt acceded to the presidency and hand-picked his Republican successor, William Taft, who won the 1908 presidential election.

Roosevelt became angry with Taft's policies and ran against Taft for the 1912 Republican presidential primary against the wishes of Republican Party bosses who supported Taft. Roosevelt bolted the Republican Party and ran as an Independent on the "Bull Moose" Party ticket. While Roosevelt out-polled Republican nominee Taft, Independent Teddy Roosevelt lost to Democrat Woodrow Wilson, the governor of New Jersey, who won the presidency in 1912 and 1916. As popular as Teddy Roosevelt was, he did not win the presidency, in part, because he ran for office as an Independent. The few legislators who do win elections as Independents caucus, or meet, with either the Republicans or the Democrats.

The Conservative Majority

Clearly, the most successful American politician of the last part of the twentieth century was President Ronald Reagan. He never apologized for calling himself a conservative. He ran for office as a Republican. He stated he was pro-life because it was a moral issue. He opposed high taxes because he thought they weakened American families. He called the Soviet Union the Evil Empire because it was. As president, he would not compromise any moral principle for political gain. He became governor of California and was twice elected president. Reagan's tactics and policies can speak volumes to us today.

After his unsuccessful presidential run in 1976, Reagan outlined his approach to politics in a February 1977 speech to the Conservative Political Action Conference—an annual meeting of political conservatives who first organized the event, known better by its acronym CPAC—in 1973:

> Despite what some in the press may say, we who are proud to call ourselves "conservative" are not a minority of a minority party; we are part of the great majority of Americans of both major parties and of most of the independents as well.
>
> A Harris poll released September 7, 1975 showed 18 percent identifying themselves as liberal and 31 percent as conservative, with 41 percent as middle of the road; a few months later, on January 5, 1976, by a 43-19 plurality, those polled by Harris said they would "prefer to see the country move in a more conservative direction than a liberal one."[3]

Forming Conservative Coalitions

Ronald Reagan recognized that there were two branches of conservatives: social (moral) and economic. He instructed:

> You know, as I do, that most commentators make a distinction between [what] they call "social"

---

[3]   Ronald Reagan, "The New Republican Party," Regan 2020, February 6, 1977, http://reagan2020.us/speeches/The_New_Republican_Party.asp.

conservatism and "economic" conservatism. The so-called social issues—law and order, abortion, busing, quota systems—are usually associated with blue-collar ethnic and religious groups themselves traditionally associated with the Democratic Party. The economic issues—inflation, deficit spending and big government—are usually associated with Republican Party members and independents who concentrate their attention on economic matters. . . .

. . . In short, isn't it possible to combine the two major segments of contemporary American conservatism into one politically effective whole?

I believe the answer is: Yes, it is possible to create a political entity that will reflect the views of the great, hitherto [unacknowledged], conservative majority. . . .

This will mean compromise, but not a compromise of basic principle.[4]

Pick a Candidate

The proximate authority for earthly civil government comes from citizens, or "we the people." A republican form of government is structured in such a way that others act in our name, on our behalf, and with our consent. Therefore, it is best to work and vote for someone who you believe would vote and act as you would in the legislature.

A citizen is not required to join a political party to support a candidate of a particular party. Anyone can work for and vote for a candidate who is already on the ballot of a political party. Many candidates have volunteers who support them

---

[4]   Ibid.

out of personal loyalty, not party loyalty. However, by signing up as a member of your local political party, your influence with the candidates will skyrocket. You will meet with other volunteers and become better informed of campaign issues, campaign events, party meetings, and opportunities to help your candidate and strengthen the overall political party effort.

Many voters, especially those who consider themselves Republican, often complain that their party's nominees are too liberal. But nominees are picked by the party activists. Those who participate in their local political party by attending monthly meetings and participating in party conventions or activities eventually become decision makers within the party that nominates candidates.

If we truly want to restore the Founders' vision, we should never volunteer for a candidate who does not respect and adhere to the Constitution or support the right to life and real marriage. If we work hard to help candidates who represent the "lesser of two evils," they will know they can count on our support no matter how they vote, and they will be less inclined to change their ways to win our support.

If more conservatives were involved in the party or candidate nominating process and they supported truly conservative candidates, our Congress would have more conservatives in office. Frankly, in most cases, there is little difference between the tax and spend Democrats and borrow and spend Republicans on big government issues. And with respect to final goals of protecting life and marriage, there is no such thing as the middle ground.

Attending candidate forums will help you find out how well your candidate answers questions without a prepared script, communicates your values, understands the issues, and makes a presentable appearance. A candidate must stay true to principle and remain cool under pressure. Do not depend upon the media to judge candidates for you. Investigate these traits yourself.

If you cannot find a candidate with the right values, experience, capacity, and ability to run, consider running for political office, or party office for that matter, yourself. Do not automatically rule this out.

In my own case, I asked several leaders in my community who shared my values and philosophy about government if they would run in the newly created state delegate district drawn after the 1990 census. None were able, so I decided to run myself after my wife agreed.

Pick a Political Party

After he lost the presidential nomination in 1976 to Gerald Ford, Ronald Reagan was confronted with disgruntled conservatives who wanted to bolt the Republican Party and form an Independent Party. Reagan was familiar with American history and knew the public rarely supported Independent parties and that Independent candidates hardly ever won elections.

His 1977 CPAC speech suggested that the Republican Party was the most practical means of securing conservative policies. Here is more from Reagan's speech:

What will be the political vehicle by which the majority can assert its rights?

I have to say I cannot agree with some of my
friends. . . .

. . . I believe the Republican Party can hold and
should provide the political mechanism through
which the goals of the majority of Americans can be
achieved. For one thing, the biggest single grouping
of conservatives is to be found in that party. It makes
more sense to build on that grouping than to break it
up and start over.[5]

Reagan also said in 1977 that the base and image of the
Republican Party had to change, not the conservative principles which united the Republican Party:

The New Republican Party . . . cannot, be one limited
to the country clubbing business image . . . [and] is
going to have room for the man and the woman in the
factories, for the farmer, for the cop on the beat and the
millions of Americans who may never have thought of
joining our party before, but whose interests coincide
with those represented by principled Republicanism.
. . . They have a say in what goes on in the party. . . .

. . . Let me say this about our friends who are now
Republicans but who do not identify themselves as
conservatives: . . . If we truly believe in our principles,
we should sit down and talk. . . .

. . . A political party is a mechanical structure created to further a cause. The cause, not the mechanism,

---

[5]   Ibid.

brings and holds the members together. And our cause must be to rediscover, reassert and reapply America's spiritual heritage to our national affairs.

Then with God's help we shall indeed be as a city upon a hill with the eyes of all people upon us.[6]

Conservative Republicans

Despite his efforts to unify conservatives within the party, Reagan knew a RINO (Republican in name only) when he saw one. In 1975, he criticized the spending policies of Republican president Gerald Ford and even said that those Republicans who cannot agree with conservative principles should just go their own way.

Conservative voters who are dissatisfied with the direction of the Republican Party will have to join or support others who join their local county or city party and run for leadership positions within the party so they can eventually nominate candidates, help to organize volunteers to win elections, or become active in the support of a conservative candidate for public office. If enough new people become involved, and each does a small share of the work, the task will not be overwhelming. At a minimum, we must convince more conservatives to work and vote in primaries to ensure conservative candidates are on the ballot in November.

Voter Registration Drives Are Not Just for Liberals

Voting as a Fundamental or Primary Right of Citizenship

The English born author Thomas Paine, who penned the 1776 pamphlet *Common Sense* that inspired many to

---

6   Ibid.

consider breaking from Great Britain, noted, "The right of voting for representatives is the primary right by which other rights are protected. To take away this right is to reduce a man to slavery, for slavery consists in being subject to the will of another, and he that has not a vote in the election of representatives is in this case."[7]

Qualifications for Voting

To vote in any federal election, a person must be at least eighteen years of age (stipulated by the Twenty-Sixth Amendment to the US Constitution) and a US citizen. Voter registration before age eighteen is allowed in some states if the registrant will turn eighteen by election day. Legal impediments to becoming a registered voter are mental incompetence and the commission of a felony. In all but two states, felons are able to restore their right to vote by undertaking certain actions. But by far the largest impediment to voting is the decision of citizens to not register to vote.

All states except North Dakota require formal voter registration. In a few states, voter registration may occur on the day of the election. Some states require that you identify your political party affiliation to register to vote. Others permit it, while others do not allow party affiliation identification when registering to vote.

---

7   Thomas Paine, *The Writings Of Thomas Paine*, vol. 3, ed. Moncure Daniel Conway (New York, 1895; Project Gutenburg, 2010), chap. 24, http://www.gutenberg.org/files/31271/31271-h/31271-h.htm.

Registration Deadlines

Except in those few states where voters are allowed to register to vote on election day, there are pre-election deadlines to register to vote. These deadlines enable election officials to compile a complete list of eligible voters who can be verified by election officials at the polls on election day.

A voter must re-register to vote:

- after a move, since voter registration is by locality in each state;
- to change party affiliation in states with party registration requirements;
- if a last name was changed by choice or by marriage.

After registering to vote, a voter registration ID card, which lists polling place, precinct name/number, congressional district, and State House and Senate legislative district, is mailed to the newly registered voter. In some states, a voter registration card or a government issued ID with a picture, such as a driver's license, will be needed to cast a vote at the polls.

Mechanics of Voter Registration Drives

Registering to vote is an easy process. Anyone can obtain voter registration information and forms for his own state from the US Election Assistance Commission via the Internet at http://www.eac.gov/nvra. These national voter registration forms are available in English, Spanish, Chinese, Japanese, Korean, Tagalog, and Vietnamese, even though naturalized citizens are expected to speak a certain amount of English. (The US Territories of Puerto Rico, US Virgin Islands, American Samoa, and Guam do not accept the national form.)

You never can tell when and where you might meet someone who shares your values but who is not registered to vote and might consider registering if asked. Everyone should carry voter registration forms in their cars or purses, when going door-to-door for candidates, shopping at the supermarket, waiting in car pool lanes, attending sporting events, and wherever a group may gather. Make sure you have an instruction sheet and an envelope pre-addressed to the voter registrar to make it easy for anyone to complete the voter registration process.

Voter Registration for Churches & Non-Profits

Churches can legally conduct voter registration drives, but they are subject to different rules as of this writing since they have tax-exempt status under the IRS, which prohibits them from engaging in partisan election politics. The reason it is a good idea to hold registration drives at churches or non-profit fraternal organizations is because generally there will be more potential voters at these locations, and generally church members have at least some conservative voters.

Without violating their tax-exempt status, churches can:

- Engage in voter registration drives that do not promote a particular candidate or political party;
- Teach via film, talks, sermons, publications, etcetera, regarding social issues, religious duty, and civic involvement;

- Educate parishioners about the mechanics of the political process;
- Distribute candidate surveys, including incumbent voting records on a wide range of issues with no editorial comments favoring positions or candidates;
- Conduct petition drives in support of or in opposition to legislation;
- Use church facilities for candidate debates provided all candidates for the same office are invited (the non-profit League of Women Voters sponsors presidential debates, with the major party candidates);
- Support or oppose the nomination of non-elected, appointed judicial, departmental, or cabinet level officers;
- Discuss Church teaching, Bible instruction, or denominational teachings or traditions on moral or cultural concerns relating to public policy topics, such as abortion, same-sex "marriage," debt, citizenship, etcetera;
- Encourage church membership to support or oppose particular legislation as long as such activity does not comprise or consume more than 5 percent of its annual revenue.

Churches, under Internal Revenue provisions initiated by then-Senator Lyndon Johnson (D-TX) in the early 1950s, can jeopardize their tax-exempt status by the following activities:[8]

---

[8]   As of July 2017, President Trump has indicated that he hopes to remove these provisions; an initiative known as the Johnson Amendment.

- Overtly campaigning for or endorsing candidates or opposing candidates;
- Making contributions to political campaigns or political action committees from church funds, although individual clerics can make personal donations to candidates;
- Using the church bulletin for the pastor or a staff member to endorse or oppose a candidate;
- Holding fund raisers for candidates;
- Using the church name to support or oppose a particular candidate;
- Supporting or opposing judicial candidates who are elected to judgeships.

Pastors, priests, rabbis, deacons, or other clerics are permitted to:

- Invite candidates or elected officials to speak at church events or services where they are not soliciting votes or speaking about their candidacy. Inviting officials from one party may raise questions;
- Hold candidate or issue forums or debates for all qualified candidates for that office;
- Personally invite the congregation to come to a voter registration drive at the church that does not promote or endorse a particular candidate or political party;
- Distribute materials on candidate positions that do not endorse or favor a particular candidate or political party.

Pastors, priests, rabbis, deacons, or other clerics may jeopardize their church tax status if they:

- Allow candidates or elected officials to ask for campaign money at a church function;
- Set up a political action committee that gives money to candidates;
- Use church donations to pay for partisan, political events;
- Allow church office machines or services to be used by a candidate for office;
- Allow the distribution of candidate or political party brochures that favor one candidate or party;
- Endorse a candidate on behalf of the church.

If your church decides to conduct a voter registration drive, you should contact officials from your local voter registrar office. Do a computer search of your state voter registrar. Some states require volunteers at such drives to be deputized (a simple process) as registrars.

If a church conducts a candidate survey to prepare a voter guide of candidates' positions on issues, the questions must be sent to all qualified candidates and cover a broad range of issues. Certified mail with return receipt requested eliminates any doubt that the survey was received by a candidate. An email that does not "bounce back" is not proof the candidate received the survey. An email could easily be filtered out as "junk" or accidentally deleted by an aide.

CHAPTER 12

Let's Vote!

Ballots

A ballot is the means by which a voter expresses a choice for a candidate, or a proposition. Ballots can be paper or the record of the mechanical or electronic machines that are used to record the vote. The vote is the actual choice by the voter of the candidate or proposition as notated or recorded on the ballot. A ballot question is a proposition put on ballot such as an amendment to a state constitution, a vote to remove an individual from office, the repeal, suspension, or passage of a law, or the approval of a bond that voters approve or disapprove. An advisory referendum amounts to an election day poll of voters to ascertain what voters favor or disfavor on a public question. The outcome of the advisory referendum is not legally binding on officials.

Types of Voting

Not everyone who intends to vote or who states they will definitely vote will actually end up voting. Elections are not decided by majorities of citizens or a majority of registered voters but by majorities or pluralities of voters who actually vote either absentee or at the polls on election day. In primaries, the voter turnout is as low as 3 percent or less of those registered to vote.

An absentee (or early ballot) is a ballot cast by a voter who does not vote at the polls on election day. The ballot may be returned by mail or in person. In twenty states, a reason is required to vote absentee, while twenty-seven states and Washington, DC, allow qualified voters to vote absentee for any reason. For voters who cannot easily get to the polls on election day, absentee voting is helpful. Some states have a permanent absentee ballot list that allows a voter to automatically receive an absentee ballot for future elections.[1]

Absentee ballots, if mailed, must arrive by a specified date, usually the day of the election. The two most common reasons that absentee ballots are rejected by election officials are that the mail arrives too late or the absence of a signature on the absentee ballot.[2]

Mail Voting occurs when a ballot is automatically sent to every registered voter before an election without the voter having to request it. This process replaces voting at your precinct on election day. Washington, Oregon, and Colorado vote in this fashion.[3]

---

[1]   "Absentee and Early Voting," National Conference of State Legislators, August 17, 2017, http://www.ncsl.org/research/elections -and-campaigns/absentee-and-early-voting.aspx.

[2]   *2008 Election Administration and Voting Survey*, US Election Assistance Commission, November 2009, p. 10.

[3]   "Absentee and Early Voting," National Conference of State Legislators.

Early Voting is a type of absentee voting allowed in thirty-three states and Washington, DC, that allows voters to vote at an election office or other designated location to cast a vote before election day without providing a special reason. This type of voting can be done in person or by mail, from forty-five days before the election to the Friday before the election.[4]

Chuck Todd, political director of NBC News, wrote, "In ten states a majority of votes was cast before Election Day . . . Democrats dominated the early vote . . . and if Republicans don't catch up quickly, they'll lose an election or two that they shouldn't simply because of the Democrats out-organizing them."[5]

In the 2008 presidential election, 133,944,538 voters cast their ballots as follows:

- 80,693,815 voters went to the polls on election day,
- 22,244,396 voters cast absentee ballots (not citizens who live overseas),
- 17,379,871 voters cast their votes in various forms of early voting.

For 2008, states reported to the US Election Assistance Commission that 26,044,388 absentee ballots were sent out to voters, and 23,733,439 were returned and counted. There were 880,995 overseas civilian and military absentee ballots cast. Another 226,438 domestic absentee ballots

---

4   Ibid.
5   Chuck Todd and Sheldon Gawiser, *How Barack Obama Won: A State-by-State Guide to the Historic 2008 Presidential Election* (New York: Vintage Books, 2009), p. 27.

were undeliverable, and 210,730 were spoiled. So roughly 2,311,000 of the absentee ballots sent out to registered voters were not returned with votes, or not returned on time.[6]

Indiana and North Carolina reported rejecting more than 10 percent of their absentee ballots. The reasons for states rejecting voters' absentee ballots varied widely. More than four hundred thousand absentee ballots were returned to state election officials as undeliverable or spoiled. States reporting high absentee voting rates were Washington (87.2 percent), Colorado (62.3 percent), Arizona (50.6 percent), Montana (42.2 percent), and California (41.7 percent).[7]

Online Voter Registration

The US Elections Assistance Commission reports that in 2008, almost seven hundred thousand Americans registered to vote using online voter registration, according to data provided by the states.[8] Also, in 2008, more than 3.6 million citizens took advantage of same day registration, and almost 1 million of these were new voters. (The others were previously registered at another location.)[9]

Provisional Voting

When a voter shows up at the polls, the election official may not have proof the person is registered within the precinct. These voters are allowed to cast a provisional ballot, which

---

6   *2008 Election Administration and Voting Survey*, US Election Assistance Commission, November 2009, p. 10.
7   Ibid.
8   Ibid., p. 8.
9   Ibid.

is set aside to be counted after election officials determine the voter is properly registered in the precinct. In 2008, 1,746,338 persons voted by means of a provisional ballot, or roughly 1.3 percent of all those who voted in 2008.[10]

Poll Watchers

Election officials, or "poll watchers," are citizens who help administer the voting process and identify eligible voters at the polls. They usually live in the precinct where they vote. They are paid a small stipend from public funds. Election judges attempt to ensure a fair election process. President Harry Truman, who liked to say that he went from "precinct to president," was the democratic clerk of Grandview precinct in Missouri where his father was the election judge.

Straight Ticket Voters

Voters choose candidates for a variety of reasons, including influence from family or friends, upbringing or personal experience, job background or education. Some choose candidates based on looks, dress, or even age. But political party and positions on issues are the deciding factors for most voters.

Most general election voters usually will vote a "straight ticket." This means they only vote for candidates of a single political party even though they may not vote for all the offices. They are called straight ticket voters even if they do not vote for all the candidates from a particular party and are popularly thought to vote only for the nominee of their

---

10   Ibid., p. 10.

party. In general, it will be nearly impossible to secure the vote of the straight-ticket voter if he is of the opposite party of your candidate.

Some states also allow voters to choose all the candidates for office from a single political party by making a single mark on a ballot. As of October 2016, ten states allow voters to vote a straight party slate by making a single mark on a ballot according to the National Conference of State Legislatures.[11]

Straight-ticket voters can be identified by examining voter lists to see their voter history in past party primary elections. These records are kept by voter registrars. Election campaigns usually identify such voters on walk and call lists. Campaigns also do polling to find party preference. It is important to remember, however, that individuals in the same household can and do vote in different primary elections, so do not assume that because one person in a house votes one way that everyone there does. You may be missing an opportunity to secure a vote and even change a mind in that house!

Voters need to be reminded of upcoming elections, especially primary elections, which do not receive the publicity of general elections. They may also need to be reminded to apply for an absentee ballot by a particular date or they may miss voting.

---

[11] "Straight Ticket Voting States," National Conference of State Legislatures, May 31, 2017, http://www.ncsl.org/research/elections-and-campaigns/straight-ticket-voting.aspx#1. Alabama, Indiana, Iowa, Kentucky, Michigan, Oklahoma, Pennsylvania, South Carolina, Texas, and Utah allow straight-ticket voting.

Split-Ticket Voters

Split-ticket voters are usually driven by a particular issue or concern rather than party loyalty. If very serious about an issue, split-ticket voters will vote for or against a candidate based on one overriding issue. Such voters are at times referred to as single-issue voters. It is not that these voters are only concerned about one issue, but that one issue overrides others in determining how they will vote.

Bypassing Legislatures—Direct Voter Democracy

The increased use of mechanisms for direct citizen-initiated legislation or rejection of statutes passed by state legislatures resulted from disclosures in the Progressive era (1900–1920) of special interest domination of state legislatures. The Progressives devised methods for bypassing state legislatures. Some of these include:

Initiative

The process of initiative allows citizens to bypass their state legislature and propose laws directly and, in a few states, place constitutional amendments on the ballot. Initiative is allowed in twenty-four states.[12] Initiative can be direct, as

---

12   "Initiative and Referendum States," National Conference of State Legislatures, December 2015, http://www.ncsl.org/research/elections-and-campaigns/chart-of-the-initiative-states.aspx. Alaska, Arizona, Arkansas, California, Colorado, Florida, Idaho, Illinois, Massachusetts, Michigan, Mississippi, Missouri, Montana, Nebraska, Nevada, North Dakota, Ohio, Oklahoma, Oregon, South Dakota, Utah, Washington, Wyoming, and the US Virgin Islands.

when citizens place a measure directly on the ballot, or it can be indirect, depending on actions taken or not taken by the legislature. In a few states, the legislature can place a similar competing proposal on the ballot alongside the one offered by voters. Six states have an indirect process.[13] In Utah and Washington, proponents may select either the direct or indirect method.

While the procedures are different for different states, certain steps are usually followed: petitions must be signed by a minimum number of registered voters, usually a percent of the total votes cast in the most recent statewide election. The petition must be written in a prescribed format and submitted to state officials who, in some states, may review the language of the proposition.

Referendum

A referendum is a policy question placed on the ballot for voters to approve or to reject. There are two types of referenda:

A *legislative referendum* includes proposals for laws, constitutional amendments or bond questions that are placed on the ballot by state legislatures or local governments and not by citizen petitions. Amendments to a state's constitution must be placed on the ballot for voter approval. Also, some bonds must be approved directly by voters through a legislative referendum.

---

[13]   "The Indirect Initiative," National Conference of State Legislatures, http://www.ncsl.org/research/elections-and-campaigns/the-indirect-initiative.aspx. Maine, Massachusetts, Michigan, Mississippi, Nevada, and Ohio.

Popular referendum involves placing a measure, passed by a state legislature, on the ballot to obtain a popular vote on a recently passed law. It can act as a "citizen veto" of the legislature's actions. Usually, opponents to the pending law circulate petitions that must be collected, normally within ninety days of passage, by the legislature. The petitions must be signed by a minimum number of currently registered voters. If enough signatures on petitions are gathered to place the pending law on the ballot, the law cannot go into effect until voters approve the law in the popular referenda. The purpose of a popular referendum is to allow voters opposed to the actions of the legislature a "second chance" to defeat a law passed by the legislature.

Recall

Recall is the removal by popular vote of a local or state elected official from office before the official's term expires. Thirty-one states do not allow for recall, and some only allow it for certain offices. A recall effort requires the collection of a minimum percent of registered voters who sign a petition to make the public official stand for recall at a special election before the normal expiration of the official's term of office. Recall of state elected officials by a citizen-voter petition and a special election before the regularly scheduled election is allowed in nineteen states.[14]

14   "Recall of State Officials," National Conference of State Legislatures, March 8, 2016, http://www.ncsl.org/research/elections-and-campaigns/recall-of-state-officials.aspx. Alaska, Arizona, California, Colorado, District of Columbia, Georgia, Idaho, Illinois, Kansas, Louisiana, Michigan, Minnesota, Montana, Nevada, New Jersey, North Dakota, Oregon, Rhode Island,

Provisions to recall members of Congress, while allowed under the Articles of Confederation from 1780–87, were not included in the US Constitution.

Recall sometimes succeeds against state officials, as it did against former California governor Grey Davis in 2003, the first success after thirty-two attempts to recall a governor via a recall ballot since 1911. In 2012, Wisconsin governor Scott Walker survived an attempt to recall him from office. Virginia and the District of Columbia also allow recall. However, Virginia's recall removes a local county or city elected official after a citizen-voter petition and a trial before a circuit court judge.

Most recall efforts are directed at school board and local elected city and county officials. Los Angeles was the first local municipality to adopt recall (1903). Recall of county or city officials is allowed in twenty-nine states.[15]

Primary Elections: Their Importance

Baltimore Sun newspaperman and historian of the Democratic Party in the early twentieth century Frank R. Kent pointed to the non-voter and the irregular general election voter as the main reason for the ills of American government:

Washington, and Wisconsin.

[15] "Recall of Local Officials," National Conference of State Legislatures, http://www.ncsl.org/research/elections-and-campaigns/recall-of-local-officials.aspx. Alabama, Alaska, Arizona, Arkansas, California, Colorado, Florida, Georgia, Idaho, Kansas, Louisiana, Michigan, Minnesota, Missouri, Montana, Nebraska, Nevada, New Hampshire, New Mexico, North Dakota, Ohio, Oregon, Rhode Island, South Dakota, Tennessee, Washington, West Virginia, Wisconsin, and Wyoming.

Machines run the country because their adherents regularly vote in primaries and general elections, and the rest of us do not. . . .

Thousands of the men and women who curse Congress for its stupidity and extravagance, who . . . shudder over the incompetence of mayors and governors . . . and the wickedness of politicians in general, are unregistered or are registered and do not vote. Actually, these voluntary non-voters are responsible for the politicians and their power. . . .

The average voter . . . groans under the mismanagement and mistakes of the politicians, but they cannot be got to interest or inform themselves about political conditions and candidates in their own wards and precincts. . . . The result is that the politicians pursue their way, serene and undisturbed, fully aware that the citizens who denounce them in mass meetings and newspapers, who clamor loudest for independent candidates . . . will be particularly absent from the polls on election day. So we have our bosses and their machines in practical control of the country. They are the real rulers of America . . . just as long as the lethargy of the average citizen lasts, and he regards primary elections as not important enough to vote in.[16]

Kent identified primaries as the key to electoral politics: "In 99 percent of all elections, the choice of the voters in the general election is limited to the choice of the voters in

---

16   Frank R. Kent, *The Great Game of Politics* (Garden City, NY: Doubleday, 1935), pp. 180, 181, 182.

the primary elections. . . . The man who votes in the general election and not in the primaries loses at least 50 percent of the value and effectiveness of his vote as compared to the man who votes in both."[17]

If the political machine is powerful, how do you beat it? Kent suggested one way: "No candidate with good sense, making a fight against the machine in the primaries, bases his hopes wholly on his appeal to the anti-machine or independent voters. He may do so publicly as loud as he pleases, but if he is politically wise, privately he devotes his real resources to the effort to split the machine."[18]

Splitting the machine is achieved by previously identifying voters who are committed to vote on select issues, increasing the size of the potential electorate by registering new voters who are identified as committed on specific issues, identifying for these voters a candidate who satisfactorily addresses those issues, and lastly, ensuring these voters go to the polls and vote in the primary on behalf of that candidate.

Because far fewer voters vote in primaries than general elections, you can have a greater impact in a primary campaign to elect a principled candidate. In fact, if you live in a district that is having a primary between moderate candidates whose views are not conservative, you can better use your time volunteering to help the principled candidate in the neighboring district. Although you will not be allowed to vote for that candidate, your volunteering may help elect someone to office who better reflects your views.

The following are the types of primary elections:

---

[17]   Ibid., pp. 7, 8.
[18]   Ibid., p. 25.

- Closed primary: Only those voters who are registered members of a particular party or who claim allegiance to the party can vote. In other words, Republicans vote for Republicans in a Republican primary, and Democrats for Democrats in the Democrat primary.[19] In some states, political parties have the option to allow unaffiliated voters to vote in a closed primary. Usually, unaffiliated voters are not allowed to vote in a closed primary, unless they give up their independent status and register in the party holding the closed primary.

- Open primary: All independent registered voters cast ballots along with voters who are registered by party. Normally, if more than one political party is holding a primary, voters will be allowed to pick which party ballot they want, but they may not vote in more than one primary.[20]

- Semi-closed primary: Voters must be registered in a particular party, but Independents are allowed to vote in some party primaries according to party rules.[21]

- Blanket primary: Registered voters vote for any person running in a political party's primary on an office-by-office basis regardless of whether they are formally registered voters of a particular political party.[22]

[19]   See "Closed Primary," Ballotpedia, http://ballotpedia.org/Closed_primary.
[20]   See "Open Primary," Ballotpedia, http://ballotpedia.org/Open_primary.
[21]   See "Semi-Closed Primary," Ballotpedia, http://ballotpedia.org/Semi-closed_primary.
[22]   See "Blanket Primary," Ballotpedia, http://ballotpedia.org/Blanket_primary.

- Runoff primary: If three or more candidates run but no candidate receives an absolute majority of votes (more than 50 percent), the two candidates who received the most votes "run off" against each other in this new election.

Conventions and Caucuses

These methods of nominating candidates are directly conducted directly by the major political parties. They are not state run. Usually, though not always, the "caucus" or "convention" method requires voters to present credentials and vote at a particular meeting. These meetings may also adopt rules and other procedures for voting and counting votes. A "weighted" vote means that individuals who come to a meeting will vote as a sub-unit of the entire convention or caucus. So, if one person comes from that sub-unit or fifty people come, the total vote from it is the same. The winners of these events are normally the candidates whose supporters stay until the last vote.

CHAPTER 13

The Building Block of American Politics: The Precinct

Or

All Politics Is Local

In a March 29, 1952 speech broadcast on TV and radio from the National Guard Armory in Washington, DC, to the attendees at the annual Jackson-Jefferson Day Dinner, President Harry Truman said, "I have been in politics more than 30 years, and I know that nothing else could have given me greater satisfaction. I have had a career from precinct to President."[1]

Precinct Description

A precinct, sometimes called a ward, is the smallest political and geographic subdivision in the United States for select-ing elected officials. It is composed of nonvoting residents as well as registered voters organized from census data and

---

[1]   Harry S. Truman, "Address at the Jefferson-Jackson Day Dinner," Harry S. Truman Presidential Library & Museum, http://trumanlibrary.org/publicpapers/viewpapers.php?pid=951.

physical boundary information. A precinct is also called a voting district, an election district, box, or polling place. State laws provide for an upper limit on the number of registered voters (not population) assigned to a precinct. When that number is reached, the precinct is divided because the precinct serves as the place where a certain number of voters vote during the time polls are open on election day. Each precinct has a specific building where voters cast ballots on election day. If a single polling place or precinct is used for more than one election district (split precinct), voters cast ballots within the polling place on specific machines designated for their election district.

Function of Precincts

Despite computers, television, automated calls, the Internet, social media, and other technical and cultural changes, the precinct is still the fundamental building block of all elections. It remains the place where votes are counted, where voters live and are registered, and the vehicle by which the system identifies voters. "Working the precinct," either by walking door to door or by making live phone calls, is still the most efficient and effective way to win elections. Frank Kent's almost ninety-year-old description of the function of the precinct and its importance is still relevant today:

> No clear idea of a party organization can be had unless you start from the bottom. To discuss Presidential politics without understanding precinct politics is an absurdity. It is like trying to solve a problem in trigonometry without having studied arithmetic.

The election precinct is the smallest political division. . . . In each precinct the party organization has a precinct executive, or captain or Committeeman. Just as the precinct is the smallest political division, so is the precinct executive the smallest unit in the political machine. While he is the smallest he is also, by long odds, the most vital. . . . He is the bone and sinew of the machine. He is its foundation and the real source of its strength. If he does not function, the machine decays. If he quits, the machine dies.

He is the actual connecting link between the people and the organization, and he is the only connecting link—the only man in the machine who has any point of direct contact with the voters, who knows anything about them, who has any real influence with them.[2]

Precinct Organizing Wins Elections

Handing out campaign brochures, making a twenty second pitch to neighbors on behalf of a candidate or ballot question at a doorstep, and keeping track of favorable voters to remind them to vote on election day, and other similar activities will win elections! That's it. Such voter contact is many times more important than TV, radio, or social media ads. Volunteers who can spend a few hours per week starting forty-five to thirty days before an election will change the outcome of that election and the direction of America.

---

[2]   Frank R. Kent, *The Great Game of Politics* (Buffalo, NY: Economics Books, Smith, Keynes and Marshall, 1959), p. 1.

In my experience going back to 1960, door-to-door efforts yielded the most extra votes compared to phoning, leafleting, leaving recorded phone messages, TV, or anything else. Political analysts have verified this approach time and again. So why aren't more campaigns run this way? Dedicated neighbors must be willing to take the time to meet others in their community. No one can buy that kind of dedication.

In the 2008 general election, the states operated 185,671 precincts.[3] If conservative Americans each took charge of one of the roughly 186,000 precincts across the nation, and worked for principled candidates, we could change the direction of our country. It is that simple! Compared to the sacrifices our Founding Fathers made, this is the least we can do to ensure our children, grandchildren, and great grandchildren are not saddled with crippling debt and moral anarchy.

The Importance of School Board Elections

It is vitally important to ensure that children receive schooling that is not hostile to the Judeo-Christian vision for man. Schooling in America is largely controlled or directed by local school boards, which, for example, hire the superintendent, develop policies for the operation of schools, select books for libraries and class curriculum, oversee school budget priorities, and in some areas have taxing authority.

A particularly difficult area for Washington liberals to implement their secular program rests with local school

---

[3]   *2008 Election Administration and Voting Survey*, US Election Assistance Commission, November 2009, p.13.

board control of public schools because of their great number and their decentralized operations. For example, California has 985 elected school boards, New York has 705, Pennsylvania has 501, New Jersey has 551, Wisconsin has 426, and Texas has 1,043.[4]

This is an area of public service where comparably it does not take a lot of votes or campaign funds to win elections. School boards are usually at the bottom of the ballot. (A few school board members are appointed by mayors, county supervisors, etc.) If the techniques outlined in this chapter were applied to school board elections across the United States, it would throw a major wrench in the secular liberal agenda by school boards who would tell the Department of Education Civil Rights Division that implementing the LGBTQ agenda will be resisted.

For example, will your local public middle and high schools have Gay Straight Alliance (GSA) clubs?[5] The GSA's describe themselves as follows:

> A Gay-Straight Alliance (GSA) is a student-run club in a high school or middle school that brings together LGBTQI+ and straight students to support each other, provide a safe place to socialize, and create a platform to fight for racial, gender, LGBTQ, and economic justice.[6]

---

4   "Local School Boards," Education Commission of the States, http://ecs.force.com/mbdata/mbquestRT?rep=K12G713.

5   "Directory of the National Association of GSA Networks," GSA Network, https://www.gsanetwork.org/national-directory.

6   "What is a GSA?," GSA Network, https://www.gsanetwork.org/what-we-do.

Will students take school surveys asking questions about sexual and drug behaviors in such a way as to make such behavior seem normal? The US Centers for Disease Control and Prevention (CDC) has been conducting such surveys for years and suggesting model questions for public school students regarding "sexual behaviors that contribute to human immunodeficiency virus (HIV) infection, other sexually transmitted diseases, and unintended pregnancy."[7]

Massachusetts public schools modified the CDC survey to ask whether students thought of themselves as heterosexual (straight), gay or lesbian, bisexual, or unsure; whether students were transgendered; ever had oral, anal, or vaginal intercourse; and the age at such initiation.[8]

The Gay Lesbian Straight Education Network (GLSEN) supports "safe schools." Who wouldn't? But their version of safe schools has a definite LGBTQ slant. The GLSEN organization seeks to use state anti-bullying laws as leverage for spreading and seeking special protections for LGBTQ youth.

---

[7]   Nancy D. Brener et. al., "Methodology of the Youth Risk Behavior Surveillance System — 2013," *MMWR* 62, no. 1, (March 1, 2013), p. 1, http://www.cdc.gov/mmwr/pdf/rr/rr6201.pdf.

[8]   "Unbelievable surveys given to children in Massachusetts -- and schools across America," MassResistance, May 5, 2015, http://www.massresistance.org/docs/gen2/15b/School-surveys/index.html. MassResistance officially organized in 1995 as Parents' Rights Coalition, although it had been active both locally and state-wide since 1993. In 2003, under the name Article 8 Alliance, it expanded to issues surrounding the same-sex "marriage" court ruling and its effects in Massachusetts. In 2006, these efforts were consolidated under the new name, MassResistance.

The long-term importance of school board elections on America is hard to overestimate. Concentration on school board elections will make other elections much easier for those who follow the Judeo-Christian ethic to return America to our natural law roots.

Why Door-to-Door Campaigns Lost Popularity

The Brookings Institute study found that the decline in door-to-door campaigns resulted from national political parties exercising control over campaigns through mass marketing techniques as the cost of mass phone and mass mailings decreased. Candidates with money but little experience with the local party were thus able to bypass the local political organization through TV, radio, and mass mailings.

In my own experience, I have found that a door-to-door effort is much more effective, as well as much less expensive than media based campaigns. Of course, some campaigns may need media, especially in the more populated areas, but absolutely nothing beats personal contact. When voters see a volunteer who appears to be a reasonable person at their doorstep speaking on behalf of a candidate, voters are much less likely to believe the negative TV and radio ads or brochures that are usually wielded against conservative candidates.

My Own Door-to-Door Experience

Visiting voters in a community by walking door-to-door provides fresh air, exercise, and helps you get to know your neighbors. It is the most labor intensive and weather dependent activity, but definitely has the best chance of winning votes. Talking to a voter one-on-one and asking for that person's vote, and later reminding him or her to vote, greatly increases the likelihood that the person will vote for your candidate.

Years ago, I regularly took my young children door-to-door with me to meet voters, and they seemed to enjoy the experience. They liked ringing doorbells and giving brochures to voters. The voters responded positively to the sight of children accompanying their dad on the campaign trail. (Today my children are in their late twenties and early thirties and help me in my campaigns with graphic design, new technology, and computer help.)

After introducing myself, I usually asked voters what issue concerned them the most. Invariably, the reply in one particular area was "transportation." One voter, when asked, said he could not decide, and his lack of response promoted my then-five-year-old son to whisper to this gentleman, "It's transportation." His seven-year-old brother promptly scolded him, saying, "You're not supposed to tell him. He has to guess." We all had a great laugh, and I did get a promise of a vote.

One of my veteran precinct captains recounted how her young grandson rode his toy car, stopped it, stepped out, picked up papers, walked, made a speech, returned to the car, and repeated the process. When asked what he was doing, he replied, "door-to-door."

Another time at an amusement park, my then-eight-year-old daughter remarked after seeing pennies at the bottom of a small pond, "Dad, I know who put that money in there. It was the Democrats. They're always throwing money away." Unfortunately, it is not just the Democrats who have become profligate spenders.

Although I try to visit as many voters as possible, I always include my cell number on my brochures. In 2009, I had about 240,000 mail pieces sent to 34,000 households, plus additional literature that I and my volunteers distributed at various events, but only thirty voters called my cell during the campaign. I started including my home or cell phone numbers on campaign brochures in 1993. Very few voters actually call. Giving out a personal cell number makes a candidate totally accessible, but will not normally overwhelm a candidate with calls. Nor will volunteers be overwhelmed with calls if they give out their cell number on a brochure they pass out for a candidate.

Occasionally, a voter has asked me how his name and voter information was obtained. Voter information is considered public information, although some states only allow political candidates to access it and states also forbid its use for commercial purposes.

The Precinct Captain

The precinct captain is in charge of gathering votes within the precinct boundaries for a political party, candidate, or ballot question. Anyone can volunteer to be a precinct captain. No formal political party affiliation is needed to help a candidate work a precinct. A volunteer can be affiliated with the local political party or can simply volunteer to help a particular candidate. Most often, the political party finds precinct captains to work for a slate of party candidates running in the same election. Some candidates recruit their own precinct captains, especially if they are not sure they will have the full support of the local political party organization.

Political parties often designate the head of a precinct as a precinct captain or precinct committee officer. In some states, political party precinct captains are elected in regular party primary elections. Their names can be placed on a primary ballot after receiving as few as five to ten registered voters on a petition from registered voters who live in the precinct. Additionally, political party precinct captains can have duties under state law related to the operation of the political party. These can include:

- Nominating or selecting candidates in certain circumstances;
- Chairing precinct convention meetings to select candidates;
- Serving on the county/city political party executive committee;
- Selecting election judges to count votes;
- Running a primary election for the political party;
- Filling vacancies on the county/city executive committee.

Precinct captains rely on other volunteers to distribute literature and contact voters for an election. Precinct captains or precinct volunteers do not need to be twenty-one years old with political science degrees. Alert, outgoing high school students have been successful precinct captains securing election victories, including my own.

A precinct captain finds "area captains" or "block captains" to distribute literature and conduct surveys of voters living in particular housing developments or neighborhoods. Precinct workers make sure there is contact between the candidate and the voter. This is accomplished through door-knocking, literature drops, live phone calls, and placing yard signs or distributing bumper strips.

The information collected must be reported back to the precinct chairman because the purpose of the effort is to collect a list of favorable voters who will be reminded to vote on election day. The reminders are important, especially for primary elections, which are not as well publicized as general elections.

Voter Contact: Walking and Talking

A volunteer who takes the time to visit someone on behalf of a candidate is as impressive, if not more impressive, than the candidate making a visit himself. A volunteer does not seek the elective office himself, but takes time out of his busy life to work on behalf of someone he trusts. When a neighbor or other friendly citizen vouches for a candidate, it is the best recommendation a candidate can get, and, in my experience, counts more with voters than a long list of endorsements from elected or party officials.

Knocking on doors is not that intimidating. It involves meeting people on their own turf. Hundreds of thousands of Americans do it every day in delivery jobs for UPS, FedEx, the US mail, retailers, girl scouts, newspapers, flower shops, furniture stores, home repair, etcetera. Visiting neighbors opens up the community and can lead to new friendships and opportunities to serve your neighbors. You may be surprised by the number of neighbors concerned about the country's direction. They may even volunteer to help you with your task.

If you are serious about throwing unethical politicians out of office, the first thing you need is a map of your own precinct! Your local political party, voter registrar, or state election board can help you locate this map.

Look at your map! How many people do you already know in the neighborhoods on your map who may volunteer to help you organize to reach other voters? You may find you have a gated community that is not accessible except to residents of the community. Do you know anyone who lives in this gated community? Are there high-rise buildings in the area? If so, you may need to find a resident who can leave brochures in a community room.

Pay special attention to the boundary lines of your precinct. If it is a street, then one side of the street could be located in a different precinct and be part of a different election district with a different candidate. Until you see the registered voter list for your precinct, you may not find out if both sides, or only one side, of the boundary street is part of your precinct.

Determine where the single-family homes are located, as well as the town home areas. Developments are easier to walk than more rural areas, which have more space between homes. Fewer condo and apartment dwellers are registered to vote. Voters who own their own homes generally move less frequently and are more often registered to vote because of family roots in their community. Voter lists will be more accurate for these homeowners.

Door-to-Door *Do's and Don'ts*

Door-to-door volunteers can travel alone, but many prefer to work in pairs. The pair can also split the street so each side is covered at the same time. Or a third volunteer can drive the door-knocking volunteers around. Never argue with a voter. Your opponent's supporters may try to argue with you just to use your time. If you come across a "no soliciting" sign, do not knock on the door, just leave a brochure on a doorstep or in a newspaper box without disturbing the occupant. Soliciting means selling products. You are not selling a product, you are asking citizens for a vote. But anyone who posts such a sign has a reason to not answer the door.

Never leave a brochure in a mailbox because it is against federal law to do so. A brochure may be left on the post that supports the mailbox. Try to avoid leaving a brochure where it is visible from the street in case the voter is out of town and a thief is tipped off that no one is home. Also, place the brochure where it will not get wet if it rains.

Avoid walking across a lawn unless motioned to do so by the homeowner. If you meet folks taking a walk in the neighborhood, offer a brochure, even if you are not sure they are registered to vote. This friendly gesture may cause a neighbor to mention your candidate to others and this can win support for your candidate.

If voters ask questions you can't answer, give contact information for the campaign. Also note on your voter walk list who needs follow-up calls. Make sure the person's questions are answered, or you may not win the person's vote.

The Door-to-Door Script

The door-to-door script can be as short and simple as: "Hi, I'm Sally Smith, a volunteer for Bob Jones who is running for State Senate. May I give you his brochure? Bob has covered some of the important issues in this flyer. If you have any questions, feel free to contact the campaign (point to the campaign phone number or email listed on the brochure). Bob hopes he can count on your support." That is all you need to say.

At least 90 percent of the people you meet will simply thank you for the brochure and make a mental note about your candidate. Personal visits leave lasting impressions. I have run into voters who moved from one location to another in the district I represent, who remembered I had stopped by to see them at their old address in a previous election.

Literature Drops

Door-to-door voter contact can involve "literature drops," or placing brochures (for a candidate or ballot question) on doorsteps without knocking on doors. A literature drop that attempts to reach every home on a street will reach both voters and non-voters. A targeted literature drop leaves brochures only at homes of registered voters with the goal of reaching the most voter homes in the shortest time.

Some volunteers prefer to not talk with voters. These volunteers might be willing to leave brochures on doorsteps or behind screen doors. Every volunteer is a valuable asset in a campaign no matter his or her level of commitment. Even though leaving a flyer on a doorstep is not as personal a gesture as talking to a neighbor, your candidate's name is still publicized. Knocking on a door and talking to a voter, or leaving a shorthand written note on the brochure if the voter is not home, is more impressive.

Where homes are spaced too far apart to walk door-to-door. One person drives, while the other places brochures in newspaper boxes or on mailbox support posts (never inside a mail box). Volunteers who have the time visit as well. Because voters living in rural areas are rarely visited in person, they will be very impressed.

In 2008, one of my sons and I delivered brochures to 2,600 homes on behalf of Republican candidates. We also dropped a brochure outlining Obama's liberal positions, in his own words, including his plan to draft women for front line military service. In precincts where we dropped the flyers, Obama either lost or won by smaller margins than in comparable precincts.

Voter Candidate Canvass to Identify Favorable Voters

Before you can identify favorable voters by phone or by visits to their homes, you must have a list of registered voters. Voter lists usually indicate which voters participated in a past primary election. A voter who supported a particular Republican or Democrat candidate in the past does not automatically vote for another Republican or Democrat in the next election, especially if the voter list indicated that the person voted in both Democrat and Republican party primaries during different election cycles. Voter canvasses are conducted to discover how voters intend to vote in the upcoming election.

Some campaigns want volunteers to directly ask voters whom they plan to vote for. Even if a volunteer is reluctant to ask the voter directly, a positive or negative response at the door without a definite commitment is a good indication of voter preference and such responses should be noted on the voter list as "leaning" favorable.

Not everyone in the same household has similar political views and may not vote for the same candidate. Identify on your turnout list only the voter(s) who favor your candidate because you do not want to notify your opponent's supporters.

One good way to conduct a voter canvass is to recruit high school or college students who will receive class credit or community service hours for their work. Most voters will respond to students to help them earn school credit. It is perfectly ethical to then pass on survey results to the campaign. Check with your local high school or college political science departments about recruiting students to participate in a voter canvass.

Do not be discouraged if you find few people home. In the average suburban neighborhood, usually there are about a third or fewer people at home or who will answer the door. Unless you are trying to identify non-registered citizens to see if they agree with protecting marriage or children in the womb, do not take time to convince people who are not registered to vote to support your candidate.

Voter preference surveys can also be conducted by phone. When favorable registered voters are identified, they should be added to the list of names to be contacted by phone or by "door hangers" (flyers placed on front door knobs right before the election as part of the "Get Out the Vote" effort to remind favorable voters to turn out to vote).

Sample In-Person Canvass Using Registered Voter List
Campaigns always want to find out what voters are thinking. Following is a sample survey to discover what issues are of the most concern to voters that could be conducted while going door to door or by phone.

"Hi! My name is _____, a student (or volunteer) conducting a survey for class (or community service or a campaign). Do you have about a minute to help me complete a two-question survey about the upcoming election?"

If the respondent declines, thank them, offer a candidate brochure, and go on to the next voter.

If the respondent answers "yes," ask if he is the individual listed on your sheet or, if not, ask which member of the family or household he is.

If the person answers that he is none of those named, continue with the survey and record the name anyway. He could be a newly registered voter. Ask if he is registered to vote, and if he is not registered but you learn the voter is favorable to your candidate, give them voter registration information.

The survey questions can be very simple, as these two examples demonstrate:

"Do you plan to vote for Candidate (name) or Candidate (name) for (office) this November (or month and day of primary)?" (If asked for which party the candidates are running, name them.)

(If there are additional candidates running for different offices in the same election, the survey will take only a few moments longer).

"What issue concerns you the most in this election?"

If you are conducting your canvass by phone but reach an answering machine, leave a short message on behalf of your candidate including the phone number and email of the campaign so the call is not wasted.

Thank the person for participating in your canvass.

Importance of Voter Contact

Personal voter contact makes the critical difference between winning and losing elections. Because we are social creatures and not hermits, walking in a neighborhood and knocking on doors forms a bond with voters, helps identify problems of a particular community, and can even help identify solutions that will promote the common good. I have learned much about traffic problems, zoning violations, and other citizen concerns by talking to voters on their doorsteps.

In 2008, Barack Obama created "temporary communities" in swing states with paid campaign "workers." In Virginia, I saw many cars with Obama bumper stickers and out-of-state license tags from the Midwest with college-age drivers and passengers. These young people went door to door in Prince William County, Virginia, to identify actual and potential Obama supporters without identifying them-selves as living out of state.

If a voter is *not* contacted by a candidate or his campaign, it leaves the impression that the candidate does not need his or her vote to win. Simply contacting a voter in person pro-duced winning campaigns. Chuck Todd, NBC News polit-ical director, writes, "Half of all Virginia voters, 51%, were contacted by the Obama campaign, while less than four in ten, 37%, said the McCain campaign contacted them. This advantage in campaign contact was important. Since six in ten voters contacted by the Obama campaign voted for the Democrat . . . and six in ten of those contacted by the McCain campaign voted Republican."[9]

Both campaigns convinced roughly the same percent of voters whom they contacted, but the victory in Virginia went to Obama because his campaign simply contacted more voters. Other than the price of literature, it costs nearly nothing for volunteers to contact voters door to door or by a live phone call.

Door-to-Door Tools

Besides a map of your precinct with clearly identified streets, an accurate list of registered voters is critical. The voter lists will usually contain the following information: street name, house number, last and first names of registered voters at each house, sex and age of voters, date voter registered, voting his-tory in general and primary elections, and phone numbers.

---

9   Chuck Todd and Sheldon Gawiser, *How Barack Obama Won: A State-by-State Guide to the Historic 2008 Presidential Election* (New York: Vintage Books, 2009), p. 95.

Not all campaigns include phone numbers on walking lists, but phone numbers are very helpful for follow-up after walking neighborhoods.

The date of a voter's registration tells you how long the voter has been eligible to vote. Often you will find different last names at the same street address. Normally the most recent registration date (if more than one voter with a different last name is listed at the same house) is the current resident, although registered voters with different last names and different registration dates can live at the same address.

One of the most effective tools we have used in our thirteen winning state campaigns is a short, handwritten note on a campaign brochure or sticky note attached to a brochure, which is prepared ahead of time. It is either signed by myself, if I am walking, or by my volunteers. The message simply says, "Sorry to miss you," or "Hope you vote for Bob," with a signature of the canvasser and sometimes a cell number written in colored ink. These personal touches show voters the candidate is "real," with genuine support in the community.

The Mechanics of Precinct Organizing

The actual mechanics of precinct organizing are not difficult. Door-to-door efforts are best done on Saturday from 11 a.m. until just before sunset or on Sunday from roughly 1:30 p.m. to just before sunset. You will need to prepare the packets of campaign brochures, names of voters to contact, and street maps for each volunteer. Volunteers do not need to live in the precinct they are walking, though it helps.

Make sure the registered voter list for your particular precinct is organized alphabetically by street name and is in ascending or descending numerical street address order. Each street should be printed on separate sheets. This is necessary so you can pick out only those streets that are near each other when you make walking packets for volunteers.

You need the walking lists to be printed in ascending or descending numerical order to make it easy for volunteers to contact voters in the same fashion that a mailman would efficiently deliver the mail. Your list should be prepared with the names of all voters at each house listed next to the address of the houses so you can easily identify your contacts. Some lists will also include the years in which the resident voted.

A telephone call list for a precinct need not be in street order, but walking lists of registered voters must be. Here is a simulated voter list arranged for walking door to door:

Adirondack Court—PRECINCT 405 Bull Run

6300	Smith, George	05 07 08	Rpri 12	R3 D0	703-111-0000
	Phyllis	05 07 08	Rpri 12	R5 D0	703-111-0000
6302	Jones, Alice	07 08	Rpri 08	R1 D0	571-111-0000
	Robert	07 08	Rpri 12	R1 D0	571-111-0000
	Staubbs, Sandra	08		R0 D0	
6304	Bell, James	05 07 08		R2 D4	703-000-0000
	Mary	05 07 08		R2 D4	703-000-0000
6307	Armour, Albert	05 12		R0 D0	703-000-1111
	Amy	05 08		R0 D0	703-000-1111
6312	Lee, Ahn	05 07 08		R0 D0	

This sample street list gives you the following information for each voter on the street named Adirondack Court. The address number is on the left, followed by the last name then first name of the registered voter, the years in which the voter voted in a general election, whether the voter voted in the 2008 Republican presidential primary or the 2012 Republican US Senate primary, the total number of times a vote was cast in a Republican or Democrat primary, and a phone number if available. Just make sure you ask for the significance of the abbreviations on the street walking sheets.

At 6302 Adirondack Court, Sandra Staubbs is listed along with Alice and Robert Jones. Unless you call or visit 6302 Adirondack Court, you will not know if the Jones family moved, or if Sandra Staubbs lives with the Jones family. She may or may not be a relative. This particular list does not give the date the voter registered.

Examine your precinct map and pick several contiguous streets. Go through your registered voter walking list and pick out those streets. Remember, one street of registered voters may be on several sheets of paper. Then, to determine how many brochures you or your volunteer will need to deliver, count out one brochure for each household on your walking list. You do not need to count brochures for every voter at the same address. One brochure per house will do. Then add a few extra brochures in case some get crumpled in the car, or voters ask for extra copies for friends.

Voter lists should be compiled to eliminate households that you do not need to visit. For example, if you are working in a primary race, you would not want to waste brochures or time on voters who never vote in primaries, or voters who regularly vote in primaries for the opposing party. To make the best use of your time, target voters who are most likely to vote in that particular election.

Some political campaigns provide walking packets already made up, complete with the street sheets of registered voters and computer drawn maps. Every packet should include a map as well as the walking sheets for the streets to be walked. Highlight the streets to be walked on the precinct map included in the volunteer packet so a volunteer knows exactly where to walk.

Keep a master voter list and two master precinct maps to keep track of areas being walked and by whom. Highlight in color the streets assigned, and highlight the second map in a different color the streets that have been walked so you can keep track of your progress. If a volunteer is unable to complete an assignment, you can easily make another packet from your master map and list.

Show on your precinct map the location of homes where yard signs have been requested and placed. A yard sign on someone's front lawn is much more impressive than one posted along a roadside because it is a personal endorsement. However, large signs on high traffic routes are also important.

No effort is too small to contribute to an election victory! Very few people do more than simply vote, so finding several volunteers to physically contact twenty-five to fifty homes each in an election could easily change the outcome of an election. Over the past twenty-six years I've been in office, volunteers (some of whom were not old enough to vote) helped me beat opponents who spent up to four times what

I spent and who had the endorsements of major newspapers. While funding is necessary, an organization on the ground can overcome a money deficit.

Phone Calls and Campaigns

Telephone calls are made in elections to survey voters for their positions on issues, to find out which candidate has the lead, to ask for support for a candidate or ballot issue, and to remind previously identified supporters to vote on election day.

Not all registered voter lists include phone numbers since voter applicants are not required to have phones, and many younger voters use cell phones. Answering machines have also reduced the ability to make phone contact with voters. Still, a live phone call from a voter who may also live in the same precinct is the next most effective way to contact voters after door-to-door contact. Automated messages can be annoying, but if left on an answering machine, they serve the same purpose as a live call.

Successful Telephone Surveys

We made phone calls to defeat two very liberal pro-abortion Democrat congressmen from Northern Virginia in 1980. A five-question phone survey executed over several months by a network of around fifty area leaders, who in turn relied on hundreds of volunteer callers, took about eighteen months to complete.

The purpose of the phone survey was to identify in two suburban Virginia congressional districts in Northern

Virginia every voter or prospective voter who was pro-life and who would vote for or against a candidate based on that issue.

We called most homes in two Northern Virginia congressional districts using commercially available street directories (sometimes called "Criss-Cross" or Haines Directories) that listed persons by street name, street number, zip code, and phone number. Such directories are often used by door-to-door salesmen.

Before the age of sophisticated computers, we simply cut up the street directory and taped the data for each street onto the left sides of copy paper, then organized the street lists into piles based on zip codes that roughly corresponded to clusters of election precincts. We then prepared packets of street lists and distributed them to volunteers who agreed to make calls over several months under the direction of area coordinators.

We made duplicates of the sheets in case some were misplaced or volunteers couldn't complete their calls. The finished product was well worth the time and effort.

The names of "positive" respondents were typed from our calling sheets into rather primitive computers. The lists were broken down by congressional district. Current registered voters who responded favorably to the survey were on one list, and another list consisted of those who responded favorably but were not registered to vote. We sent voter registration information to favorable persons who were not yet registered to vote. Later we followed up to encourage them to register.

About a third of the roughly nineteen thousand favorable pro-life person households we identified had not been previously registered. Ultimately, this effort produced a list of roughly eleven thousand voter households in one congressional district and about eight thousand voter households in the other congressional district who told us they would vote for a candidate based on his position on the right to life. The total possible pro-life voter pool was nineteen thousand multiplied by 1.4 to 1.6 voters per household or 26,600 to 30,400 pro-life voters. Remember those figures included from 8,800 to 10,100 newly registered voters.

We asked for stamps, envelopes, and brochures from the pro-life candidates we were supporting. We inserted a brochure that compared the candidates' positions on right to life. We included a general brochure from the candidate. This effort helped to defeat two liberal Democrats and elect two pro-life Republicans in November 1980.

Similar efforts could be undertaken across the US with a short survey on life, real marriage, or the so-called transgender controversy. Lists of pro-life or pro-marriage registered voters and not-yet-registered voters could be compiled for future elections. Supporters not yet registered to vote could be encouraged to register, or even given forms to register. Voters could be informed which candidates support these policies.

Voter Marriage, Family, & Life ID Poll

The following surveys can be conducted by phone calls or door-to-door interviews. You and your friends could ask all three questions, two questions, or just one of the questions.

Sample Survey Using Registered Voter List

"Hello, Mr. (or Mrs.) X. I am (first name) with (name of your civic group, such as Roanoke Good Government Group).

"We are conducting a civic awareness survey. It will only take a minute to participate. May I ask you a few questions?"

If answer is "no," thank them and hang up. If answer is "yes," continue with survey.

"Do you believe marriage should only be between one man and one woman?"

Yes ( ) No ( ) If "no," stop the survey and say, "Thank you very much."

If "yes," continue with survey.

"Would you only support a candidate for office who supported marriage between one man and one woman?"

Yes ( ) No ( ) If "no," stop the survey and say, "Thank you very much."

If "yes," continue with survey.

"Do you believe all preborn children deserve legal protection?" (If asked from what point in pregnancy, say, "from conception to birth.")

Yes ( ) No ( )

"Would you only support a candidate for office who would protect these children by law?"

Yes ( ) No ( )

"Would you support a candidate for office if they would *not* permit boys in public school to use girls restrooms, showers, changing areas, or sleep in girls' rooms on overnight field trips?"

Yes ( ) No ( )

"Do you consider yourself Conservative ( ), Moderate ( ), or Liberal ( )?"

"This survey is complete, Thank you!" (You could also ask, "Would you like to receive email information about legislation on these topics?")

If "yes" ( ), take down email. If "no" ( ), say, "Thank you very much," and hang up.

Sample Survey Using Criss-Cross Directory Names

"Hello, Mr. (or Mrs.) X. I am (first name) with (name of your civic group, such as "Roanoke Good Government Group").

"We are conducting a civic awareness survey. Do you have a minute to participate?"

If answer is "no," thank them and hang up. If answer is "yes," continue with survey.

"Do you think that marriage should be only between one man and one woman?"

Yes ( ) No ( ) If "no," stop the survey and say, "Thank you very much."

If "yes," continue with survey.

"Would you only support a candidate for Congress who supported marriage between one man and one woman?"

Yes ( ) No ( ) If "no," stop the survey and say, "Thank you very much."

If "yes," continue with survey.

"Do you believe all preborn children deserve legal protection?" (If asked from what point in pregnancy, say, "from conception to birth.")

Yes ( ) No ( )

"Would you only support a candidate for office who would protect these children by law?"

Yes ( ) No ( )

"Would you support a candidate for office if they would *not* permit boys in public school to use girls restrooms, showers, changing areas, or sleep in girls' rooms on overnight field trips?"

Yes ( ) No ( )

"Are you registered to vote?"

Yes ( ) No ( ) If "no," this person should be sent voter registration info.

"Do you consider yourself Conservative ( ), Moderate ( ), or Liberal ( )?"

"This survey is complete, thank you!" (But you could ask, "Would you like to receive email information about legislation on these topics?")

If "yes" ( ), take down email. If "no" ( ), say, "Thank you very much," and hang up.

After completing your survey using the Criss-Cross directory (or other list), make sure voter registration information is sent to the favorable responders to help them register to vote. It is also helpful to organize your names into precincts to help in future elections.

Election Day Voting

"Get Out the Vote" (GOTV) refers to the efforts to remind favorable voters to vote. Usually calls or visits are made in the three or four days before election day. You may also offer to provide rides to the polls for those who need them.

After going through all the work to identify your favorable voters, it would be a shame if these voters simply forgot to vote. Because we all lead busy lives, some people do forget to vote, especially for primaries or special elections, or find it difficult to fit voting into their schedule. They might have a car in the shop and need a ride to the polls. Elections have been won and lost by a single vote per precinct, so do not dismiss even one possible vote.

Remind voters to vote, especially in primary elections, which are usually less publicized than general elections. Your last contact with a voter may have been six or eight weeks earlier. So a phone call or a "door hanger" left on the doorstep will remind them to vote.

GOTV phone calls should start the Wednesday or Thursday before a Tuesday election and finish by the Monday immediately before election day. Avoid making phone calls past 8:30 p.m. If you reach an answering machine, include the candidate's name, the office for which he is running, and why their vote is important. Give the day and date of the election, times polls are open, and location of their polling place.

GOTV efforts often use a "door hanger" made of cardstock with a hole to attach it to a doorknob. If the door hanger is specific to a precinct, make sure the election date and location of the polling place are accurate. Mistaken or unclear instructions could direct voters to the wrong polling place.

Volunteers can make phone calls or walk to "Get Out the Vote." Campaigns usually have a headquarters where volunteers gather to make GOTV calls to ensure calls are completed. Computer technology makes it possible to make calls from home or cell phones. Just make sure the calls are completed or the door hangers are delivered.

Your GOTV list will never match exactly the number of favorable voters who show up to vote, because despite your best efforts, some of your favorables will end up not voting, and it is not possible to identify every single possible favorable voter. Some voters will not be home when you drop by, and others may not answer their phone or the answering machine may not work. Some favorable voters may not want to divulge their vote preference.

In the last ten years, GOTV efforts have competed with the phenomenon of early voting, especially as states expand the reasons for absentee voting. The US Election Commission reported that in 2008, only 60 percent of all voters cast their ballots on election day. This makes late summer and early fall precinct door knocking all the more important, because many voters are making up their minds earlier and casting their votes before election day.

Judicial Supremacy Reconsidered

Today, too many members of Congress and the vast majority of citizens believe that Congress has no authority over the Supreme Court, that the Supreme Court has more authority than the Congress, the president, and the states, and that it has the exclusive and final authority to determine the meaning of the Constitution and the operations of the national government and the several states. This concept is called judicial supremacy.

Proponents of judicial supremacy usually take the position that "the only political process which can be constitutionally used for the purpose of overcoming an undesired judicial interpretation of the Constitution is that of constitutional amendment, . . . [but] . . . this simply begs the question whether the Constitution needs amending, and in view of the extremely undemocratic method which the Constitution provides for amendment, such question-begging is extremely hazardous."[1]

---

[1]   Edward S. Corwin, *Court Over Constitution: A Study of Judicial Review as an Instrument of Popular Government* (Princeton, NJ:

But is the Supreme Court the final and exclusive inter-
preter of the Constitution, and are constitutional amendments the only way around Supreme Court decisions? Did
the Founders really give power to judges of the Supreme
Court to definitively decide that states must provide for
so-called marriage between two men or two women or
remove legal protection for the lives of children before birth?
Is such authority to be found in the written Constitution?
Let's investigate.

The Supreme Court—More Infallible than the Pope

Judicial review is the power of a court to decide on the validity or constitutionality of acts of a legislature or executive
agency. Judicial supremacy incorporates both the practice
of judicial review and the proclamation of that review as
the last word over the other branches of government, both
federal and state, once the Supreme Court has spoken. But
since state and federal legislators, as well as governors and
presidents, also take an oath to the US Constitution, how
is it that judges, and Supreme Court judges only, have been
determined to have the final word on the constitutionality
of a statute?

Commentator Edward Corwin analyzed the presump-
tions of judicial supremacists:

> In other words, owing to some clairvoyant faculty
> which enters into a man when he becomes a justice
> of the Supreme Court, or on account of some mysti-
> cal connection between Court and Deity, the Court

Princeton University Press, 1938), p. 80.

is able at all times to speak the authentic Constitution. . . . But there are some facts . . . that furnish grounds for skepticism. To recur once more to the phenomenon of overruled cases: which Court was it that enjoyed divine inspiration—the one that did the overruling, or the one that was overruled? . . . And when a decision disallowing an act of Congress is a five to four decision, is the inspiration enjoyed by all the majority judges, or only the odd man?[2]

Corwin is referring to decisions in which the Supreme Court had previously held that a law or policy is constitutional and later concludes that the identical law or policy is unconstitutional (or the reverse). Corwin's observations are illustrated by Supreme Court justice Kennedy's 2003 majority opinion in the *Lawrence v. Texas* case striking down all state criminal anti-sodomy laws, which, in 1986, had previously been held constitutional in *Bowers v. Hardwick,* a 5-4 Supreme Court decision upholding a Georgia law criminalizing oral and anal sex between consenting homosexual adults.[3]

In *Lawrence*, Kennedy noted that the Georgia legislature based its assumptions of criminality on Judeo-Christian moral and ethical standards. Kennedy based his own 2003 reversal of *Bowers* in *Lawrence* on the 1986 minority dissenting opinion of Justice Stevens in *Bowers*.

---

2   *American Constitutional History, Essays by Edward S. Corwin,* ed. Alpheus Mason and Gerald Garvey, (New York: Harper and Row, 1964), pp. 127–8.

3   Bowers v. Hardwick, 478 U.S. 186 (1986).

> The fact that the governing majority in a State has tra-
> ditionally viewed a particular practice as immoral is
> not a sufficient reason for upholding a law prohibiting
> the practice. . . .
>
> Justice Stevens' analysis, in our view, should have
> been controlling in *Bowers* and should control here.
> . . . *Bowers* was not correct when it was decided, and
> it is not correct today. It ought not to remain binding
> precedent. *Bowers v. Hardwick* should be and now is
> overruled.[4]

Note that Justice Kennedy does not resolve for citizens how to know which (and when) Supreme Court decisions are "correctly" applying the Constitution. So, in the light of current events, we may legitimately ask which LGBTQ decision reflects the true meaning of the Constitution since the Supreme Court has reversed itself on the question of what is or is not constitutional.

Every congressional office has a large volume prepared by the Library of Congress that documents, from 1808 through July 1, 2014, the Supreme Court has reversed itself on the meaning of the Constitution 233 times, ruling either that what the court held to be unconstitutional is now constitutional or what previously was held to be constitutional is ruled in the later decision to be unconstitutional.[5]

How should changes to the Constitution be made? George Washington, at the end of his second presidential

---

4   Lawrence v. Texas, 539 U.S. 558 (2003).
5   "The Constitution of the United States of America: Analysis and
       Interpretation," S. Doc. No. 112-9, at 2595 (2014).

term, noted, "The basis of our political systems is the right of the people to make and to alter their constitutions of government. But the Constitution which at any time exists, till changed by an explicit and authentic act of the whole people, is sacredly obligatory upon all."[6] Courts do not have the authority to change the Constitution, but the Supreme Court has extracted opposite meanings from the same constitutional provisions on 233 occasions.

Why should the public believe that the Supreme Court is authentically applying the Constitution and should have the final word on what is ultimately constitutional when the court moves like a weather vane in a storm, anchored to nothing other than its own judicial will?

Considering there have been so many Supreme Court reversals, it should be interesting to find out how at least some Supreme Court judges arrive at their decisions.

The Supreme Court and the True Meaning of the Constitution

Corwin, one of the more incisive critics of the claim that the Supreme Court is the sole arbiter of the Constitution, wrote, "The juristic conception of judicial review involves a miracle. It supposes a kind of transubstantiation whereby the Court's opinion of the Constitution . . . becomes the very body and blood of the Constitution. This dogmatic assumption of the identity of the law with the judicial version of it,

---

6   George Washington, "Washington's Farewell Address 1796," The Avalon Project, Yale University, http://avalon.law.yale.edu/18th_century/washing.asp.

is not, however, coeval with the Constitution."[7]

Corwin's point was demonstrated in a 1937 letter from Supreme Court justice Felix Frankfurter to President Franklin Roosevelt about the role of the US Supreme Court and the veneration it enjoyed: "A majority of the Court . . . have been exploiting the mystery which so largely envelops the Court. People have been taught to believe that when the Supreme Court speaks it is not they who speak but the Constitution, whereas, of course, in so many vital cases, it is they who speak and not the Constitution. And I verily believe that that is what the country needs most to understand."[8]

Frankfurter brought Roosevelt's attention to a decision of Justice Oliver W. Holmes, who never hesitated to infuse his own agnostic views into decisions. In the opinion cited, Holmes wrote, "The ever increasing scope given to the Fourteenth Amendment in cutting down . . . the constitutional rights of the states. . . . I see hardly any limit but the sky to the invalidating of those rights if they happen to strike a majority of this Court as for any reason undesirable. I cannot believe that the Amendment was intended to give us *carte blanche* to embody our economic or moral beliefs in its prohibitions."[9]

So, according to Justice Felix Frankfurter, his predecessor Justice Oliver Wendell Holmes, who wrote a Supreme Court decision saying it was constitutional to forcibly sterilize individuals thought to be less than geniuses, himself hesitated

---

[7]   Corwin, *Court Over Constitution*, pp. 68–9.
[8]   "Frankfurter letter to Roosevelt, 2/18/37," New Deal Network, http://newdeal.feri.org/court/ff02.htm.
[9]   Baldwin v. Missouri, 281 U.S. 586 (1930).

at the thought that he and his fellow justices were given such latitude that the Fourteenth Amendment amounted to a complete blank check for them to write anything they wished! Yes, he hesitated . . . for a moment, but he went along with the continuous judicial power grabs.

The late Justice William O. Douglas relates in his autobiography that Chief Justice Charles Evans Hughes once told him:

> "Justice Douglas, you must remember one thing. At the constitutional level where we work, ninety percent of any decision is emotional. The rational part of us supplies the reasons for supporting our predilections."
>
> I had thought of the law of Moses, principles chiseled into granite. . . . I had never been willing to admit to myself that the "gut" reaction of a judge at the level of constitutional adjudications dealing with . . . due process, freedom of speech and the like was the main ingredient of his decision. The admission of it destroyed in my mind some of the reverence for the immutable principles. . . . No judge at the level I speak of was neutral. The Constitution is not neutral. It was designed to take the government off the backs of people.[10]

Douglas is saying here that judges were not impartial arbiters of abstract justice divorced from interests and outcomes, and that they came to the bench with notions they would

---

[10]   William O. Douglas, *The Court Years: 1939-1975* (New York: Random House, 1980), p. 8.

weave into their decisions. And as for taking government off the backs of the people, Douglas is not talking about eliminating a nanny state run by nosy, meddlesome bureaucrats. No, judicial elites would make decisions for the rest of us down to who would be favored and who would not receive favors, who would be given a break before the law and who would not be given a break, who would live and who would die. In other words, the judges would select themselves as platonic guardians and make decisions with vast social consequences for the rest of us.

Douglas concludes, "In time I came to realize that Hughes was right when he said that a Justice's decisions were based 90 percent on emotion."[11] Why the gut feelings of appointed federal judges are more important, authoritative, constitutional, legal, and social moorings than the visceral leanings or ethical dispositions of elected officials or even average citizens, Douglas does not explain.

Douglas also relates how Justice Frankfurter privately called Chief Justice Hughes "Bushy." One day Frankfurter told Douglas, "If we can keep Bushy on our side, there is no amount of rewriting of the Constitution we cannot do."[12]

The court as a self-validating constitutional weather vane did not escape notice by its own sitting members. Referring to past controversial decisions of the Supreme Court, Chief Justice Earl Warren (1953–69) commented in 1962 on the World War II Japanese internment cases that "the fact that the Court rules in a case like Hirabayashi that a given program is constitutional, does not necessarily answer the

---

[11]   Ibid., p. 33.
[12]   Ibid., pp. 7–8.

question whether, in a broader sense, it actually is."[13]

The sweeping usurpations of state legislative authority by the justices of the court would eventually become fodder for commentary by popular writers like Watergate reporter Bob Woodward and colleague Scott Armstrong, who commented on the *Roe* and *Doe* abortion cases: "The clerks in most chambers were surprised to see the Justices, particularly Blackmun, so openly brokering their decision like a group of legislators. . . . There was something embarrassing and dishonest about this whole process. It left the Court claiming that the Constitution drew certain lines at trimesters and viability. . . . As a constitutional matter it was absurd."[14]

Some of the more self-deluding justices apparently believe they are agents of some great commission that only they understand. Justice Anthony Kennedy was asked in a 2005 interview if he ever second-guessed himself. He responded, "Not often. You can't be effective if you're always worrying about the last decision. You sometimes wonder how your decisions will play out, but I think the major decisions that I've made are correct over the course of time." When Justice Kennedy was asked which qualities are most important for a judge, he answered, "To have an understanding that you have the opportunity to shape the destiny of this country. The framers wanted you to shape the destiny of the country. They didn't want to frame it for you."[15]

---

[13]   Earl Warren, "The Bill of Rights and the Military," *Air Force Law Review* 60, pp. 16–17.

[14]   Bob Woodward and Scott Armstrong, *The Brethren: Inside the Supreme Court* (New York: Simon and Schuster, 1979), p. 233.

[15]   "Anthony Kennedy Interview," Academy of Achievement, last modified June 8, 2017, http://www.achievement.org/achiever/

Reading a quote like that, a citizen could be forgiven for thinking that, instead of deciding cases, Justice Kennedy and others like him are always looking beyond the litigants and issues presented in the courtroom and arranging their decisions to alter the future, according to what they consider the callings of destiny. Burdened with such heavy responsibilities, it is a wonder that Kennedy manages to take into account what the Constitution means at all.

Kennedy's response to decisions that are met with waves of rejection by citizens who see their moral beliefs uprooted like weeds is strikingly defensive for someone who has an exalted view of his own mental prescience and morals. He gives the unwashed a pat on the head for their ignorance of the higher law that federal judges issue like the oracle at Delphi: "So if there's a decision people don't like, of course, we're pressured about it. I think it's unfortunate that sometimes people ascribe improper motives to judges. They don't understand the tradition."[16]

Yet Kennedy shows no hesitance in his majority opinions to ascribe improper motives to anyone who differs with his goal to make America safe for sodomy as he clearly did in the 1996 case of *Romer v. Evans, Lawrence v. Texas* citing *Romer*, and the 2013 *United States v. Windsor*, all cases that advanced homosexual claims.

Justice Kennedy ruled in *Romer* that "laws of the kind now before us raise the inevitable inference that the disadvantage imposed is born of animosity toward the class of

---

[16]   anthony-m-kennedy/#interview.
       Ibid.

persons affected."[17] (Does Justice Kennedy think Moses and Christ were motivated by animosity?)

Think about Kennedy's claim. How did he know what 814,000 individual Colorado voters were thinking on one day in November four years prior when they voted for the referendum in question? Yet he concludes every last one of them marched into polling booths and allegedly voted because of their animosity toward homosexuals!

Justices previously would not question motives of 535 congressional lawmakers, much less assume powers of clairvoyance regarding the personal motives of voters. For example, in 1919 Justice Louis Brandeis wrote, "No principle of our constitutional law is more firmly established than that this court may not, in passing on the validity of a statute, inquire into the motives of Congress."[18]

Yet the Congress allows Justice Kennedy to remain on the bench after pretending he can read minds and the thoughts of 814,000 voters from the past. If this is indicative of good judicial behavior, what would constitute bad judicial behavior?

Calling the Judicial Bluff

Actually passing legislation curbing the court was not always necessary to effect a change in Supreme Court decisions. Referencing FDR's Court Packing Plan, the "history of Court-congressional conflicts in general, and that of 1937 in particular, had shown that the *passage* of a Court curb was not necessary to effect a change in the judicial mind.

---

17   Romer v. Evans, 517 U.S. 620 (1996).
18   Hamilton v. Kentucky Distilleries 251 U.S. 146 (1919).

The threat of congressional action could work wonders in shuffling alignments on the High Bench."[19]

And in the mid-1950s, the Supreme Court issued a number of decisions that alarmed Congress with respect to its own power of investigation, the ability of the FBI to secure prosecutions of Communists under the Smith Act, and an uncritical and seemingly novel expansion of civil liberties that prompted congressional hearings as well as threats to pass bills directed at those areas of judicial activism in which the court seemed to challenge the prerogatives of Congress. This produced a "retreat of the Warren Court" from rejecting civil liberty claims in only 26 percent of cases in 1956, to rejecting 48.8 percent of such claims in the 1958 term.[20]

Shortly before he was appointed chief justice in 1969, Warren Burger noted, "A Court which is final and unreviewable needs more careful scrutiny than any other. Unreviewable power is most likely to self-indulge. . . . No public institution, or the people who operate it, can be above public debate."[21]

Curbing Federal Court Jurisdiction or Impeaching Judges

Civics 101 courses regularly note that the Constitution set up a system of checks and balances between the legislative, judicial, and executive branches. One tool the Founders gave

---

[19]   Walter F. Murphy, *Congress and the Court: A Case Study in the American Political Process* (Chicago: University of Chicago Press, 1962), p. 260.

[20]   Ibid., p. 246.

[21]   Woodward and Armstrong, *The Brethren*, p. 5.

to Congress to rein in erring presidents and judges was that of impeachment, which provided for their removal from office for any actions or omissions significant enough to impede discharge of their duties. Impeachable offenses did not have to be criminal acts.

Impeachment itself is the act of the presentment of charges by the US House of Representatives by a majority vote. Impeachment is *not* the conviction by the Senate, which requires a two-thirds vote. While the Constitution provides that judges are appointed "for good behavior," in practice and in the absence of Congress abolishing an entire level of the judiciary, as was done under President Thomas Jefferson, judicial appointments have lasted as long as the judges wished to remain on the bench.

The first use of impeachment was brought against federal judge John Pickering of New Hampshire, not for any one particularly odious legal decision; it was his general demeanor and courtroom behavior on the federal bench. "In 1803, District Judge Pickering was removed from office by the process of impeachment on account of drunkenness and other unseemly conduct on the bench. The defense of insanity was urged in his behalf, but unsuccessfully."[22]

The next impeachment came in 1804 with charges against Samuel Chase, a signer of the Declaration of Independence from Maryland and a Supreme Court justice. "Chase had been the target of an impeachment attempt earlier in his career as a state court judge in Maryland. His vocal Federalism and his judicial excesses in handling politically sensitive

---

[22]   Edward S. Corwin, *The Constitution and What it Means Today* (Princeton: Princeton University Press, 1974), p. 13.

trials led the House to draft eight articles of Impeachment against him."[23]

Chase's judicial demeanor was not restrained. Today, he would be called a transparently political judge. He engaged in behavior that would be prohibited by the rules of professional conduct for attorneys or judges. For example, the Supreme Court term for August 1800 was delayed "because Justice Chase remained in his home state of Maryland to campaign for the reelection of John Adams as President. . . . While charging a grand jury in Baltimore, Chase spoke disparagingly of some Republican [Jefferson] policies, sharply criticized at least one act of Congress passed after Jefferson became president, and also criticized proposed changes in the Maryland state constitution."[24]

Thomas Jefferson, both as president and party leader of the Democratic-Republicans, wrote to Maryland congressman Joseph Nicholson of Chase's intemperate charge to the grand jury:

"You must have heard of the extraordinary charge of Chase to the grand jury at Baltimore. Ought this seditious and official attack on the principles of our Constitution, and on the proceedings of a State, to go unpunished? And to whom so pointedly as yourself will the public look for the necessary measures?"[25]

---

[23]   Emily Field Van Tassel and Paul Finkelman, *Impeachable Offenses, A Documentary History from 1787 to the Present* (Washington: Congressional Quarterly, 1999), p. 102.

[24]   William H. Rehnquist, *Grand Inquests: The Historic Impeachments of Justice Samuel Chase and President Andrew Johnson* (New York: William Morrow and Co., 1992), p. 22.

[25]   *The Jeffersonian Cyclopedia*, ed. John P. Foley (New York: Funk & Wagnalls, 1900), no. 1204.

Jefferson's fellow Virginian John Marshall was chief justice at this time. He was troubled by the effect Chase's impeachment would have on the stature and position of the Supreme Court in the newly formed government.[26]

Marshall wrote a letter to Chase in January 1804 at the time of the House impeachment vote opining that Congress should rely on removing appellate jurisdiction rather than impeachment: "The present doctrine seems to be that a Judge giving a legal opinion contrary to the opinion of the legislature is libel to impeachment. I think the modern doctrine of impeachment should yield to an appellate jurisdiction in the legislature. A reversal of those legal opinions deemed unsound by the legislature would certainly better comport with the mildness of our character than (would) a removal of the Judge who has rendered them unknowing of his fault."[27]

The Senate voted Chase not guilty on five of the eight charges and guilty by a majority vote on three, but not by the two-thirds majority needed to remove Chase from the court.[28] As a result of this defeat, Jefferson would conclude that impeachment was "not even a scarecrow," that the "Judiciary is independent of the nation," and that it would be a "difficult task in curbing the Judiciary in their enterprises on the Constitution. . . . Impeachment therefore is a bugbear which they [judges] fear not at all."[29]

---

[26]   Rehnquist, *Grand Inquests*, p. 126.

[27]   Albert J. Beveridge, *The Life of John Marshall*, vol. 3, *Conflict and Construction, 1800-1815* (Boston and New York: Houghton Mifflin Company, 1919), p. 177.

[28]   Van Tassel and Finkelman, *Impeachable Offenses*, p. 103.

[29]   Foley, *The Jeffersonian Cyclopedia*, nos. 4178, 4179, 4182.

Presidential Appointment of Supreme Court Justices

Or

Put Not Your Faith in Princes (or Their Nominations to the Supreme Court)

Waiting for justices of the Supreme Court like Justice Kennedy to "save" marriage, or reverse their abortion-on-demand decisions, has not worked. Republican Ronald Reagan, whose pro-life credentials were genuine, appointed three justices to the court: Antonin Scalia, Sandra Day O'Connor, and Anthony Kennedy. The record shows that only Scalia ruled in support of state or federal legal protection for children before birth. O'Connor and Kennedy advocated for a type of liberty that included the choice to kill a child before birth without state prohibitions. Ronald Reagan also elevated Justice Rehnquist to be chief justice. But that fact changed no decisions.

Ronald Reagan nominated district court judge Vaughan Walker, the federal district court judge who struck down California's one-man, one-woman Proposition 8. The nomination stalled, and President George Bush nominated Walker in 1991. President Bush also nominated Justice David Souter to the Supreme Court in 1991. Souter agreed with the majority in *Lawrence v. Texas*, the decision striking down state criminal anti-sodomy laws. Justice Clarence Thomas, who opposes liberal homosexual rights policies and supports protecting children before birth, was nominated to the Supreme Court by President Bush in 1991.

Republican president George W. Bush nominated Chief Justice John Roberts and Samuel Alito. Both of these Justices dissented in the 2013 *United States v. Windsor*, the decision striking down the federal Defense of Marriage law that had allowed states to refuse to recognize out-of-state so-called same-sex marriages.

Republican president Gerald Ford nominated Justice John Paul Stevens in 1975. Stevens regularly supported abortion and homosexual rights. Republican president Richard Nixon nominated Justice Harry Blackmun in 1970 and Chief Justice Warren Burger to the Supreme Court in 1969. Blackmun wrote the disgraceful *Roe v. Wade* decision in 1973, and Chief Justice Burger wrote a companion decision for *Doe v. Bolton* striking down hospital requirements for abortion. He said health should be understood in a broad context.

Whatever expectations were, the bottom line is that judges rule their own way once appointed to the bench. Experience shows that relying on presidents to choose judges who will defend marriage and life has not been a winning formula.

Constitutionalizing Homosexual "Marriage"

On June 26, 2015, the US Supreme Court ruled that the Fourteenth Amendment prevented states from not recognizing so-called same-sex marriages. Two Virginia attorneys, William Olson and Herb Titus, commented on the inconstancy in the Supreme Court's *Obergfell v. Hodges* decision, which purported to find a right of same sex couples to "marry." They noted:

> The opinion by Judge Sutton of the U.S. Court of Appeals for the Sixth Circuit — upholding traditional marriage against five challenges in four states . . . points out that *"nobody in this case . . . argues that the people who adopted the Fourteenth Amendment understood it to require the States to change the definition of marriage."* *DeBoer v. Snyder*, 772 F.3d 388, 403 (6th Cir. 2014) (emphasis added).
>
> Laymen logically deduce that if the Fourteenth Amendment as written had nothing to do with same-sex marriage, that's the end of the matter. . . .
>
> But for those lawyers who want unelected judges to set the public policy of our nation, it simply doesn't matter what the Framers intended. . . .
>
> Recently, Justice Alito observed that "same-sex marriage presents a highly emotional . . . question . . . but not a difficult question of constitutional law." *United States v. Windsor*, 570 U.S. ___, 133 S.Ct. 2675, 2714 (2013) (Alito, J., dissenting): "The Constitution does not guarantee the right to enter into a same-sex marriage. Indeed, no provision of the Constitution speaks

to the issue. It is beyond dispute that the right to same-sex marriage is not deeply rooted in this Nation's history and tradition." [Id. at 2714-15.]

Therefore, Justice Alito explained that challengers to traditional marriage: "seek . . . not the protection of a deeply rooted right but the recognition of a very new right, and they seek this innovation not from a legis- lative body elected by the people, but from unelected judges." [Id. at 2715.]

If we are now considering a new right, one could legitimately ask when and where did this new right come from. Indeed, during oral argument in the case of *Hollingsworth v. Perry*, Justice Scalia asked this very question to same-sex marriage champion lawyer Ted Olson.

Justice Scalia: "When did it become unconsti- tutional to prohibit gays from marrying? . . . Was it always unconstitutional?"

Ted Olson: "It was [un]constitutional when we — as a culture determined that sexual orientation is a characteristic of individuals that they cannot control . . ."

Justice Scalia: "I see. When did that happen? . . ."

Ted Olson: "There's no specific date in time. This is an evolutionary cycle."[1]

---

[1]   William J. Olson and Herbert W. Titus, "The 14th Amendment is no mandate for same-sex marriage," MercatorNet, June 10, 2015, https://www.mercatornet.com/conjugality/view/the-14th- amendment-is-no-mandate-for-same-sex-marriage2/16314.

The *Obergefell* ruling provokes unusual dissents. Justice Roberts noted:

> The Court takes the extraordinary step of ordering every State to license and recognize same-sex marriage. . . . Five lawyers have closed the debate and enacted their own vision of marriage as a matter of constitutional law. Stealing this issue from the people will for many cast a cloud over same-sex marriage, making a dramatic social change that much more difficult to accept.
>
> The majority's decision is an act of will, not legal judgment. The right it announces has no basis in the Constitution or this Court's precedent. . . . The Court invalidates the marriage laws of more than half the States and orders the transformation of a social institution that has formed the basis of human society for millennia, for the Kalahari Bushmen and the Han Chinese, the Carthaginians and the Aztecs. Just who do we think we are?[2]

Justice Antonin Scalia wrote:

> Today's decree says that my Ruler, and the Ruler of 320 million Americans coast-to-coast, is a majority of the nine lawyers on the Supreme Court. The opinion in these cases is the . . . furthest extension one can even imagine—of the Court's claimed power to create "liberties" that the Constitution and its Amendments neglect to mention. This practice of constitutional

---

[2]   Obergefell v. Hodges, 576 U.S. ___ (2015).

revision by an unelected committee of nine, always accompanied (as it is today) by extravagant praise of liberty, robs the People of the most important liberty they asserted in the Declaration of Independence and won in the Revolution of 1776: the freedom to govern themselves. . . .

. . . The five Justices who compose today's majority are entirely comfortable concluding that every State violated the Constitution for all of the 135 years between the Fourteenth Amendment's ratification and Massachusetts' permitting of same-sex marriages in 2003. They have discovered in the Fourteenth Amendment a "fundamental right" overlooked by every person alive at the time of ratification, and almost everyone else in the time since. . . . They are certain that the People ratified the Fourteenth Amendment to bestow on them the power to remove questions from the democratic process when that is called for by their "reasoned judgment." These Justices *know* that limiting marriage to one man and one woman is contrary to reason; they *know* that an institution as old as government itself, and accepted by every nation in history until 15 years ago, cannot possibly be supported by anything other than ignorance or bigotry.[3]

The Supreme Court ruling means that persons like Jesus, Moses, Mother Teresa, or the Reverend Rick Warren—who gave the invocation at Barack Obama's first inaugural—are now "haters" and "bigots" and will be marginalized or even

---

[3]   Ibid.

excluded from the public life of this nation by future decisions and applications of this decision whether by courts, legislatures, governors, or presidents.

This is a most unwise decision attempting to coerce citizens to choose between their country and their faith or conscience, and by doing so make them enemies of the state for following the laws of nature and of nature's God. It is not heartless conservatives who would prevent same-sex "marriage," it is nature itself.

The *Roe* and *Doe* decisions of the court in 1973 did not settle the abortion issue. This deplorable *Obergefell* decision will not settle what marriage means.

The legal walls that protected children from dismemberment and destruction, as well as protecting marriage from attack and ruin, have been torn down. The prophet Nehemiah petitioned Artaxerxes, the king of Persia, for permission to rebuild the walls of Jerusalem. But in America, when we petition Caesar, we petition for ourselves through our agents in public office. At least since 1973, federal judges have propounded rulings attacking the value of human life and marriage, values derived from Judeo-Christian traditions, and the Founders' reliance upon the "Laws of Nature and of Nature's God."

New presidential appointments to the Supreme Court from real or ostensible pro-life presidents have not reversed the *Roe* and *Doe* abortion on demand decision, and now the justices have given us the biological anomaly and the moral contradiction of same-sex "marriage."

Just as Nehemiah did, we too must start rebuilding the walls of legal protection to defend and protect children and traditional marriage and remove federal court jurisdiction over these areas so that laws protecting pre-born children and real marriage cannot be struck down by federal judges, at whatever level, who are accountable to no one but themselves.

To do so, we must restrict the power of unelected lifetime judicial appointees who seek to mold society and remake man in their image rather than God's. In so doing, we will restore representative government "of the people, by the people, and for the people."

Transgender: The Next Domino to Fall . . . Unless We Act

Parliament can do everything but make a woman a man and a man a woman.
Jean-Louis de Lolme, The Constitution of England, 1771

George Orwell, author of *1984*, once stated, "Political language . . . is designed to make lies sound truthful and murder respectable, and to give an appearance of solidity to pure wind."[1] The term *transgender* is a contrived misnomer in the mold of Orwell's observation.

The Latin preposition or equivalent English prefix *trans* means "across, through, over, to, or on the other side of."[2] Gender is a classification of words (nouns, pronouns, and modifiers) to describe the word's sex attribute: either male, female, or neuter. The term *transgender* is meant to convey that a male or female can cross over to the other sex.

---

[1]   Sonia Orwell and Ian Angus, eds., *The Collected Essays, Journalism and Letters of George Orwell*, vol. 4, *In Front of your Nose: 1945-1950* (New York: Harcourt, Brace, Jovanovich, 1968,), p. 139.

[2]   *The Oxford Universal Dictionary*, 3rd ed. (1955), s.v. "trans."

This appendix will discuss political ramifications of the transgender (TG) efforts, and not the individual psychological experiences of persons who perceive themselves to be "in the wrong body." "Such persons do not doubt their anatomical identity, but they are convinced it is the wrong one and therefore desire their anatomy to correspond with their perceived gender identity. The condition can become acutely painful, leading to severe disruption of their lives and even suicidal tendencies."[3]

Current political efforts to affirm the transgender agenda by allowing confused minors to receive sex change hormones and surgery—as opposed to helping the gender-confused recognize reality, as we do in the case of anorexic persons—should be considered a form of child abuse. Castration and surgery to form essentially functionless genital organs and the administration of synthetic hormones can change the appearance of a body but cannot alter XX or XY chromosomes that have always determined the two sexes apparent in nature: male and female. Female reproductive organs do not spontaneously form in men who take female hormones and dress like women. A male can act or look like a female, and a female can act like or look like a male, but that likeness does not change the actual sex of the person as evidenced by DNA.

Obviously, those who claim to be "transitioning" end up conforming themselves to the appearance and behavior of

3   Donald McCarthy and Edward Bayer, eds., *Handbook on Critical Sexual Issues* (Garden City, NY: Image Books, 1984): pp. 164, quoted in John F. Harvey, *The Homosexual Person: New Thinking in Pastoral Care* (San Francisco: Ignatius Press, 1987), pp. 29–30.

the sex they wish to "become" while at the same time decrying sexual stereotypes and proclaiming gender fluidity. Their attempt to imitate nature, albeit of the opposite sex, cannot be denied.

Transgender advocates, as if claiming clairvoyance, gratuitously attack the moral character of those who disagree with their agenda as having personal animus, insensitivity, bigotry, and low intelligence. Not using trans-approved pronouns is considered a violation of TG rights called "misgendering," deserving of apologies, and prohibited by school speech codes.

TG advocates want their opposition silenced, perhaps to pretend there is no public disapproval of their behavior. "The cynic who ridicules conscience forgets that his own cynicism has its reasons not unrelated to his own conscience."[4]

Media Controversy over Transgender Policy

Much of the public debate on TG has centered on North Carolina's so-called bathroom bill, which attempted to keep bathrooms segregated by sex. The Obama administration was very clear that opening up restrooms to either sex was merely the initial demand for compulsory TG compliance. The Obama administration's 2016 "guidance letter" sent to every public school board in the United States threatened withdrawal of federal education money unless schools complied with the broad TG agenda:

---

[4]   Edmund Bergler, *The Battle of the Conscience* (Washington: The Washington Institute of Medicine, 1948), quoted in Fulton Sheen, *Peace of Soul* (Garden City, NY: Garden City Books, 1951), p. 76.

Gender identity refers to an individual's internal sense of gender. A person's gender identity may be different from or the same as the person's sex assigned at birth.

Sex assigned at birth refers to the sex designation recorded on an infant's birth certificate. . . .

. . . A *transgender male* is someone who identifies as male but was assigned the sex of female at birth; a *transgender female* is someone who identifies as female but was assigned the sex of male at birth.

. . . Transgender individuals may undergo gender transition at any stage of their lives, and gender transition can happen swiftly or over a long duration of time. . . .

. . . There is no medical diagnosis or treatment requirement that students must meet as a prerequisite to being treated consistent with their gender identity. . . .

. . . A school must treat students consistent with their gender identity even if their education records or identification documents indicate a different sex. . . .

. . . When a school provides sex-segregated activities and facilities, transgender students must be allowed to participate in such activities and access such facilities consistent with their gender identity.

Restrooms and Locker Rooms. A school may provide separate facilities on the basis of sex, but must allow transgender students access to such facilities consistent with their gender identity. . . .

Athletics. . . . A school may not . . . adopt or adhere to requirements that rely on overly broad generalizations or stereotypes about the differences between transgender students and other students of the same sex (*i.e.*, the same gender identity) or others' discomfort with transgender students. . . .

Housing and Overnight Accommodations. . . . A school must allow transgender students to access housing consistent with their gender identity and may not require transgender students to stay in single-occupancy accommodations or to disclose personal information when not required of other students.[5]

The congressionally chartered US Institutes of Medicine, a branch of the National Academy of Sciences, points out that even in the scientific community the term *transgender* has a broad meaning that makes legal codification virtually impossible, thus enabling government enforcement easier. For example, the Institute of Medicine states that the term *transgender* includes:

- transsexuals, which includes persons who have had hormone therapy and/or surgery to take on feminine or masculine attributes;
- cross-dressers or transvestites, who wear clothes and present themselves as persons of the complementary sex for emotional or sexual gratification;
- bi-gender persons, who claim both male and female attributes;
- transgenderists, who live full time as the opposite sex;

---

5   "Dear Colleague Letter on Transgender Students," U.S. Department of Justice and U.S. Department of Education, May 13, 2016, https://www.justice.gov/opa/file/850986/download.

- drag queens or kings, who dress in clothes that exaggerate masculine or feminine appearance;
- and gender queer or two-spirit, which describes Native Americans with or without hormones or surgery who assume both male and female roles.[6]

Such classifications are expressed as attraction, behavior, identity, or combinations of these.[7] School boards that assure parents they merely want transgender rights protected are giving a green light to completely arbitrary regulations. For example, Harvard University's Office of BGLTQ Student Life attempts TG definitions but suggests that Americans who do not use proper TG pronouns could be guilty of assault:

> Sex assigned at birth, gender identity, gender expression, sexual orientation, hormonal makeup, physical anatomy . . . are not necessarily related. There are more than two sexes. . . . Gender is fluid and changing, and can be affirmed and/or expressed in many ways. . . . Self-understanding can change from day to day. . . . Transphobic misinformation is a form of systemic violence. Fixed binaries and biological essentialism, manifest in gendered language, misgendering someone . . . threaten the lives of trans people.[8]

---

6   See *The Health of Lesbian, Gay, Bisexual, and Transgender People: Building a Foundation for Better Understanding*, Institute of Medicine (Washington, DC: National Academies Press, 2011), p. 26.
7   See Ibid., p. 27.
8   Flyer published by Harvard Office of BGLTQ Student Life, Spring 2017, bgltq.fas.harvard.edu/.

Media Confusion

Reporting on the subject has become unintelligible:

- The *New York Times* seriously writes, "The case the Supreme Court agreed to hear concerns Gavin Grimm, who was designated female at birth but identifies as male. He attends Gloucester High School in southeastern Virginia."[9]
- The *New Republic* describes in all earnestness a prisoner convicted of murder, born male, who sought a tax-paid sex change operation as follows, "To suffer from gender dysphoria . . . is to exist in a real state for which our only frame of reference may be science fiction. You inhabit a body that other people may regard as perfectly normal. . . . *But it is not yours*. . . . She . . . tried to castrate herself by tying off her testicles."[10]
- The *Associated Press* states with no apparent irony that "a transgender man sued a Roman Catholic hospital in New Jersey on Thursday after he says it cited religion in refusing to allow his surgeon to perform a hysterectomy procedure he said was medically necessary as part of his gender transition."[11]

---

9   Adam Liptak, "Supreme Court to Rule in Transgender Access Case," *New York Times*, October 28, 2016, https://www.nytimes.com/2016/10/29/us/politics/supreme-court-to-rule-in-transgender-access-case.html.

10   Nathaniel Penn, "Should This Inmate Get a Sate-Financed Sex Change Operation?," *New Republic*, October 30, 2013, https://newrepublic.com/article/115335/sex-change-prison-inmate-michelle-kosilek-should-we-pay.

11   Associated Press, "Transgender man sues Catholic hospital in Paterson for refusing hysterectomy," New Jersey On-Line, January

- *NBC Out* proudly notes that "Actor Kelly Mantle is making Academy Awards history this year. The gender-fluid performer is eligible for Oscar nominations in both male and female categories, which is a first for the Academy of Motion Picture Arts and Sciences."[12]
- "Transgender people find it offensive to be referred to by their pre-transition gender, because they point out that they always were their current gender."[13]
- "A transgender man is speaking out about his shocking pregnancy, which came a decade after transitioning from womanhood — a process he was still undergoing when he learned he was carrying a 21-week-old baby."[14]

Special Protections for Transgendered Students Are Not Needed

As during the early years of the campaign to normalize homosexuality, the transgender agenda includes tactics such

---

5, 2017, http://www.nj.com/passaic-county/index.ssf/2017/01/transgender_man_sues_catholic_hospital_in_paterson.html.

[12] Alamin Yohannes, "Gender-Fluid Actor Kelly Mantle Makes Oscars History," *NBC Out*, December 12, 2016, http://www.nbcnews.com/feature/nbc-out/gender-fluid-actor-kelly-mantle-makes-oscars-history-n694926.

[13] Eliza Gray, "Transitions," *New Republic*, June 23, 2011, https://newrepublic.com/article/90519/transgender-civil-rights-gay-lesbian-lgbtq.

[14] Melanie Dostis, "Transgender Man Opens up on Learning About Shocking Pregnancy Halfway Through Sex Change," *New York Daily News*, November 15, 2015, http://www.nydailynews.com/news/national/transgender-man-opens-shocking-pregnancy-article-1.2435731.

as exaggerating threats, seeking protected class status, and lying. In 2016, I filed a Freedom of Information request asking for the number of founded cases of discrimination based on sexual orientation or gender identity for the previous five years in our Prince William County public school system from its eighty-eight thousand students, staff, or contractors. The response: "There were no founded cases of discrimination filed against Prince William County Schools or its employees on the basis of sexual orientation or gender identity in the last 5 years by its students, employees, or contractors."[15]

The claim that TG students were bullied and teased was given by the Prince William County Schools as the reason to change its policy. However, any kind of bullying is already banned in Virginia public schools for any reason. In fact, I drafted the 2005 law giving schools authority to address bullying, establish character education and student conduct codes, and require mandatory reporting to parents if their child had been bullied or attacked.[16] While no law can change hearts, bullying laws can address harassment of gender-confused children. But TG advocates seek no shield for themselves. *Rather, they seek a club to use against those who simply want common sense privacy for their children in school locker rooms, showers, bathrooms, hotel rooms on overnight school trips, and sports teams.*

Since there were no discrimination cases in the last five years in Prince William County Schools, and laws were already on the books to address bullying, there was no valid

---

15   Tanisha Holland, email message to author, September 16, 2016.
16   VA HB 2879 (2005).

reason to add sexual orientation or gender identity protections to the School Non-Discrimination Code. Additionally, four Democrat attorneys general, three Republican attorneys general, and the Virginia Supreme Court all ruled that local government bodies cannot add protected classes unless enacted by the General Assembly.[17]

The school policy was changed despite hundreds of parents testifying against it. School Board members voted 5-3 to add the "protections" without any definitions or regulations. Progressive social liberals usually rely on their own moral authority and ignore the usual requirement for legal or constitutional authority. One more traditionally-minded school board member voting against would have defeated the measure on a tie vote, another reason why elections—especially "down ballot" elections—are so important.

Transgender School Bullying Data Is Speculative

While bullying of any student for any reason is wrong, TG advocates often cite suspect surveys to prove LGBTQ students are bullied more than non-TG or non-LGBTQ students. The findings of the Youth Risk Behavior Surveillance System (YRBSS), a survey developed by the US Centers for Disease Control and reported in a 2016 publication of the National Academy of Sciences suggests that such data is hard to accurately establish:

---

[17] Attorneys General Gerals Baliles (D-1982), William Broaddus (D-1985), Mary Sue Terry (D-1986), Stephen Rosenthal (D-1993), Richard Cullen (R-1997), Jerry Kilgore (R-2002), Ken Cuccinelli (R-2010), and VA Supreme Court, 2,000.

The data captured by the national YRBS reflect self-report surveys from students enrolled in grades 9-12 at public or private schools. . . . It does not identify many subpopulations that are at increased risk for bullying such as lesbian, gay, bisexual, and transgender (LGBT) youth and overweight children. . . .

A growing body of research has aimed to assess the experiences of transgender youth specifically. . . . For instance, in a sample of 5,542 adolescents sampled online, 82 percent of the transgender or gender non-conforming youth reported any bullying experience in the past 12 months, compared to 57 percent among cisgender [non LGBTQ] boys and girls. . . .

Given the absence of measures of gender identity . . . , estimates of the prevalence of bullying among transgender youth are not currently available. . . .

The four major national surveys that include bullying do not uniformly address all age groups and school levels. . . . A majority of prevalence data collection is done through self-reports or observation."[18]

The absence of verifiable facts about the incidence of bullying does not stop TG advocates from making claims or presenting emotional anecdotal stories to win approval for their policies; perhaps ironically, given their expressed opposition to bullying, name calling and bullying of their opponents is perfectly acceptable and is used effectively at hearings, public forums, and in the liberal media.

---

[18]   Frederick Rivara and Suzanne Le Menestrel, eds., *Preventing Bullying Through Science, Policy, and Practice* (Washington, DC: The National Academies Press, 2016), pp. 36, 48, 49, 59.

Opposition to Transgender Policies Is *Not*
About Liberal Versus Conservative Ideology

Mary Dillard Smith, a liberal democratic African American woman, resigned her position as head of Georgia's ACLU (American Civil Liberties Union) chapter in mid-2016 over transgender restrooms. Smith said she was met with hostility and feared being branded a homophobe for merely questioning the pro-TG policy. Smith recounted an incident in which three transgendered women with deep voices used the women's restroom: "My kids were visibly frightened. I was scared. And I was ill-prepared to answer their questions."[19]

Time magazine reported in 2016 that "girls from a swim team in New York City's Upper West Side are too scared to use the women's locker room. . . . The girls, who range in age from about seven to 18, became concerned after they saw a 'bearded individual' in the women's changing room."[20]

A voter survey of the 2018 Pennsylvania governor's race found significant opposition to Democrat incumbent Governor Wolf stemming from his support for transgender school policies. Prospective voters were told, "Governor Tom Wolf supports school policies that force children to share shower facilities with members of the opposite sex." Voters were then asked if, based on that information, they were

---

[19]   Greg Bluestein, "Georgia ACLU director resigns over transgender fight," Atlanta Journal Constitution, June 4, 2016, http://politics.blog.ajc.com/2016/06/02/georgia-aclu-director-resigns-over-transgender-fight/.

[20]   Belinda Luscombe, "Even in Liberal Communities, Transgender Bathroom Laws Worry Parents," *Time*, May 13, 2016, http://time.com/4324687/even-in-liberal-communities-transgender-bathroom-laws-worry-parents/.

"more likely, less likely or it makes no difference" to vote for Governor Wolf in the 2018 governor's race. Ninety-two percent of Republicans, 51 percent of Democrats and 66 percent of Independents said they were less likely to re-elect democratic governor Wolf. While all "parties support parental notification if a child notifies a teacher that they identify as transgender . . .", the percent saying they were less likely to support re-electing Governor Wolf was smaller than the group refusing to re-elect Wolf because of the mixed shower policy.[21]

The Transgender Movement Creates
Fears for Personal Safety

In the fall of 2016, a Prince William County middle school female student told the Prince William School Board, "If a boy would walk into the locker room while I was changing my clothes, I would feel violated and embarrassed. Do you really think that a class of 7th grade girls in the locker room would like it if a boy walked into the locker room and started taking off his clothes? All the girls would feel violated!"[22]

Her concerns were echoed by a West-Coast mom, Kristen Quintrall Lavin, who found a bearded man in a Disneyland women's restroom.

---

21   "American Principles Project: Party Messaging Analysis, 2018 Pennsylvania Governor's Race," Revily Political Insights Co., https://thenationalpulse.com/wp-content/uploads/PA_ExecutiveSummary.pdf.

22   Testimony presented before Prince William School Board, September 2016, transcribed by Robert Marshall.

There was a man in the bathroom. Not transgender. There was a man who felt entitled to be in the [women's] restroom, because he knew no one would say anything. There were 20-25 people by the time I left. . . . And the only thing stopping us was our fear of political correctness. . . .

. . . Gender must be clearly defined to keep women safe. . . . We can not coddle this small fraction of . . . people who are men, [who] identify as women. . . . We can not put doubt in women's minds regarding their ability to recognize and identify a man. In a world where 99.9% of sexual assault is done by men, we must have the right to "assume someone's gender."[23]

Ms. Lavin is no social conservative and makes clear in her blog post that she is very accepting of the transgender phenomenon. She would not have had any problem if the man in question had been clearly transgender or "transitioning." Her blog post simply decries the fact that there was a man not making any apparent effort to look like a woman in the women's restroom. Where is the common sense here we might ask? So, presumably, had the man in question been wearing a skirt instead of a Lakers jersey, she would have felt more comfortable. In this profoundly confused era, however, what is to stop any man with malicious designs from dressing like a female and going into the ladies' bathroom? Fathers and mothers, ask yourselves and even ask your liberal

23   Kristen Quintrall Lavin, "A Man in the Women's Restroom at Disneyland," *The Get Real Mom* (blog), March 13, 2017, http://www.thegetrealmom.com/blog/womensrestroom.

friends if they are comfortable letting their pre-adolescent or even older daughters go to the bathrooms unaccompanied anymore.

Since males commit the overwhelming percentage of sexual assaults, allowing biological males more opportunities to find women in vulnerable situations will place more women at risk of sexual or other assault. A 2011 study in Sweden of transsexuals undergoing conversion therapy from female to male found "a shift to a male pattern regarding criminality and that sex reassignment is coupled to increased crime rate."[24]

Transgender Recruiting in Kindergarten and Pre-K

Portraying morally objectionable actions under the guise of novel, "fun" learning for little children is the perfect way to gain converts and increase "tolerance" for a lifetime of deviancy. Self-described drag queens now read books on changing one's sex to three- and four-year-olds, and new toys to brainwash youth will soon be marketed.

Billed as a toy to stop transphobia before it starts in families, a Canadian toy company is making a nesting doll, "Sam," a collection of six dolls that change sex before the real Sam happily finds his/her true self and lives happily ever after. "The tiniest, innermost version of Sam begins as a happy baby, blissfully unaware of what gender even is—although

---

[24]   Cecilia Dhejne et. al., "Long-Term Follow-Up of Transsexual Persons Undergoing Sex Reassignment Surgery: Cohort Study in Sweden," *PLOS*, February 22, 2011, http://journals.plos.org/plosone/article?id=10.1371/journal.pone.0016885; see also "Crime in Virginia 2015," Virginia State Police, 2016.

Sam is already dressed in a pink onesie. The other dolls show Sam exploring gender norms and displaying confusion as Sam questions his identity and cuts off his long hair, as well as isolation as he separates himself from others as a result of not feeling accepted. But the largest, final Sam is happy and presenting as male after his family and friends accept him."[25]

Instead of grandparents reading to grandchildren, TG apostles promote the Drag Queen Story Hour (DQSH), which "is just what it sounds like—drag queens reading stories to children in libraries, schools, and bookstores. DQSH captures the imagination and play of the gender fluidity of childhood and gives kids glamorous, positive, and unabashedly queer role models. In spaces like this, kids are able to see people who defy rigid gender restrictions and imagine a world where people can present as they wish, where dress up is real."[26]

This "educational" novelty is not just for San Francisco. TG ideology has also received adulatory coverage from the highbrow *Smithsonian* magazine coverage of a drag queen reading to children in a May 18, 2017, article:

> "Drag Queen Story Hour," . . . brings in drag queens
> to read stories to kids. . . . Stories that show the things
> kids and drag queens have in common—like a love of
> drama, sass and sparkle.

---

[25]   Nicole Lyn Pesce, "Meet Sam, a transgender nesting doll who teaches kids about gender identity," *Moneyish* (blog), June 28, 2017, https://moneyish.com/heart/meet-sam-a-transgender-nesting-doll-who-teaches-kids-about-gender-identity/.

[26]   "About Drag Queen Story Hour," Drag Queen Story Hour, https://www.dragqueenstoryhour.org/.

"Drag Queen Story Hour captures the imagination and play of the gender fluidity in childhood and gives kids glamorous, positive, and unabashedly queer role models," the library writes on its website. . . .

. . . The drag queens of Brooklyn Public Library aren't just campy or glam—they're giving the act of reading some much-needed sparkle.[27]

For those not familiar with the *Smithsonian* magazine, its seventeen member governing board of regents as of this writing includes such individuals as US Supreme Court chief justice John Roberts, Jr., chancellor of the board of regents for the Smithsonian Institution; Vice President Michael Pence; Senator Patrick Leahy (VT); Senator David Perdue (GA); John Fahey, chairman of the National Geographic Society, which published a cover story with a young "girl-to-boy" in 2017; and past chairman, president, and CEO of Time Life Inc. Risa J. Lavizzo-Mourey, MD, now the president and CEO of the Robert Woods Johnson Foundation; David Rubenstein, co-founder and co-CEO of The Carlyle Group, one of the largest private equity firms in the world; and Steve Case, co-founder and chairman of AOL to name a few.[28]

Christ, in Matthew 18:6, reminded those who corrupt children: "But whoever causes one of these little ones who

---

[27]   Erin Blakemore, "Drag Queens Are Public Libraries' Newest Storytellers: Early reading just got a lot more glamorous," *Smithsonian*, May 18, 2017, http://www.smithsonianmag.com/smart-news/drag-queens-are-public-libraries-newest-storytellers-180963341/.

[28]   "Members of the Board of Regents," Smithsonian, accessed Oct. 13, 2017, https://www.si.edu/regents/members#DavidRubenstein.

believe in me to sin, it would be better for him to have a great millstone fastened around his neck and to be drowned in the depth of the sea."

Parental Rights Deliberately Curtailed and Denied in Schools

A number of public school districts across the country that have approved TG friendly policies have also already approved speech codes. Such a code may list a compilation of speech "no, no's" for staff when addressing students. What is perhaps most alarming is that parental involvement in their child's education in such districts is subject to a series of yellow caution lights by school staff, the gratuitous working assumption being that school personnel, not parents, have the best interests of children at heart. Further sexual exploitation between teacher, staff, and student will be enhanced by isolating sexually confused children from their parents.

The TG movement is but one spinoff of so-called gay marriage. There will be others unless persons motivated by the ethics and moral teachings of Moses and Christ animate the political and social order. For example, in 2015, St. Louis County, Minnesota usurped the parental rights of Anmarie Calgero to initiate tax-paid hormone treatment of her fifteen-year-old son so he could "transition" from male to female. Calgaro stated, "Last year, without my knowledge or consent, without any court hearings . . . , a legal aid group that gives free services to low income people created a 'Notice of Emancipation' for my 15 year old son. . . . My son

. . . was no longer under my supervision. . . . The St. Louis County Health and Human Services treated him as an adult. I couldn't get any information regarding my son, even the school refused to allow me to access his records."[29]

Consider, what will parents do when their 115-pound daughter is run over on a soccer or lacrosse field or basketball court by a 200-pound male "transitioning" to female? This is already happening in different areas of the country and causing no small amount of controversy. Will the climate of political correctness stifle common sense on this issue? Of course, there are more serious issues at stake than who wins or loses an athletic competition.

It is no exaggeration to say that your children and grand-children's future for family formation, employment, and every other aspect of life is being decided today by LGBTQ and TG zealots. Will the future belong to those who follow Moses and Christ or to those who follow and/or endorse a sexual ethic absolutely opposed to that of nature and nature's God and insist that Christians betray their baptismal promises by acquiescing in this ongoing revolution? The outcome will be decided by what you and others with the gift of faith decide to do or not do today. It is your decision. As written above, what is at stake is not merely who wins or loses a game, but the republic itself. Let's reclaim it before it is too late.

---

[29]   Anmarie Calgaro, "Anmarie Calgaro Statement," Minnesota Child Protection League, November 16, 2016, http://mnchild-protectionleague.com/protect-childrens-privacy-and-mental-health-fund/.

Bibliography

Books

The Annals of America. Chicago: Encyclopedia Britannica, 1968.

Beveridge, Albert J. *The Life of John Marshall*. Vol. 3, *Conflict and Construction, 1800-1815*. Boston and New York: Houghton Mifflin Company, 1919.

Blackstone, William. *Commentaries on the Laws of England*. New Haven: Yale University, 1765.

Blechschmidt, Erich. *Beginnings of Human Life*. New York: Springer Verlag, 1977.

———. *The Ontogenic Basis of Human Anatomy*. Translated by Brian Freeman. Berkeley, CA: North Atlantic Books, 2004.

Carey, George, and James McClellan, eds. *The Federalist*. Indianapolis, The Liberty Fund, 2001.

Chaput, Charles. *Render Unto Caesar: Serving the Nation by Living Our Catholic Beliefs in Political Life*. New York: Image Books, 2008.

Cooley, Thomas M. *The General Principles of Constitutional Law in the United States* Bridgewater, VA: American Foundations Publications, 2001.

Corwin, Edward S. *The Constitution and What it Means Today*. Princeton: Princeton University Press, 1974.

Mason Alpheus T. and Gerald Garvey, eds. *American Constitutional History: Essays by Edward Corwin*. New York: Harper and Row, 1964.

————. *Court Over Constitution: A Study of Judicial Review as an Instrument of Popular Government*. Princeton, NJ: Princeton University Press, 1938.

DeLee, Joseph B. and J. P. Greenhill, eds. *1940 Yearbook of Obstetrics and Gynecology*. Chicago: The Year Book Publishers, 1941.

Douglas, William O. *The Court Years: 1939-1975*. New York: Random House, 1980.

Driesbach, Daniel. *Thomas Jefferson and the Wall of Separation between Church and State*. New York: New York University Press, 2002.

Farrand, Max, ed. *The Records of the Federal Convention of 1787*. Vol. 2. New Haven: Yale University Press, 1966.

Fisher, Louis. *Religious Liberty in America: Political Safeguards*. Lawrence, KS, University Press of Kansas, 2002.

Foley, John P., ed. *The Jeffersonian Cyclopedia*. New York: Funk and Wagnalls, 1900.

Gillespie, Michael Allen and Michael Lienesch, eds. *Ratifying the Constitution* Lawrence, KS: University Press of Kansas, 1989.

Green, Donald and Alan Gerber. *Get Out the Vote*. Washington, DC: Brookings Institution Press, 2008.

Hamburger, Philip. *Separation of Church and State*. Cambridge, MA: Harvard University Press, 2002.

Koch, Adrienne and William Peden, eds. *The Life and Selected Writings of Thomas Jefferson: Including the Autobiography, the Declaration of Independence & His Public and Private Letters*. New York: Random House, 1944.

Kent, Frank R. *The Great Game of Politics*. Garden City, NY: Doubleday, 1935.

————. *The Great Game of Politics*. Buffalo, NY: Economics Books, Smith, Keynes and Marshall, 1959.

Kirk, Marshall and Hunter Madsen. *After the Ball: How America Will Conquer its Fear and Hatred of Gays in the 90's*. New York, Penguin Books, 1989.

Farrand, Max, ed. *The Records of the Federal Convention of 1787*. Vol. 2. New Haven: Yale University Press, 1937.

Rakove, Jack, ed. *James Madison, Writings*. New York: Library of America, 1999.

Marlin, George, Richard Rabatin, and John Swan, eds. *The Quotable Fulton Sheen: A Topical Compilation of the Wit, Wisdom, and Satire of Archbishop Fulton J. Sheen*. New York: Doubleday, 1989.

Miller, Marion M., ed. *Great Debates in American History*. Vol. 4. New York: Current Literature Publishing Company, 1913.

Moore, Keith L. and T. V. N. Persaud. *Before We Are Born: Essentials of Embryology and Birth Defects*. Philadelphia: W. B. Saunders, 1993.

Murphy, Walter F. *Congress and the Court: A Case Study in the American Political Process*. Chicago: University of Chicago Press, 1962.

Rehnquist, William H. *Grand Inquests: The Historic Impeachments of Justice Samuel Chase and President Andrew Johnson*. New York: William Morrow and Co., 1992.

―――. *The Supreme Court: How it Was, How it is*. New York: William Monroe and Company, 1987.

Hickok, Jr., Eugene, ed. *The Bill of Rights: Original Meaning and Current Understanding*. Charlottesville, VA: University Press of Virginia, 1991.

Sadler, T. W. *Langman's Medical Embryology*. 7th ed. Baltimore: Williams & Wilkins, 1995.

Shirer, William L. *The Rise and Fall of the Third Reich: A History of Nazi Germany*. New York: Simon and Schuster, 1959.

Stokes, Anson Phelps and Leo Pfeffer. *Church and State in the United States*. New York: Harper and Row, 1964.

Kurland, Philip and Ralph Lerner, eds. *The Founder's Constitution*. Vol. 5. Chicago: University of Chicago Press, 1987.

Story, Joseph. *A Familiar Exposition of the Constitution of the United States*. Washington, DC: Regnery Publishing, 1986.

Todd, Chuck and Sheldon Gawiser. *How Barack Obama Won: A State-by-State Guide to the Historic 2008 Presidential Election*. New York: Vintage Books, 2009.

United States Catholic Conference. *Catechism of the Catholic Church*. New York: Doubleday, 1991.

US Election Assistance Commission. *2008 Election Administration and Voting Survey*. Washington, DC, 2009.

Van Tassel, Emily Field and Paul Finkleman. *Impeachable Offenses, A Documentary History from 1787 to the Present.* Washington, DC: Congressional Quarterly, 1999.

Veit, Helen, Kenneth Bowling, and Charlene Bickford, eds. *Creating the Bill of Rights: The Documentary Record from the First Federal Congress.* Baltimore, Johns Hopkins University Press, 1991.

Witte, Jr., John. *Religion and the American Constitutional Experiment: Essential Rights and Liberties.* 2nd ed. Boulder, CO: Westview Press, 2004.

Woodward, Bob and Scott Armstrong. *The Brethren: Inside the Supreme Court.* New York: Simon and Schuster, 1979.

Organizations and Documents Cited

Guttmacher Institute. "Refusing to Provide Health Services." September 1, 2017. https://www.guttmacher.org/state-policy/explore/refusing-provide-health-services.

Ballotpedia. "Blanket Primary." http://ballotpedia.org/Blanket_primary.

―――. "California Proposition 8, the 'Eliminates Right of Same-Sex Couples to Marry' Initiative (2008)." http://ballotpedia.org/California_Proposition_8,_the_%22Eliminates_Right_of_Same-Sex_Couples_to_Marry%22_Initiative_(2008).

―――. "Closed Primary." http://ballotpedia.org/Closed_primary.

―――. "Semi-Closed Primary." http://ballotpedia.org/Semi-closed_primary.

————. "Open Primary." http://ballotpedia.org/
      Open_primary.

Blackstone, William. *Commentaries on the Laws of England.*
      Avalon Project, Yale University. http://avalon.law.yale.
      edu/18th_century/blackstone_intro.asp#1.

Washington, George. "Washington's Farewell Address
      1796." The Avalon Project, Yale University. http://
      avalon.law.yale.edu/18th_century/washing.asp.

Jefferson, Thomas. "Thomas Jefferson Second Inaugural
      Address." The Avalon Project, Yale University. http://
      avalon.law.yale.edu/19th_century/jefinau2.asp.

Jackson, Andrew. "President Jackson's Veto Message
      Regarding the Bank of the United States: July 10, 1832."
      That Avalon Project, Yale Law School. http://avalon.law.
      yale.edu/19th_century/ajveto01.asp.

Lincoln, Abraham. "First Inaugural Address of Abraham
      Lincoln." The Avalon Project, Yale Law School. http://
      avalon.law.yale.edu/19th_century/lincoln1.asp.

Centers for Disease Control and Prevention. " CDC Fact
      Sheet: Incidence, Prevalence, and Cost of Sexually Trans-
      mitted Infections in the United States." http://www.cdc.
      gov/std/stats/sti-estimates-fact-sheet-feb-2013.pdf.

GSA Network. "Directory of the National Association
      of GSA Networks." https://www.gsanetwork.org/
      national-directory.

————. "What is a GSA?" https://www.gsanetwork.org/
      what-we-do.

Gallup News. "Party Affiliation." http://www.gallup.com/
      poll/15370/party-affiliation.aspx.

Human Rights Campaign. "Corporate Partners." http://
www.hrc.org/the-hrc-story/corporate-partners.
————. "2015 Dinner Gala, EVOLVE-LOVE." http://
www.hrcladinner.com/confirmed-sponsors/, https://
www.boxofficetickets.com/go/event?id=287133.
————. "The Need for Full Federal LGBT Equality."
http://www.hrc.org/fullfederalequality/.
Jefferson, Thomas. "Jefferson's Letter to the Danbury Baptists." The Library of Congress, https://www.loc.gov/loc/
lcib/9806/danpre.html.
MassResistance. "Unbelievable surveys given to children
in Massachusetts -- and schools across America." May
5, 2015. http://www.massresistance.org/docs/gen2/15b/
School-surveys/index.html.
National Conference of State Legislatures. "2015 State and
Legislative Partisan Composition." February 4, 2015.
http://www.ncsl.org/Portals/1/Documents/Elections/
Legis_Control_2015_Feb4_11am.pdf.
————. "Absentee and Early Voting." August 17, 2017.
http://www.ncsl.org/research/elections-and-campaigns/
absentee-and-early-voting.aspx.
————. "The Indirect Initiative." http://www.ncsl.org/
research/elections-and-campaigns/the-indirect-initiative.
aspx.
————. "Initiative and Referendum States." December
2015. http://www.ncsl.org/research/elections-and-
campaigns/chart-of-the-initiative-states.aspx.
————. Recall of Local Officials." http://www.ncsl.org/
research/elections-and-campaigns/recall-of-local-officials.
aspx.

———. "Recall of State Officials." March 8, 2016. http://www.ncsl.org/research/elections-and-campaigns/recall-of-state-officials.aspx.

———. "Straight Ticket Voting States." May 31, 2017. http://www.ncsl.org/research/elections-and-campaigns/straight-ticket-voting.aspx#1.

New Deal Network. " Frankfurter letter to Roosevelt, 2/18/37." http://newdeal.feri.org/court/ff02.htm.

Paine, Thomas. The Writings of Thomas Paine. Vol. 3. Edited by Moncure Daniel Conway. *Project Gutenberg*, 2010. http://www.gutenberg.org/files/31271/31271-h/31271-h.htm.

Reagan, Ronald. "The New Republican Party." Regan 2020. February 6, 1977. http://reagan2020.us/speeches/The_New_Republican_Party.asp.

United States Conference of Catholic Bishops. "Marriage and the Supreme Court." 2015. http://www.usccb.org/issues-and-action/marriage-and-family/marriage/promotion-and-defense-of-marriage/upload/Bulletin-AFTER-Scotus-brown.pdf.

———. "One Man, One Woman, for Life." http://www.usccb.org/issues-and-action/marriage-and-family/marriage/promotion-and-defense-of-marriage/upload/Marriage-Redefinition-Lead-Messages-5-6-13.pdf.

United States Election Assistance Commission. *2008 Election Administration and Voting Survey*. November 2009.

Geyh, Charles Gardner. *Judicial Disqualification: An Analysis of Federal Law*. Second Edition. Federal Judicial Center, 2010. https://www.fjc.gov/sites/default/files/2012/JudicialDQ.pdf.

United States Census Bureau. *Age and Sex Composition in the United States.* 2012.

United States National Archives and Records Administration. The Virginia Declaration of Rights. https://www.archives.gov/founding-docs/virginia-declaration-of-rights.

Roberts, John. "Proposals to Divest the Supreme Court of Appellate Jurisdiction: An Analysis in Light of Recent Developments." National Archives and Records Administration. https://www.archives.gov/files/news/john-roberts/accession-60-89-0172/006-Box5-Folder1522.pdf.

United States Department of State. "Terrorist Designations of Boko Haram and Ansaru." November 13, 2013. https://www.state.gov/j/ct/rls/other/des/266565.htm.

Harry S. Truman Presidential Library and Museum. "Address at the Jefferson-Jackson Day Dinner." http://trumanlibrary.org/publicpapers/viewpapers.php?pid=951.

Print and Electronic News Media

Robberson, Todd. "Is anyone really trampling on Craig James' religious freedom." *The Dallas Morning News*, August 4, 2015. http://dallasmorningviewsblog.dallasnews.com/2015/08/is-anyone-really-trampling-on-craig-james-religious-freedom.html/.

Torres, Zahira. "Civil Rights Commission Says Lakewood Baker Discriminated Against Gay Couple." *The Denver Post*, May 30, 2014. http://www.denverpost.com/news/ci_25865871/civil-rights-commission-says-lakewood-baker-discriminated-against.

Fox News. "Boko Haram leader says kidnapped girls married off, converted to Islam." November 2, 1014. http://www.foxnews.com/world/2014/11/02/boko-haram-denies-truce-kidnapped-girls-married/.

Starnes, Todd. "DC Comics Faces Boycott over Anti-Gay Writer." Fox News, February 13, 2013. http://nation.foxnews.com/anti-gay-comics/2013/02/12/dc-comics-faces-boycott-over-anti-gay-superman-writer.

Lewis, Andy and Borys Kit. "'Ender's Game' Author's Anti-Gay Views Pose Risks for Film." *The Hollywood Reporter*, February 20, 2013. http://www.hollywoodreporter.com/heat-vision/enders-games-orson-scott-cards-422456.

Terkel, Amanda. "Apple Breaks Ties with Anti-Gay Lobbyist." *The Huffington Post*, February 19, 2015. http://www.huffingtonpost.com/2015/02/17/_n_6699054.html.

Uribarri, Jamie. "Fox Sports Southwest Charged with Discrimination Over Craig James Firing." *New York Daily News*, March 6, 2014. http://www.nydailynews.com/sports/college/fox-sports-charged-discrimination-craig-james-firing-article-1.1713059.

Bruni, Frank. "Bigotry, the Bible and the Lessons of Indiana." *New York Times*, April, 3, 2015. http://www.nytimes.com/2015/04/05/opinion/sunday/frank-bruni-same-sex-sinners.html?_r=0.

Holmes, Stephen. "Report Says Census Bureau Helped Relocate Japanese." *New York Times*, March 17, 2000. http://www.nytimes.com/2000/03/17/us/report-says-census-bureau-helped-relocate-japanese.html.

Egelko, Bob. "Judge Vaughn Walker tells his side of Prop. 8 trial." *SFGate*, April 19, 2014. http://www.sfgate. com/lgbt/article/Judge-Vaughn-Walker-tells-his-side-of-Prop-8-5416851.php.

Saletan, William. "Purge the Bigots." *Slate*, April 4, 2014. http://www.slate.com/articles/news_and_politics/frame_game/2014/04/brendan_eich_quits_mozilla_let_s_purge_all_the_antigay_donors_to_prop_8.html.

WMAZ TV 13. "EEOC Backs Mount de Sales Band Director in Discrimination Case." March 30, 2015. http://www.13wmaz.com/story/news/local/macon/2015/03/30/eeoc-backs-mount-de-sales-band-director-in-discrimination-case/70680918/.

US Supreme Court Cases Cited

Adkins v. Children's Hospital, 261 U.S. 525 (1923).

Bowers v. Hardwick, 478 U.S. 186 (1986).

Doe v. Bolton, 410 U.S. 179 (1973).

Dred Scott v. Sanford, 60 U.S. 393 (1856).

Everson v. Board of Education of the Township of Ewing, 330 U.S. 1 (1947).

Hamilton v. Kentucky Distilleries, 251 U.S. 146 (1919).

Harris v. McRae, 448 U.S. 297 (1980).

Lawrence v. Texas, 539 U.S. 558 (2003).

Minersville School District v. Board of Education, 310 U.S. 586 (1940).

New York v. United States, 488 U.S. 1041 (1992).

National Federation of Independent Business v. Sebelius, 567 U.S. __ (2012).

Obergefell v. Hodges, 576 U.S. __ (2015).

Prigg v. Pennsylvania, 41 U.S. 16 Pet. 539 (1842).

Printz v. United States, 521 U.S. 898 (1997).

Roe v. Wade, 410 U.S. 113 (1973).

Romer v. Evans, 517 U.S. 620 (1996).

Rust v. Sullivan, 500 U.S. 173 (1991).

Sherbert v. Verner, 374 U.S. 398 (1963).

Ableman v. Booth, 62 U.S. 506 (1858).

Torcaso v. Watkins, 367 U.S. 488 (1961).

Korematsu v. United States, 323 U.S. 214 (1944).

Turner v. Bank of North America, 4 U.S. 8 (1799).

United States vs. Windsor, 570 U. S. __ (2013).

Wallace v. Jaffree, 472 U.S. 38 (1985).

West Coast Hotel v. Parrish, 300 U.S. 379 (1937).

West Virginia State Board of Education v. Barnette, 319 U.S. 624 (1943).

Miscellaneous Court Cases and Legal Opinions

DeBoer v. Snyder, 772 F.3d 388, 403 (6th Cir. 2014).

Kody Brown vs. Jeffrey B. Buhman, United States District Court of Utah, Central Division, Case No. 2:11-cv-0652-CW.

George Mason, Robin v. Hardaway, 2 VA (2 Jefferson) 109, 114, (1772).

Obergefell v. Hodges, Brief of 379 Employers and Organizations, (2015).

Papal Encyclicals

Pope Leo XIII. *Diuturnum* (1881).

———. *Rerum Novarum* (1891).

Pope Pius XI. *Mit Brennender Sorge* (1937).

————. *Quadragesimo Anno* (1931).

Pope John Paul II. *Evangelium Vitae* (1995).

————. *Veritas Splendor* (1993).

Miscellaneous Articles and Law Reviews

Chaput, Charles. "Disability: A Thread for Weaving Joy." *Public Discourse*, January 24, 2012. http://www.thepublicdiscourse.com/2012/01/4575/.

Currie, David. "The Constitution in Congress: The Federalist Period, 1789-1801." *The University of Chicago Law Review* 61, no. 3 (Summer 1994).

Gilson, Etienne. "Dogmatism and Tolerance." *International Journal* 8, no. 1 (Winter 1952/1953).

Academy of Achievement. "Anthony Kennedy Interview." Last modified June 8, 2017. http://www.achievement.org/achiever/anthony-m-kennedy/#interview.

Mason, George. "George Mason's Objections to the Constitution." Gunston Hall. http://gunstonhall.org/library/archives/manuscripts/objections.html.

Montagna, Diane. "US Won't Help Fight Boko Haram Until Nigeria Accepts Homosexuality, Birth Control, Bishop Says." *Aleteia*, February 17, 2015. http://www.aleteia.org/en/religion/article/us-wont-help-fight-boko-haram-until-nigeria-accepts-homosexuality-birth-control-bishop-says-5344466437144576.

Olson, William J. and Herbert W. Titus. "The 14th Amendment is no mandate for same-sex marriage." MercatorNet, June 10, 2015. https://www.mercatornet.com/conjugality/view/the-14th-amendment-is-no-mandate-for-same-sex-marriage2/16314.

Warren, Earl. "The Bill of Rights and the Military." *Air Force Law Review* 60 (2007).

Federal Acts, Statutes, and Congressional Legislative Reports

Freedmen & Southern Society Project. "Law Enacting Emancipation in the Federal Territories." http://www.freedmen.umd.edu/freeterr.htm.

Comm. on Appropriations, Financial Services and General Government Appropriations Bill, 2016, H.R. Rep. No. 114-194.

Disqualification of federal Judges and Magistrates from litigation, 28 U.S.C. § 455 (2012).

Exec. Order No. 9066 (1942).

Marriage Protection Act of 2004, House of Representatives, Judiciary Committee Report, 108th Congress, 2nd Session, Report No. 108-614, July 19, 2004.

Oath of Office, Pub. L. No. 89–554, 80 Stat. 424 (1966).

Money and Finance, 31 U.S.C.

State Statutes

Massachusetts Personal Liberty Act of 1855, Acts and Resolves Passed by the General Court of Massachusetts in the Years 1854-5.

Virginia Prohibition on Co-operation with the Unlawful Detention of United States Citizens, HB 1160, passed April 18, 2012.

Virginia Statute for Religions Freedom, January 16, 1786.

 TAN·BOOKS

TAN Books is the Publisher You Can Trust With Your Faith.

TAN Books was founded in 1967 to preserve the spiritual, intellectual, and liturgical traditions of the Catholic Church. At a critical moment in history TAN kept alive the great classics of the Faith and drew many to the Church. In 2008 TAN was acquired by Saint Benedict Press. Today TAN continues to teach and defend the Faith to a new generation of readers.

TAN publishes more than 600 booklets, Bibles, and books. Popular subject areas include theology and doctrine, prayer and the supernatural, history, biography, and the lives of the saints. TAN's line of educational and homeschooling resources is featured at TANHomeschool.com.

TAN publishes under several imprints, including TAN, Neumann Press, ACS Books, and the Confraternity of the Precious Blood. Sister imprints include Saint Benedict Press, Catholic Courses, and Catholic Scripture Study.

For more information about TAN,
or to request a free catalog, visit
TANBooks.com

Or call us toll-free at
(800) 437-5876